CITROËN

HAYNES CLASSIC MAKES SERIES

CITROËN

DARING TO BE DIFFERENT

JOHN REYNOLDS

First published in May 2004

A catalogue record for this book is available from the British Library

ISBN 1 85960 896 5

Library of Congress catalog card no 2002117290

Published by Haynes Publishing, Sparkford, Yeovil, Somerset BA22 7JJ, UK.
Tel: 01963 442030 Fax: 01963 440001
Int. tel: +44 1963 442030 Int. fax: +44 1963 440001
E-mail: sales@haynes.co.uk
Website: www.haynes.co.uk

Haynes North America Inc.
861 Lawrence Drive, Newbury Park,
California 91320, USA

Edited by Jon Pressnell
Page layout by Chris Fayers
Printed and bound in Great Britain by J. H. Haynes & Co. Ltd, Sparkford

contents

Introduction
André Citroën and the conventional cars

A rare photo of André Citroën (wearing his customary bowler hat) with the Traction Avant, in one of his last public appearances. It was shot in October 1934 at the finish of a Paris-Moscow-Paris endurance run. The driver was François Lecot, on Citroën's left. (Citroën)

Today, almost 80 per cent of popular family cars produced world-wide have front-wheel drive. Yet as recently as a mere 30 years ago, fwd was regarded with suspicion, if not downright opposition, by the automobile industry at large, having been rejected completely by the great majority of manufacturers.

That this situation has been reversed, so that fwd has been adopted almost universally for use on passenger cars and light commercial vehicles, has amounted to an overthrow of established prejudice on a scale unprecedented in the history of the automobile. Much of the credit for bringing about this change can be attributed to the pioneering work of Automobiles Citroën. Consistently

The Citroën name

In a practice that some might think disrespectful of the wishes of the marque's founder, Citroën UK Ltd insists on referring to itself in its TV commercials as 'Cit-ron', as if the word had only two syllables. In fact, it has three and thus should correctly be pronounced 'Cit-ro-en', as in France, as is shown by the dots over the 'e', called a diaeresis, which indicate that the last syllable should be stressed.

The name has its origins in the Netherlands, in the early years of the 19th century, when the country was under Napoleonic occupation. It was decreed that all citizens had to have a family name, and André Citroën's forebears, who were then active as costermongers, selling lemons and other tropical fruit in and around Amsterdam, took the patronym Limoenman or 'Lemonman'. When his father moved to France in 1871, this was transliterated into 'Citroen' – initially without the accent. By the time André Citroën entered the Lycée Condorcet in Paris in 1885, the diaeresis had appeared on the family name, bringing with it the change in pronunciation, in accordance with French custom.

André Citroën, 1878–1935, the founder of the marque. (Citroën)

throughout its 85-year history, Citroën has dared to differ from convention by introducing a succession of innovations that represent milestones in the evolution of automobile design and construction. The revolution really began in 1934, when Citroën introduced the Traction Avant, the world's first mass-produced fwd car and the vehicle that is nowadays acknowledged to have set the technical pattern for the modern automobile.

For a pioneer who made such a profound and enduring impact on the history of motoring, André Citroën was not, strictly speaking, a specialist automobile engineer or designer, nor even a practical hands-on mechanic or inventor. Indeed, he was not even a very keen motorist. He rarely drove a car for pleasure and certainly never put his products through their paces in person on the test track or the racing circuit, as did so many other leading constructors of his day. Instead, he preferred to regard himself as an industrialist and entrepreneur whose mission was to provide a benevolent and progressive working environment in which other gifted engineers could flourish. Certainly, Citroën possessed an uncanny ability to find and recruit a staff of exceptionally talented individuals, and

then to retain their loyalty and devotion by encouraging and inspiring their creativity in an atmosphere of high achievement. Few other motor magnates of any era were able to establish so remarkable an esprit de corps among their employees, at every level.

Urbane, sophisticated and highly intelligent, André Citroën was born in Paris in February 1878, the third son of a Dutch diamond merchant who seven years earlier had moved from Amsterdam, via Warsaw, adopted French nationality and settled in the city with his Polish wife. In 1898, aged 20, he won a place at the prestigious Ecole Polytechnique, the technical academy of the French army and the recognised training ground for ambitious high-flyers seeking successful careers in the engineering branches of the French military and civil service. Today, the graduates of the Polytechnique (known as *les Xs* because of the crossed swords on their cap badges) continue to dominate France's scientific and technical elite, and indeed the present chairman of Automobiles Citroën, Jean-Martin Folz, is among their number.

In 1900, while on leave from the Ecole Polytechnique, André Citroën visited Poland, where he made a chance discovery that was to change

his life. At a foundry near Lodz he was shown a set of novel double-helical-pattern gearwheels, cast in iron from a pattern carved from wood. Realising the commercial potential that this invention would offer if manufactured from high-quality steel, machined to precise dimensions that would permit a perfect mesh, Citroën purchased the patents on the spot.

Two years later, after completing the period of national service then compulsory for all male French citizens, he established a small workshop in the rue Faubourg St Denis, Paris, with the aim of perfecting the double-helical gear principle and developing a process for its manufacture. The unique feature of these strong and silent-running Citroën helical-cut reduction gears was that since they produced no axial thrust, greater power could be transmitted with minimal loss of efficiency due to friction. This advantage made them superior in many important heavy-duty industrial applications, for example in pumping, mining or milling machinery.

Thanks largely to André Citroën's flair for marketing and publicity, by 1913 his gear-cutting business had

10 HP CITROËN Torpedo série Luxe
4 PLACES

Usines Citroën – 115 à 145 Quai de Javel - Paris

Citroën's first car was the 10CV Type A, the first mass-produced, mass-marketed European automobile: 24,000 were built between 1919 and 1921. (Citroën)

André Citroën's first direct connection with the automobile industry began in 1908 when he became a director of the old-established Mors company, which was then experiencing severe financial difficulties. By instituting a complete reorganisation, including the introduction of new designs, he was able to transform its affairs. Within five years, sales and production had increased ten-fold, from 120 to 1200 vehicles per annum.

In 1912, in connection with his work for Mors, André Citroën made his first journey to the United States, a fact-finding trip that was to have a profound impact on his thinking. On a visit to the Ford factory in Detroit, he saw the advanced machine tools and moving production-line assembly methods that Henry Ford had developed in order to increase output and bring down the prices of his cars. Impressed with the energy and enterprise of Ford's operations, Citroën understood immediately that these same techniques of automobile mass-production had to be brought across the Atlantic at the earliest opportunity.

On the outbreak of war in 1914, however, Citroën was recalled to military service with the rank of captain in the artillery, but when joining his regiment he found that its fighting strength was severely weakened by a shortage of ammunition. Realising that his personal contribution to the war effort would be far better directed at producing shells than firing them off at the enemy, he quickly drew up far-reaching proposals for the mass-production of ammunition, which were accepted with alacrity by the military authorities. With the active backing of the Armaments Ministry and in partnership with the key associates in his gear-cutting business, he then acquired 30 acres of market gardens at the Quai de Javel in Paris, adjacent to the site of his gear-cutting business, and there built up a mighty ordnance factory utilising the latest machinery from the USA. Employing over 12,000 workers, most of them female, this

grown sufficiently to have moved to a new factory located at the Quai de Grenelle on the left bank of the Seine, not far from the Eiffel Tower. It had also established numerous European sales offices, including a branch opened in Queen Victoria Street, London, in 1910. This long tradition is still celebrated symbolically in the famous Citroën double-chevron company logo. Devised by André Citroën personally, it is derived directly from the herringbone pattern of the teeth of his double-helical gears.

factory was capable of producing 55,000 shells per day. By the end of the war he had manufactured over 28 million shells.

With the ending of hostilities in 1918, demand for munitions ceased as abruptly as it had begun. So André Citroën decided that the plant would be converted to an automobile factory and that he would enter the motor car business, not as a specialist constructor of expensive, elaborately engineered luxury cars intended for the amusement of the rich, as was the case at Mors, but as the mass-producer of simple, robust and practical popular cars, priced to suit the purposes and pockets of the middle classes.

In May 1919 the first Citroën car – the 1,327cc 10hp Type A, designed by Jules Salomon – rolled off the new assembly line at the Quai de Javel. Priced at 11,000 francs, it was not only cheaper than anything offered by Citroën's competitors but was also more economical to run. The first European car to be built using American mass-production techniques, the Type A came ready for the road. Unlike other cars that were supplied as a rolling chassis plus engine for completion by a specialist coachbuilder, it left the factory fully finished and fitted-out, complete with bodywork, hood, wheels, tyres, electric lights, horn, and even a starter. Available in a choice of three body styles and capable of 38mpg and a top speed of 40mph, the Type A was an instant success. Within a fortnight of its debut, over 16,000 advance orders had been taken. At first, 30 vehicles left the factory daily, but soon this had risen to 100 cars a day, so that by the end of 1920 a full 15,000 Citroëns were on the road.

In 1921 the Type A was replaced by the B2, equipped with a more powerful 1,452cc four-cylinder engine. Then the following year the famous 856cc 5CV Type C joined the range. An outstandingly robust and reliable light car, available initially as either an open-bodied two-seater tourer, a cabriolet or a van, the *Petite Citron* or Little Lemon (so called because of its

customary yellow paintwork) later evolved into the C2 and C3 *Trèfle* or Cloverleaf three-seater, produced between 1923 and 1926. The 5CV was perhaps the first car in the world to be aimed at the woman driver. It also broke new ground in sales techniques, at least in France, the buyer being offered a driver's manual and a list of approved Citroën repairers together with a tariff of standard service charges and replacement parts.

By 1924 Citroën output of all types had reached 250 cars a day, an

Citroën's next big popular success was the famous 5CV, introduced at the 1921 Paris Motor Show and available between 1922 and 1926. This is an early example, built in 1921 and painted canary yellow, as was customary. (Neill Bruce)

The Petite Citron *(as the 5CV was nicknamed) was specifically aimed at female drivers. (Citroën)*

La femme moderne ne circule qu'en Cabriolet

The Citroën badge

The famous Citroën double-chevron insignia, which was reputedly devised by André Citroën himself, was inspired by the pattern of the teeth of his patented double-helical gears that were manufactured by the Société des Engrenages Citroën, incorporated in 1913. When he turned his hand to building automobiles in 1919, it was only natural that he should continue to use this already familiar trademark to brand his vehicles. In January 1933 this double-chevron badge was actually incorporated into the design of the radiator grille itself, almost as if it were a heraldic motif emblazoned on a shield. In this form it was first seen on the last of the Rosalie models before becoming a feature of the new Traction Avant.

With the arrival of the DS19 and ID19, which had no radiator grille to which the double chevrons could be attached, the Citroën badge was redesigned by Flaminio Bertoni into the small faceted double-arrowhead form that was fastened to the boot lids of these two cars. Bertoni's version of André Citroën's badge is still used today, for every aspect of the company's corporate identity including signage and literature. However, the original blue and yellow colour scheme (which dated from the André Citroën era) was changed to red and white in 1985.

The B2 Grand Luxe landaulet of 1925; saloon, open tourer and taxi versions were also produced. (Citroën)

astonishing rate of production for the time. Sustaining such output called for more than organisational genius, and so André Citroën brought another of his remarkable talents to bear – his flair for marketing, publicity and promotion. A network of franchised dealerships was established throughout France, Western Europe and North Africa, the first example of this now universal method of distributing and selling cars; Citroën credit finance and insurance schemes were introduced; full-page advertising campaigns were mounted; a fleet of Citroën taxis was set up in Paris; Citroën road signs were erected at seemingly every crossroads in France; endurance trials and record-breaking marathon runs were staged – all kinds of novel marketing initiatives were employed to establish the Citroën marque and foster brand loyalty. Later, André Citroën was to have the ultimate bright advertising idea. For ten years, every night between 1924 and 1934, his name was flashed before the public in letters 100-foot high, by 250,000 electric light bulbs wired to the Eiffel Tower.

The Paris Motor Show of October 1925, meanwhile, saw the introduction of the B12 model which although it used the chassis and 1,452cc engine of the old B2 model brought another important technical innovation to the marketplace – the first use in Europe of closed, saloon-type pressed-steel bodies, spray-painted with quick-drying synthetic lacquer, a technology licensed from the Budd Manufacturing Company of Philadelphia, USA, and the outcome of André Citroën's second visit to America, made the previous year. At the 1926 Paris show, the B12 was replaced by the B14, an entirely new and improved all-steel bodied vehicle which had a larger 1,538cc engine and also drum brakes on all four wheels, for the first time on a Citroën. Yet despite the continuing popularity of the little 5CV, in September 1926 this was discontinued, as Citroën decided that its construction was uneconomic. By switching to all-steel bodies throughout his range, he could build bigger, better, stronger cars for the same cost, and by selling them at higher prices, make bigger profits.

Thanks to the enthusiastic reception given to the B14 and its successors the B14F and B14G of 1927, Citroën's wealth and confidence grew in equal measure. Consequently, at the October 1928 Paris *salon* he introduced two new models to replace the B14, the four-cylinder AC4 and the six-cylinder

AC6, each available in up to 16 different standard body styles, plus seven utility versions of the AC4 and four of the AC6. Together these cars marked the seventh change in the line begun less than a decade earlier, and both were a move up-market, offering greater technical refinement and a higher degree of performance and comfort. The AC4 – which duly became the first European car to exceed 200,000 units – was derived directly from the earlier B14, but featured an all-new, high-revving 1,628cc engine while the 2,442cc AC6 – Citroën's first six-cylinder car – was entirely new in every respect. Completely American in style and concept, this long, spacious, opulent and stylish vehicle lay somewhere between a popular mass-produced model and a coachbuilt luxury car, and consequently it offered the middle-class customer remarkable value for money.

Indeed, the success of the AC4 and AC6 served to reinforce André Citroën's reputation as the Henry Ford of France. But unlike Ford and his own great French rival, Louis Renault, Citroën was not by nature a

conventional industrialist. Although he was undoubtedly a dynamic and resourceful entrepreneur, his attitude to money and the bankers who provided it was adventurous in the extreme. Clearly, his love of gambling at the casino and the racetrack spilled over into his business affairs, as is surely borne out by his famous remark 'the moment an idea proves desirable, its price becomes of no importance'. By the end of the decade, just ten years after starting-up his motor-manufacturing business, André Citroën had achieved his initial objectives with spectacular success. With annual production now exceeding 100,000 units and with almost half a million Citroën vehicles having been sold, his company had by now overtaken all rivals to become the largest and most successful motor manufacturer in Europe. Employing 30,000 workers and capable of turning out 400 cars and lorries every day, the Citroën company had established a service network of 5,000 agents in France plus ten subsidiary sales companies and four independent factories abroad.

A B14G saloon of 1928, featuring the all-steel bodywork that André Citroën introduced from the USA in 1924, on the B10. Produced at the rate of 400 a day, the 1,538cc B14 was available in no fewer than 28 different body styles. (Neill Bruce)

André Citroën was not publicity-shy. Between 1924 and 1934 his name was beamed out across Paris by 250,000 electric light bulbs fixed to the Eiffel Tower. (Citroën)

The four-cylinder C4 series was André Citroën's greatest success – over 240,000 were built between 1928 and 1934. This is a right-hand-drive C4G, built at Slough for the British market in 1931. (Neill Bruce)

Yet despite this success André Citroën was no more immune than other European industrialists to the devastating effects of 1929's Wall Street Crash. Sales fell away in the early thirties; worse, his current range looked old-fashioned. To stay ahead of his competitors he decided to throw convention to the wind and produce a new car of radically innovative design, incorporating front-wheel drive and unitary construction.

Even then, there was nothing new about front-wheel drive. Although no other mainstream manufacturer had marketed a mass-produced fwd vehicle, already a variety of different designs had been commercialised in limited numbers by small specialist firms, beginning in France with the 1927 Tracta, designed and built by Jean-Albert Grégoire. This was closely

followed in the US by the Cord and Ruxton in 1928, the Alvis in Great Britain the same year, and ultimately the DKW and Adler in Germany, in 1931 and 1932 respectively.

Because so high a proportion of his output was sold to drivers new to car ownership, André Citroën was always keen to simplify the controls of his cars and to ease the task of driving, for women in particular. Consequently, he was well aware that the principle of fwd offered important customer benefits. Even though both Renault and Peugeot considered it to be undesirable, he understood that front-wheel drive could deliver greater stability, manoeuvrability and safety. Due primarily to its tendency to understeer, a fwd car required less experience and skill to control, allowing even the most clumsy novice to drive with confidence.

Front-wheel drive also offered numerous other advantages for the manufacturer, Citroën observed. Firstly, by concentrating the engine and transmission at the front of the car, assembly was simplified.

Secondly, by eliminating the propshaft and rear differential, space and weight would be saved and the cost of materials reduced, a process that would also be enhanced by the adoption of unitary construction, which rendered a supporting chassis unnecessary. And, thirdly, the absence of chassis, propshaft and conventional semi-elliptic springing would allow the floorline to be lowered, and with it the centre of gravity, so permitting a much more spacious, stable and aerodynamically efficient body. The one drawback was that whereas most of his previous products had been closely related to their predecessors, this new car, the Traction Avant, would inevitably be unique, having virtually nothing in common with any existing Citroën model.

But before this adventurous new car could be introduced, a further stop-gap range of conventional rear-wheel-drive vehicles would be required. Consequently three new models, the four-cylinder 8CV (1,452cc) and 10CV (1,767cc), plus the six-cylinder 15CV (2,650cc) saloons, were duly

introduced at the October 1932 Paris show. These cars were simply re-engineered versions of the old C4 and C6 designs, fitted with new all-steel bodies mounted on a traditional ladder chassis.

Constructed using the latest Budd technology, these 'Monopiece' bodies were formed by joining together five large pre-formed sections rather than by welding-up numerous smaller stampings as before. All three vehicles also featured an innovative vibration-damping engine mounting, acquired by Citroën under licence from Chrysler, and marketed as the 'Floating Power' system.

The following year the range was augmented by two further cars, the 10 Légère and the 15 Légère, using existing bodies and engines in a new combination: the former was produced by fitting the 1,767cc four-cylinder 10CV engine into the 8CV body, while the latter was a sports edition of the 15CV, with the 2,650cc six-cylinder engine in a long-wheelbase version of the 10CV. This new range was also well received, and

ultimately over 95,000 examples were sold, so reversing the fall in sales in 1931 and 1932 and enabling Citroën to recover a 45 per cent share of the French market during 1933. Eventually these cars became known as the Rosalie range, in honour of the 8CV nicknamed *Petite Rosalie*, which, circulating non-stop on the Montlhéry test track between 15 March and 27 July 1933, clocked up 300,000km (close on 186,500 miles) in 134 days at an average speed of 57.8mph during an endurance trial organised by the Yacco oil company. In doing so, the car broke 132 international and 78 world endurance records, achievements unbeaten for thirty years.

In January 1934 the Rosalie range was restyled with a raked-back radiator shell and streamlined semi-enclosed front wings; this new look was referred to as the *Nouvel Habillage*. Lastly, early in April 1934, a modified final series of Rosalie cars was introduced, the 8B, 10B and 15B, available in various body styles and all featuring independent front suspension by torsion bars, in line

One of the last conventional Citroëns – a 6-cylinder 15AL coach built in 1933. These Rosalie cars were the first Citroëns to carry the double-chevron emblem on their radiator grilles, from January 1933 onwards; previously the Citroën emblem had been confined to an enamelled badge on the radiator shell. (Citroën)

with the arrangements adopted for the revolutionary new Traction Avant front-wheel-drive model, which after less than two years of development was by now on the point of being revealed to the world at large.

In fact, the existence of the Traction Avant was announced to the press in April 1934, when it met with a rapturous reception. It entered series production the following month, initially in one form only, the Citroën '7', a light saloon powered by a 1,303cc four-cylinder engine rated at 7CV.

Alas, throughout 1934 André Citroën had been shaken by a series of calamitous events, which resulted in his physical and financial collapse and, ultimately, his death. Early in

The Citroën-Kégresse

In 1920 Citroën acquired the rights to a novel lightweight caterpillar track system, designed by Adolphe Kégresse, which replaced the rear wheels of a car with an endless flexible rubber band instead of the heavy hinged metal plates of a crawler tractor. To exploit this device he formed the Société Citroën-Kégresse-Hinstin, which manufactured and marketed a range of *autochenilles* or caterpillar-tracked vehicles, built at a factory at Levallois on the northern outskirts of Paris where, 30 years later, the 2CV was to be assembled.

Employing the engine and chassis of Citroën's B2 car, the earliest Citroën-Kégresse light tractor, the Type P2, proved an immediate success, thanks to the famous series of endurance expeditions or *Raids* which the master publicist staged to demonstrate the vehicle's remarkable cross-country abilities. The first of these expeditions, led by André Citroën's associates Georges-Marie

Haardt and Louis Audouin-Dubreuil, took place in the winter of 1922–23. Accomplished in 22 days, this 2,000-mile journey from Touggourt in Algeria to Timbuktu in Mali by a convoy of five Citroën-Kégresse half-tracked vehicles was the first complete crossing of the Sahara by motor vehicle.

Above: The Citroën-Kégresse caterpillar car was indeed an impressive machine. But none left the factory looking quite so splendid as this highly restored example. (Neill Bruce)
Below: A Citroën-Kégresse of the Citroën Central Asian Expedition seen crossing the Burzil Pass in the Himalayas during July 1931. (Citroën)

It attracted so much favourable newsreel and newspaper coverage that Citroën immediately decided on an even more remarkable trail-blazing adventure – a full-scale 12,500-mile Trans-African crossing from Algiers to Mombasa (and then on by sea to Madagascar) by way of the Sahara, Niger and the Sudan, again by a convoy of P2 half-tracks. Undertaken in 18 months between October 1922 and March 1924, this expedition, known as the *Croisière Noire*, was a journey of research and exploration over unpaved paths and tracks, traversing deserts, savannah, swamps and tropical rain-forests and venturing into uncharted territory; all eight vehicles and 16 crew (including a zoologist, a geologist, an artist and a cinematographer) came through unscathed. During the journey, the expedition shot about 90,000 feet of film and 8,000 photographs, produced over 300 botanical drawings and 15 books of sketches, and collected samples of over 300 mammals, 800 birds and 1,500 insects, many of which were unknown to science at that time.

Later, during 1931 and 1932, came the third such project – the Citroën Trans-Asiatic expedition or *Croisière Jaune*, led once more by Haardt and Audouin-Dubreuil. A genuine scientific, geographical and archaeological expedition sponsored by the French and British governments and also by the National Geographic Society of the USA, this mission covered the 8,000 miles from Beirut to Peking in just under nine months, traversing the Himalayas and the Gobi desert, a journey so difficult and dangerous that it has never been attempted again. The Citroën-Kégresse company ceased trading in 1935, but its products inspired the American M35 military half-tracks of WW2, units of the US Army having been equipped earlier with Citroën-Kégresse vehicles.

1933, after viewing the improvements that had recently been carried out at the Renault factory at Billancourt, he had decided that he too would build a super-modern assembly plant, but even bigger and better than that of his rival, in which to build the Traction Avant. Accordingly, between March and July that year, a third of the entire Quai de Javel site was torn down and reconstructed without any interruption to output, in a remarkable feat of industrial planning and organisation.

Unfortunately, with his usual over-optimism Citroën had underestimated the financial burden involved in changing both his factory and his product simultaneously, and at an adverse moment. As a result, in the autumn of 1934, his firm encountered a severe cash-flow crisis and was unable to meet its short-term obligations and debts. A creditor's moratorium was established, but when this was broken by a bankruptcy petition presented by an impatient minor creditor, the Citroën firm was declared insolvent by the commercial court of Paris, on 21 December 1934, and placed under the administration of a committee of creditors.

Over the following seven months Citroën lost not only his firm, his fortune and the rights to use his own name, but also his life. With his health gravely weakened by the struggle for survival, he gave up the fight to remain master of the Quai de Javel and on the 18 January 1935 he was admitted to hospital with a stomach tumour, which proved incurable. He died on 3 July 1935, aged only 56, and later that month the Societé Anonyme André Citroën was taken over completely by its principal creditor, the Michelin tyre company.

It was originally intended that the Rosalie models would be permanently withdrawn in September 1934; certainly no Rosalies were exhibited at the October 1934 Paris Motor Show, where the Citroën stand was devoted exclusively to the Traction Avant. However, to cater for traditionally-minded customers who hesitated to order the new front-wheel-drive car,

the conventional Rosalies were re-introduced in January 1935 in two versions, the 7UA and 11UA, powered by either the 1,628cc 9CV or the 1,911cc 11CV engines from the Traction Avant, installed in a reversed direction to drive the rear wheels. In addition to several light commercial vehicle variants, various passenger body styles were offered: two for the 7UA, a standard-wheelbase four-light saloon and a commerciale with rear tailgate, and three for 11UA, a long-wheelbase six-light saloon, a seven-seater familiale and a commerciale. These products remained in the catalogue until the spring of 1938 when the Citroën company finally abandoned rear-wheel drive forever on its passenger cars and light-commercial vehicles, as its founder had planned.

So it was that, for almost 30 years, the Citroën firm stood alone. It was not until the arrival of the Mini in 1959 that another major company recognised the advantages of front-wheel drive and adopted it for use on a truly mass-produced car. In France, despite the early post-war use of front-wheel drive by small firms such as Panhard, Citroën's great rival, Renault, took until 1961 to bring out its first front-wheel drive car, the Renault 4. Eventually even the arch-conservative Ford Motor Company was converted, producing its first front-wheel-drive design, the Taunus 12M of 1962, and then only for the German market. Ford's first global front-wheel-drive car, the Fiesta, was not introduced until 1976. But by then Citroën had already demonstrated the validity of the concept beyond all doubt, having produced at least two and a half million front-wheel-drive vehicles over the previous three decades – including many of the long series of pioneering cars examined within this book.

Clearly, by daring to be different Andre Citroën had shown the way ahead, placing the company that bears his name at the spear-head of the avant-garde and establishing the reputation for originality and innovation that it still enjoys today.

The four-cylinder
Traction Avant

One of the very first examples of the Traction Avant produced, a 7A with the original 1,303cc engine, built in the summer of 1934. The Traction saloons of this period all had chromed grilles and were available in a wide choice of colour schemes. (Citroën)

Although it is nowadays hailed as a French cultural icon, the Traction Avant was as much transatlantic in inspiration as any of André Citroën's previous conventional cars. When travelling in the USA in 1931 he had visited the Budd Manufacturing Company of Philadelphia, the suppliers of the presses and tooling for his C4 and C6 cars, and had been shown a front-wheel-drive car designed by Budd's chief engineer, Joseph Ledwinka, to demonstrate the advantages of the new chassis-less unitary construction system which Budd had recently patented.

Citroën realised that this revolutionary monocoque system made mass-production of a fwd car a practical proposition. Because the bodyshell could alone support the engine, transmission and suspension, no chassis would be required, and at last it would be possible to bring the car's weight – and its ride-height and centre of gravity – down to the levels he desired. Better still, the large savings in steel would reduce costs, providing that the car could be produced and sold in sufficient quantities to absorb the investment in expensive presses and tooling. An output of over 1,000 units per day would be required, he estimated.

On André Citroën's return to France, therefore, his engineers began adapting the Budd design for a much smaller vehicle, more suited to European conditions. The specification laid down was for a small four-seater weighing no more than 15½cwt, capable of 60mph and an average fuel consumption of 40mpg, and priced to sell at 15,000 francs. Even at this early stage, Citroën realised that the new car would have virtually nothing in common with any existing model. At a stroke, his new model would make all other cars – his own included – out of date.

In 1932 Citroën was given the opportunity to manufacture under licence a medium-sized front-wheel-drive design, which had just appeared in Germany, the Adler Trumpf. But being jealous of his reputation for innovation and independence, he chose instead to press ahead with his own *Petite Voiture* (or 'Small Car'). However, by the end of that year it had become clear to the impatient motor magnate that the project was well behind schedule; if the new car was to be ready for 1934, as intended, then fresh energies would be required. He therefore began a head-hunt, and consulted his friend the French aircraft and automobile engineer Gabriel Voisin. As luck would have it, Voisin knew of the right man for the job – André Lefèbvre, an engineer who had been his assistant, but who was currently employed by Citroën's great rival Louis Renault. Lefèbvre had been working privately on a design for a front-wheel-drive car at his own initiative, following an experimental fwd Voisin with which he had been involved, and was thus an ideal choice.

So it was that André Citroën

appointed the brilliant 39-year-old Lefèbvre as overall manager of his *Petite Voiture* project, giving him carte blanche get the car ready on time. Lefèbvre joined Citroën's *Bureau d'Etudes* or Design Office in March 1933. Elements of the car's construction must already have been established well before Lefèbvre's arrival, borrowing perhaps from Budd blueprints that Citroën is said to have brought back from the USA in 1931, but it was only at the end of June 1933 that the definitive plans for the vehicle were agreed. Despite this, within another two months two hand-built working prototypes were ready to be shown to André Citroën and his wife, for their approval. The styling of these prototypes was by Flaminio Bertoni, an Italian designer and sculptor then only thirty years old, who had joined the Citroën design office in July 1932.

Just four months later, in November 1933, a mission departed for Philadelphia bearing the full-scale drawings required to produce the tooling for the body presses. Only Budd possessed the technology to supply these dies, required in conjunction with the presses and flash-welding machines purchased earlier from the USA to fabricate the Rosalie's monopiece steel body.

In the meanwhile, however, in September 1933, Citroën threw the design into the melting pot once again. In place of the conventional gearbox and clutch of the first two prototypes, he decided to use a novel, fully automatic transmission employing a hydraulic torque converter, this being the creation of Spanish-Brazilian inventor Dimitri Sensaud de Lavaud. In effect, this 'turbine' relieved the driver of the work of changing gear by constantly synchronising the speed of the wheels with the speed of the engine. As already noted, Citroën disliked the physical effort of driving, and so the notion of eliminating the gearshift and clutch pedal altogether was a highly attractive proposition – especially as so many potential customers for the new car would be inexperienced drivers, new to motoring.

Traction Avant 11CV (post-war)
1945–1957

ENGINE:

Four-cylinder in-line, water-cooled	
Capacity	1,911cc
Bore x stroke	78mm x 100mm
Valve actuation	Pushrod
Compression ratio	6.2:1
Carburettors	Single-choke Solex downdraught
Power output	56bhp SAE at 3,800rpm
	60bhp SAE at 4,000rpm (11D)
Torque	90.4lb ft at 2,200rpm

TRANSMISSION:
Front-wheel drive
Three-speed, second and top synchronised

SUSPENSION:
Front: Independent, longitudinal torsion bars, upper and lower arms, telescopic dampers
Rear: Beam axle, transverse torsion bars, telescopic dampers

STEERING:
Rack-and-pinion, unassisted
2½ turns lock-to-lock

BRAKES:
Drum, hydraulically operated

WHEELS/TYRES:
Michelin 'X' radial, 150x400

BODYWORK:
Four-door steel monocoque
Available as Légère and Normale saloons and six-light Familiale and Commerciale

DIMENSIONS ('Big Boot' Slough Normale):

Length	15ft 6½in
Wheelbase	10ft 1½in
Track	4ft 10½in
Width	5ft 10in
Height	5ft 1in

WEIGHT:
23.5cwt (with 5 galls fuel)

PERFORMANCE:
(Source: *The Autocar*)

Max speed	70.3mph
0–50mph	17.9sec
0–60mph	29.1sec

PRICE INCLUDING TAX WHEN NEW:
£1,153 (March 1953)

NUMBERS BUILT:
620,455 (11 Légère and Normale)

André Lefèbvre

André Lefèbvre, chief designer at Citroën for 25 years between 1933 and 1958, was a unique figure in motoring history. The creator of the 2CV and the DS19 as well as the Traction Avant, he was one of very few people ever to succeed at the highest level as both a racing driver and designer. In 1923 he finished fifth in the French GP, at the wheel of a two-litre, six-cylinder Voisin of revolutionary conception that he had helped to design. Later, in 1929, he took part in a famous series of high-speed, long-distance non-stop

André Lefèbvre, 1894–1964, the brains behind the Traction Avant, the 2CV and the DS19. He was the only engineer ever to reach the highest levels of achievement in automobile design and Grand Prix motor racing simultaneously. (Citroën)

endurance runs staged by Gabriel Voisin at the Montlhéry circuit near Paris, at which many long-lasting world records were set.

Born in 1894, he trained to be an aircraft designer at the Ecole Supérieure d'Aéronautique in Paris, before beginning his career with Gabriel Voisin in 1916, constructing bombers for the French airforce. After the war, when Voisin became a manufacturer of luxury cars, Lefèbvre worked as Voisin's joint chief assistant designer and chief test driver for 15 years. When the market for Voisin's expensive products collapsed after the Wall Street Crash, Lefèbvre was obliged to leave and join Renault, as deputy to the chief engineer of its *Bureau d'Etudes*. Not surprisingly, in view of Louis Renault's conservatism, he found the position uncongenial. Consequently, when André Citroën offered him a job at the Quai de Javel to take charge of his front-wheel-drive project, Lefèbvre accepted with alacrity, having already produced his own design for a fwd car, which Renault had refused to produce.

During his quarter-century of service as de facto Chief Engineer and Designer at Citroën's *Bureau d'Etudes*, Lefèbvre held no official rank or title yet he was regarded nonetheless as the supreme authority on all technical matters. After André Citroën's departure in 1935, he reported directly to Citroën's new owners, the Michelin family, who gave his advanced thinking and adventurous policies their total support and endorsement, allowing their resident genius *carte blanche* to follow whatever lines of research seemed most interesting and promising to him personally, almost regardless of cost or ultimate commercial viability. 'The most important person in this factory is Monsieur Lefèbvre,'

explained Pierre Boulanger to a new recruit to the research department. 'He isn't the director of the *Bureau d'Etudes* because he has better things to do. He uses his imagination to conceive and create the cars that the factory produces.'

Bored by administrative matters, and totally uninterested in the symbols of power and status that motivate many lesser men, Lefèbvre left the day-to-day running of the department to others and concentrated on solving engineering problems, working at all hours and in all places. A tall, dark, elegant, somewhat bohemian figure who dressed with style and reputedly drank nothing but water or champagne, he was the archetypal artist-engineer, worshipping novelty for its own sake and taking a perverse delight in doing things differently, refusing to copy proven techniques used successfully elsewhere.

Nothing seemed impossible to him. The more audacious, unconventional and complex a solution, the greater its appeal. Throughout his career, both with Voisin and with Citroën, he was obsessed with the idea of adapting the principles of aeronautics to the automobile. Yet he never went in for the phoney streamlining that was so fashionable in the thirties and which, as often as not, was aerodynamically unsound – a thin veneer of spurious sophistication concealing as likely as not a crude chassis.

Although he was forced through ill health to retire from the company prematurely in 1958, André Lefèbvre continued to serve the marque until the end of his life. Having suffered a stroke which left him partially paralysed, he learnt to draw with his left hand and went on designing for Citroën, working from his home, until he died in May 1964, a mere 70 years old.

This is a 7C model, equipped with a 1,628cc engine, built in late 1934. This viewpoint shows clearly the absence of an opening boot on the earliest examples. (Citroën)

In February 1934, the engineers returned from the USA with the Budd tooling; it seemed that the project was back on schedule. But by then it had became obvious that the Sensaud de Lavaud transmission was utterly unreliable. Although its performance was satisfactory on the flat or even up gentle slopes, as soon a steep hill was climbed the oil in the torque converter overheated and traction was lost completely until it had cooled down. The matter came to a head when the device was demonstrated at a secret preview for Citroën's technical and commercial staff, the first time that the *Petite Voiture* had been viewed beyond the confines of the design office or the Montlhéry proving circuit. The event was an embarrassing disaster, marred by repeated failures of the transmission. Another test run a week later on public roads near Paris confirmed the problem beyond doubt. Of the five cars that set out to cover the circular course, which included several steep hills, only one did not break down. Early in March 1934 Citroën finally admitted defeat, ordering that the 'turbine' be abandoned and replaced immediately by a conventional clutch and gearbox – using the casing of the Sensaud de Lavaud device, which had already been manufactured in large numbers. The engineers having predicted this outcome, the task was achieved within a couple of weeks. To operate the new three-speed gearbox was a dashboard-mounted lever that was soon nicknamed 'the mustard spoon' and which became one of the car's most idiosyncratic features.

On 24 March 1934, almost exactly one year after the arrival of André Lefèbvre at the Quai de Javel, the *Petite Voiture* was unveiled to the firm's 40 leading concessionaires. By all accounts, the dealers were astounded at their first glimpse of the car, called the '7', and were particularly impressed by the absence of running boards. Three weeks later, on 18 April, the new Citroën was revealed to the world at large at a press reception and banquet where it received a rapturous welcome. The reports that appeared the following day extolled Citroën's latest achievement to the point of ecstasy. 'The front-wheel-drive Citroën 7 is so up-to-the-minute, so audacious, so rich in original technical solutions, so different from all that has been done before, that it truly

The fall and rise of Citroën

On the 8 October 1933 André Citroën inaugurated his rebuilt factory by holding a gargantuan banquet, as was his custom. No fewer than 6,333 guests attended the celebrations held in the vast Quai de Javel delivery hall. To the revellers it must have seemed as if the patron had reached the absolute summit of his power, wealth and prestige, and that his position was unassailably secure.

But beneath all the merry-making, the situation was grim. The huge financial burden imposed by the development of the Traction Avant had been made quite insupportable by the extra weight of debt incurred by this massive rebuilding programme, at a time of reduced sales, and the company was suffering severe financial difficulties. Citroën was under pressure from all directions, and a race against time had begun to get the new car onto the market as soon as possible, to revive sales and restore cash flow.

As the Traction Avant approached its launch, the company's financial position worsened by the hour. The crisis came to a head at the end of February 1934 when Citroën was unable to pay the interest due on the loan that he had obtained to finance his ambitious expansion plans. There was only one course of action remaining open to him. To save his firm and put the Traction Avant on the road he had no alternative but to appeal for help to Edouard Michelin, patriarch of the Michelin tyre firm of Clermont Ferrand which was now his largest trade creditor, having been the sole supplier of wheels and tyres since 1919. Citroën had known the Michelin family for almost thirty years, since his days at Mors, and in the past they had promised him money should he ever need it.

In response to Citroën's appeal, Edouard promptly sent his two deputies, his son Pierre and his right-hand man Pierre-Jules Boulanger, to Paris to inspect the factories and examine the Traction Avant,

accompanied by engineers from Michelin's own design office. Their visit, which marked a turning point in the affairs of the Citroën firm and of its founder, took place on the 25 July 1934. Fortunately, the Michelin men recognised the great potential of the Traction Avant. In fact, they were deeply impressed by the vehicle and soon gave their thumbs-up to a rescue scheme.

Edouard Michelin agreed to advance Citroën a short-term loan in addition to the existing debt, on the condition that he was given an option to buy the company. Moreover, André Citroën was also required to allow Michelin to assume a role in the management of the company, in order to implement immediately a programme of drastic economies and redundancies and to set up a system of quality control to overcome the evident manufacturing deficiencies affecting the Traction Avant. Thus the exploratory visit of Pierre Michelin and Pierre-Jules Boulanger was soon extended into a permanent stay.

deserves to be described as sensational,' gushed one paper.

The Traction Avant was indeed a technical tour de force, introducing not only front-wheel drive to the popular mass-produced car but also a host of other important engineering features never previously united in a single car, such as independent front suspension by torsion bars, hydraulic brakes and – from 1936 – rack-and-pinion steering.

In its earliest version, the Citroën 7, it was powered by a 32bhp 1,303cc four-cylinder water-cooled engine rated at 7CV. This was the first example of the classic long-stroke power-plant designed by Maurice Sainturat which, in a succession of improved and uprated versions, was to remain in production for more than 40 years, longer than almost any other automobile engine. An outstandingly

robust and reliable design, it boasted numerous advanced features including overhead valves and interchangeable wet liners, which could be removed and replaced with the engine in situ. Together with its transmission, front suspension and steering gear, the engine formed a complete, self-contained assembly, on an easily detachable cradle or subframe, which could be built up and tested separately, or withdrawn as one unit to facilitate maintenance and repair.

The other notable innovation was the torsion-bar suspension, a feature not seen before on a mass-produced European car. The choice of torsion bars, mounted longitudinally at the front and transversely at the rear, was particularly interesting in that they allowed the ride-height of the car to be reduced to the very minimum, and with it the centre of gravity.

The Traction Avant also featured the world's first use of a true monocoque bodyshell. Its manufacture involved two separate elements, the infrastructure and the superstructure, which were fabricated independently and then welded together. The infrastructure comprised the two frontal box members, left and right, which formed the engine bay, the scuttle or firewall bulkhead, and the floorpan, which was strengthened by two substantial box-section side-rails, while the superstructure comprised the visible exterior pressings, including the two large single-piece side panels, which incorporated the door and windscreen pillars, and the front, rear and roof closing panels. In its earliest form the Traction Avant had a roof-closing panel made of fabric rather than metal, as was the case in most conventional steel-bodied cars

of that era. It also lacked an opening boot, access to the luggage space being by lifting the rear seat back. The *Sept* weighed 20.1cwt, about 300lbs less than its predecessor, the 10CV Rosalie. This weight was distributed so that 56 per cent was concentrated at the front and 44 per cent at the rear, in contrast to the Rosalie, which had 48 per cent of its weight resting on its front axle and 52 per cent on the rear.

The first series-production examples went on sale at the beginning of May 1934 at a price of 17,700 francs – 2,700 francs more than the target figure, but not much more than the cost of the by now obsolete Rosalie 10CV model which the '7' was intended to supersede. Expected to give its creator a five-year lead over his rivals, the new model remained in production for almost 25 years. Even when its production ceased in 1957 it

was still considered by many experts to be technically superior to most other popular cars then available.

However, the Traction Avant was not exactly an immediate success: due to its hurried development and premature launch it exhibited a catalogue of faults including knocking driveshafts, sticking brakes, snapping torsion bars and even splitting body seams. Moreover, it was also apparent that its 1,303cc power unit was insufficient. So in June 1934 the 7A (as it was retrospectively labelled) was replaced by the 7B, equipped with an enlarged 1,529cc engine rated as a 9CV for taxation purposes. In addition, a new, more powerful version, the 7 Sport, was introduced that same month, equipped with a 1,911cc engine of 11CV rating. By this time the saloons had been joined by a soft-topped roadster and a hard-

Pre-production 11CV – retrospectively called the 11A – with the enlarged 1,911cc engine, photographed in September 1934. Wider rear quarters and less cutaway rear doors identify it as having the larger Onze Normale *body. (Citroën)*

topped *faux cabriolet* or coupé, both being two-seaters with a two-person dickey seat in the rear deck.

Although there were now eight different versions of the new model, this was by no means enough to satisfy André Citroën, despite the financial problems besetting his firm, and which were shortly to cause his personal downfall. Accordingly, in September 1934, just before the Paris *salon*, he announced a further range of vehicles with larger, heavier bodies, their track increased from 4ft 4in to 4ft 8in and their wheelbase from 9ft 6½in to 10ft 1½in. Powered by the

The 11A fixed-head coupé (known in France as the Faux Cabriolet), *introduced in autumn 1934, here photographed by Pierre Louÿs, Citroën's talented in-house photographer.* (Citroën)

The Michelin succession

On 30 December 1937, tragedy struck Citroën once again when its new *patron*, Pierre Michelin, was killed at the wheel of a Traction Avant while travelling from Paris to Clermont-Ferrand. For the following 13 years, the responsibility for running the company fell on Pierre-Jules Boulanger alone, though under the overall direction of, initially, Edouard Michelin, and then, latterly, Edouard Michelin's son-in-law Robert Puiseux, who assumed control of the entire conglomerate following Edouard's death in 1940.

11CV 1,911cc engine of the 7 Sport, the new 11 series comprised seven different models. Three of these – a six-seater saloon, a fixed-head coupé and a roadster – were simply longer and wider versions of the existing body styles, but another three were ultra-long (10ft 9in wheelbase) variants: a six-seater limousine, a nine-seater familiale with six-light body, and a coupé de ville with internal division, two jump seats and blanked-off rear quarters. Finally, there was a coupé de ville version of the regular standard wheelbase saloon. The two coupé de ville models, however, were soon deleted. To coincide with the arrival of the '11' (or

Onze Normale), the 7 Sport was renamed the 11 *Légère* (or Light Fifteen when produced in Slough in RHD form), and the regular '7' received its final upgrade, being given a 1,628cc engine and re-named the '7C'.

Throughout 1934 and 1935, Lefèbvre and his fellow engineers struggled to solve a succession of unforeseen difficulties. Only Maurice Sainturat's robust and reliable wet-liner ohv engine gave complete satisfaction from the start, and without it the Traction Avant would surely have proved a complete fiasco. Fortunately, however, one of the first emergency measures taken by Pierre Michelin on assuming control had been to recruit a first-class automobile engineer from Michelin, Antoine Hermet, to study the various technical problems besetting the new car and make recommendations on how it could be improved. Had Hermet's

report, produced early in 1935, been unfavourable, there can be no doubt that André Citroën's brain-child would have been unceremoniously killed off, and replaced by something more conventional. But his verdict was that the vehicle's numerous deficiencies could be remedied, and that it would be profitable to do so.

Under his supervision, a constant stream of improvements was made to the original design, until by the end of 1936 few parts were interchangeable with those from one of the early cars. By January 1935 a completely redesigned front suspension and transmission had been introduced, including a different type of driveshaft. Next, in May 1935, an entirely reworked bodyshell was introduced, outwardly unchanged but massively reinforced to increase rigidity and overcome its tendency to deform. Then, at the October 1935 Paris *salon*, came an opening boot lid, while the original chromed radiator grille was replaced by a painted shell.

The next, and perhaps greatest, technical improvement introduced by the new management took place in May 1936 when the original steering box with its over-complicated linkages was replaced by an entirely new

system working on the rack-and-pinion principle, for the first time on a mass-produced model. With the vagueness and slackness that had compromised the handling of earlier versions eliminated, the driving qualities of the Traction Avant were transformed, giving it an enduring reputation for positive and responsive handling. At the same time, the instrument cluster was moved from the centre of the dashboard to a new binnacle located behind the steering wheel.

The range for the 1937 season offered few changes from the previous year, except that the '11' was renamed the '11B', all previous 1,911cc cars being referred to henceforth as the '11A' series. The 1938 season saw a new arrival, the long-wheelbase, six-light '11B' Commerciale, a dual-purpose utility version aimed at rural users. Thanks to its two-part tailgate the Commerciale was a family people-carrier that doubled as a trade vehicle. Capable of carrying a 500kg (9.8cwt) payload, it was specifically intended for use by farmers, winegrowers and smallholders, or by country merchants, shopkeepers and tradesmen such as butchers and bakers.

The final pre-war change of note was the arrival in January 1938 of Michelin's low-profile Pilote tyres and associated wide-rim Pilote wheels, with their slatted spokes that were designed to cool the brake drums. Normally painted in the body colour, these Pilote wheels were finished in yellow (on the 7C and 11BL) and red (on the 11B) when the car was black; they were accompanied by wider wings. In the spring of 1938, meanwhile, the remaining rear-wheel-drive Citroëns were finally withdrawn from sale. From this point onwards the company built and sold only front-wheel-drive cars, and as such was the first major motor

The prototype of the 11A roadster/cabriolet, produced in July 1934 and fitted with the 1,911cc version of Maurice Sainturat's ohv engine. Note that the roadster's wings were generally painted in the same colour as the body. (Ludvigsen Library)

manufacturer in the world to abandon rear-wheel drive completely. By now, the development of the Traction Avant had at last reached a state of maturity. The teething troubles had largely been overcome and it was an established success, recognised as an exceedingly robust, reliable and safe means of transport. It can therefore be argued that the 'New Concept in Motoring' – as it was billed – was as much a Michelin achievement as solely the creation of André Citroën.

The *faux-cabriolet* coupé versions of the 7C, 11BL and 11B were deleted in September 1938, and in February 1939 the 7C became the 7C Economique –

An 11B Normale *roadster of 1938, showing the characteristic features of that era, such as the Michelin Pilote wheels and the painted radiator shell. (Ludvigsen Library)*

A 1939 11B *saloon: The Pilote wheels fitted to Normale cars were always painted red if the coachwork was black; those of black Légères and 15-Sixes were yellow and ivory respectively. (Citroën)*

or '7 Eco' – on account of various engine modifications which reduced its fuel consumption by a claimed 10 per cent without affecting performance; at the same time the 11BL and 11B were equipped with an uprated *Performance* engine, with output raised from 46bhp to 56bhp.

With the coming of war, the production of civilian vehicles was severely curtailed. No roadsters were made after September 1939; the only colour available for the saloons,

familiales and commerciales was black. The invasion of France by Germany in June 1940 saw Traction Avant production for the civilian market cease, although manufacture for official government or military use continued sporadically until November 1941 – with three further *Onze Légeres* assembled in 1942.

Following the liberation of France, the first post-war Traction Avant came off the assembly lines in June 1945, one month after hostilities in Europe had

ended. During the first year of post-war production, only the 11BL (*Onze Légère*) was manufactured, and indeed the 7C, with its 1,628cc engine, was never reintroduced. The '11B' or *Onze Normale* saloon was to return in 1947.

Considering its long career, the technical evolution of the Traction Avant was much less complicated than that of most other Citroën models. At first the post-war car was more or less identical to pre-war examples, the only important visual difference being that

The Slough-built Traction Avant

Few motorists today would credit that Citroën's assembly plant at Slough was once one of the largest and most important car factories in England. Opened by André Citroën in February 1926 as the first of his foreign subsidiaries, for exactly forty years, until February 1966, the Slough factory assembled both French and British components into British-made Citroëns subtly modified to appeal to Anglo-Saxon tastes. The aim was to take advantage of the system of preferential tariffs then governing trade within the British Empire and latterly the Commonwealth. The company could thus gain entry into valuable overseas markets otherwise denied to French products.

To qualify for British-made status, at least 51 per cent of the total content value of an imported vehicle, including labour, material and overhead costs, had to be of British origin. At first the Slough factory produced Citroën's conventional rear-wheel-drive cars but from 1934 until 1940, and again from 1945 until 1955, a right-hand-drive version of the Traction Avant was built. In contrast to the situation in France, in post-war years the Slough factory produced a far greater number of the *Onze Légère* (called Light Fifteen in the UK) than of the *Onze Normale* (Big Fifteen in Slough parlance) – 16,801 of the former and 1,053 of the latter, plus 1,194 of the Six-Cylinder or Big Six, as the 15-Six was variously called. A grand total of 19,048 Tractions were assembled post-war, of which 13,952 were exported.

It is hardly surprising that by incorporating such a high proportion of British-made components, the Slough-built *Tractions* differed from their continental counterparts in a number of highly visible ways. Most noticeable was their use of chromed grilles, headlamps and sidelamps throughout, even when

Paris switched to painted items, and by their leather-upholstered interiors and polished wooden dashboards in the British tradition. Moreover, after the war, when Paris cars could only be obtained painted in black, the Slough cars were available in a range of three additional colours – regal red, mist green and silver grey, teamed with either red or brown leather and leathercloth interiors. A sliding sunshine roof was also available as an option.

Slough-built Tractions used Lucas 12-volt electrics, while tyres came from Michelin's Stoke-on-Trent plant, of course, but were fitted on Rubery Owen disc wheels with large chrome hubcaps. The chromed bumpers, supplied by Pyrene, were also quite different in style from those seen on Paris-built cars. Lastly, Slough cars featured a script-lettered 'Citroën' badge on the boot lid.

Above: This rhd 11CV roadster was made in England in 1940 and has the chromed grille always fitted to Slough-built cars. Those with 1,911cc engines and Légère-type bodies (such as this example) were known as Light Fifteens, and those with Normale bodies as Big Fifteens. (LAT) Below: Late 'big boot' Slough Light Fifteen: the boot badge, trafficators and the different bumpers and wheels are all clearly visible. Inside are leather seats and a wooden dashboard, in contrast to the cloth upholstery and metal dash of Paris cars. The post-war Slough Traction Avant was available in a choice of four colours – regal red, mist green and metallic silver-grey as well as black. (LAT)

A 7C Légère *saloon of 1939; note the*
ventilation flaps in the bonnet that were a
feature of all pre-war models except the 15-
Six. (Citroën) *Right: Dashboard of 1951*
11BL, showing gold-faced speedo introduced in
mid-1949 and horizontal brightwork
(1950–52) in dash centre. (LAT)

from May 1946 the pivoting vents on
the bonnet were replaced by louvres,
as seen on the 15-Six (see next
chapter) from the outset. Even the
distinctive Michelin Pilote wheels were
retained for a while, until replaced by
the new plain-disc Michelin BM design
during 1947. Initially, these BM wheels
were shod with Michelin SP Pilote
cross-ply tyres, but from the end of
1949 onwards as an optional extra the
Traction Avant could be ordered
equipped with Michelin's new steel-
belted radial tyre, the 'X', launched at
the Paris *salon* that year.

On post-war cars the headlamps
were painted rather than chromed,
and the interior was trimmed and
equipped in a more austere and sober
style than hitherto. The elaborately
decorative interior flourishes inherited
from the André Citroën era

disappeared and the car's seats,
headlining and door panels were
trimmed in plain grey cloth, although
the tubular framed seats dating from
1935 were retained until 1949, when
they were replaced by a new type of
seating referred to as Pullman; these
seats were individual and non-
reclining at the front. In August 1946,
the characteristic cast aluminium-alloy
sabots or wing spats appeared for the

first time on certain examples and by
1947 had become a standard fitting
right across the range. By the end of
1947, with 21,153 *Tractions* having
been assembled that year, production
had reached about 40 per cent of
pre-war levels.

In July 1952 came the first and only
major change to the appearance of
the Traction Avant. As a result of a
widespread demand for greater
luggage space, the original downward-
hinging boot lid with its external
spare-wheel housing was replaced by
a new rectangular lid that opened
upwards. At the same time certain
other minor modifications were
introduced: most noticeably, the
windscreen wipers were mounted
below the windscreen rather than
above, and front and rear direction
indicators appeared for the first time,
along with new rear lamps. Inside, the
layout and colour scheme of the
dashboard was revised again and
there was a new type of metal internal
window surround, painted grey to
match the new dashboard, while the
tops and sides of the seats and the
bottoms of the door cards of the 11BL

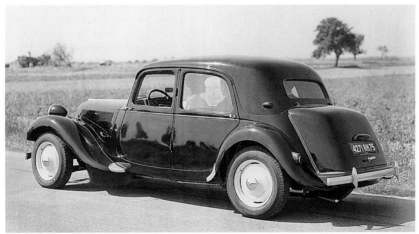

Top: In October 1953 a choice of colours became available at last for the entire Traction Avant range, including mist grey, pearl grey, midnight blue and airforce blue, all with matching wheels but with wheel embellishers painted in contrasting grey, as seen here. Even so, the traditional black with contrasting pale yellow wheels remained the most popular choice. (Ludvigsen) Left: In July 1952 all models received a built-out boot that greatly increased luggage capacity. Note that the wheel embellishers fitted to French four-cylinder models after the demise of Pilote wheels had small chromed centres rather than the large chromed hubcaps seen from 1949 on the six-cylinder cars. (Citroën)

and 11B were given grey plastic inserts, to protect the grey cloth upholstery.

In July 1953 came the return of the long wheelbase, six-light Familiale version of the four-cylinder 11B, which had been absent since 1940. This was a full nine-seater, thanks to the row of three folding occasional seats located in the footwell of the rear passenger compartment Although its impending return was announced in 1953, it was not until April 1954 that the 11B Commerciale made its reappearance.

The new version featured a one-piece top-hinged tailgate.

From October 1953 onwards as an alternative to the customary black finish, two new colours, pearl grey and iceland blue, were introduced across the Traction Avant range. The following year the shade-card was further enhanced by the addition of midnight blue, airforce blue (also known as RAF blue), mist grey and heather grey.

The final chapter was written in May

1955, when all four versions of the 11CV were equipped with an uprated version of the original 1,911cc engine, which by now had been in production for over twenty years. This new engine, the 11D, showed an increase in power output from 56bhp to 60bhp, and offered higher performance and better flexibility. It also benefited from various modifications including a revised cast-iron cylinder head with larger inlet passages and a raised compression ratio, a strengthened crankshaft, and

Driving a 1,911cc Traction Avant

You should not be deceived by the pre-war looks of the Traction Avant: this is a car that drives far more like a 'modern car' than any other classic vehicle designed in the 1930s. Above all, it has an extraordinary feeling of stability and security about its handling, cornering precisely and with no roll. The steering, although not as heavy as legend would have it, is not over-light, and you'll find that the lock is pretty poor, but otherwise the dynamics are excellent. The brakes are reassuringly effective.

Although the ride is on the firm side – at least by French standards – and the three-speed gearbox is a handicap, the torque of the 'big four' helps to overcome this disadvantage. The Traction has a natural 60mph cruising speed which can be maintained almost constantly – but don't try to push it above 4,000rpm!

And that 'mustard spoon' gearchange? It's actually a delight, moving tightly across the gate so that it's difficult to fluff a change. You shouldn't rush it, but you'll find that with a naturally gentle movement, pausing in neutral on the way through, you will engage gear cleanly each time. With an *Onze Légère*, finally, be prepared to be surprised by how compact the car seems; the *Normale*, on the other hand, feels altogether a bigger beast.

On the road in a late 11BL – note the straight bumpers that came in with the big boot. (LAT)

The final style of dashboard, with a grey top rail incorporating the speedo surround, was introduced in mid 1952. (LAT)

shell-type main and big-end bearings – along with revised pistons and valve gear and a cast-alloy sump. In fact, the new unit was derived from the engine that had been developed to power the Traction Avant's replacement, the DS19 saloon, which was to be launched later that year.

The adoption of the 11D engine was really the only major revision to be incorporated in the Traction Avant's mechanical specification throughout its long post-war career. Strangely, in view of its extended production life, no move was ever made to upgrade the electrical system from 6 volts to 12 volts, or even to replace its frail and inadequate three-speed gearbox, which was widely acknowledged to be the car's Achilles Heel.

Naturally the arrival of the DS19 signalled the demise of the Traction Avant. However, although it had originally been intended that the DS would supersede the Traction immediately and entirely, in fact the two cars continued to be assembled side by side for almost another two years, until the advent of the ID19. In the course of 1956, 39,395 *Tractions* were made, but only 9,936 DS19s. Even so, the end was now inevitable. The last car, an 11B Familiale, left the assembly line on 25 July 1957, bringing to a close an era that stretched back over three decades to the days of André Citroën.

Production of the Traction Avant had lasted for a total of 23 years, 4 months and 15 days, a world record for longevity at that time, though, as we shall see, this feat was later bettered by the 2CV. Between 1934 and 1957, a total of 700,961 examples were built at the Quai de Javel: 81,295 '7's of all types, 105,109 11AL & 11BL *Légères*, 53,856 11A & 11B *Normales* and 2,424 15-Sixes pre-war, plus 219,719 11BL *Légères*, 193,311 11B *Normales* and 45,247 15-Sixes post-war. To this tally can be added the 56,750 cars of all types built at Citroën's Belgian and British factories, making a grand combined total of 759,111 examples.

Buying Hints

1. The Familiale and Commerciale are rare, and the roadster and coupé even more so – and highly expensive too. Fake roadsters have been built over the years, consequently approach all examples with caution.

2. Buying a car in France is almost certain to be cheaper than buying in the UK, but be warned that some French restorations can be distinctly suspect. Remember, too, that although a British-sourced Slough-built car will be more expensive, it will also have a higher level of internal appointments.

3. Although the mechanical elements are robust, the *Traction* bodyshell is prone to corrosion, particularly the front and rear floors, the inner and outer sills, and the crossmember on which the front seats are mounted. A rippled roof or cracks in the body, in particular at the bottom of the screen pillars, are clues to a weakened body, as are binding doors. Check also for corrosion of the forward extensions to the body structure, either side of the engine bay.

4. Less serious rust-points are the bottom of the wings, the wing flanges where the wings are bolted to the body, the door bottoms, and the boot lid and the trough at the rear of the boot on small-boot models. On Slough cars with a sliding roof, the roof channels can rot, while defective drain tubes can cause rusting of the windscreen pillars.

5. The engine is sturdy and unproblematic; water pumps quite often leak, but rebuilding is straightforward.

6. Clicking on full lock indicates worn driveshaft outer UJs, whereas a drumming sound when the car is underway suggests worn inner joints. Some cars will have been fitted with modified driveshafts using modern CV outer joints and improved inner joints – an excellent updating.

7. The gearbox suffers from fading synchromesh and jumping out of gear. A whining transmission indicates final-drive problems – a weakness of the Traction Avant. You can check for excessive play by jacking up the front and seeing how much slop there is when you turn a wheel with the car in gear. Note that some cars will have been fitted with a four-speed gearbox from a later ID Citroën – perhaps even with an ID engine. These conversions are offered by respected specialists, and if you are not a purist they have much to be recommended.

8. Clutch judder may be nothing of the sort: it could be a defective rear engine mount or worn front suspension bushes. Judder under braking is another sign that these substantial rubber-and-metal bushes may have started to break up.

9. The steering should not be stiff, and it should not creak; if this is the case, the lower swivels may have seized.

10. Wear in the lower swivels can be checked by jacking the car up by each bottom arm, and then atempting to rock the wheel from top to bottom. Noisy suspension and judder under braking suggest worn inner bushes on the upper front suspension arms. If a sharp rearward kick to the front tyres provokes a 'clack', the diagnosis is confirmed; another test is to tug at the top of the front wheels.

11. Don't worry too much about a shabby interior on Paris-built cars: everything for a re-trim is available from French and Dutch specialists. Re-trimming a Slough car in leather is likely to be somewhat more costly.

In so far as it introduced (though not simultaneously) such key features as front-wheel drive, all-steel monocoque construction, hydraulic brakes, independent torsion-bar suspension, rack-and-pinion steering and radial tyres (a combination of features once unique to Citroën, but which have since been adopted almost universally elsewhere), the Traction Avant's significance was international. Among the most influential automobile designs ever produced, it is surely the linear ancestor of the modern family car.

At the end of 1953, the 11CV Commerciale, last seen in 1941, was also re-introduced. An ambulance version was available. (Citroën)

The six-cylinder
Traction Avant

A *rhd 15-Six built at Slough for the British and Commonwealth market in 1949. British-made examples always had chrome grilles and headlamps. (Brian Scott-Quinn)*

With the establishment of the Traction Avant range, no other French manufacturer offered so comprehensive a selection of variations on a single theme; rivals such as Renault preferred to continue producing a multiplicity of individual designs intended to appeal to different types of customer, a practice that André Citroën considered to be wasteful and uneconomic. Yet on the eve of the 1934 Paris *salon*, he revealed a further addition to the Traction Avant family, a high-performance V8 model

described as the fastest yet safest series production vehicle in the world.

The new car was the fabulous 22CV, a flagship model powered by a brand new 3,822cc ohv 90-degree V8 developing 79bhp at 3,500 rpm and claimed to be capable of 140kph or 87mph. Intended as André Citroën's riposte to Ford's flathead V8 introduced in 1932, the engine was effectively a doubled-up version of the 1,911cc 'four', with pushrod valve gear actuated by a single central camshaft located in the apex of the 'vee'.

Intended to include the same range of seven body styles as the '11', whose basic shell it shared, the '22CV' stood apart on account of its revised frontal appearance, with headlamps integrated into the wings in streamlined housings incorporating stylised horn grilles, and a wider grille with a prominent '8' motif. Listed at 32,000 to 38,000 francs, the 22CV cars would have been roughly twice the price of the basic 7CV saloon.

Unfortunately, André Citroën's plans for the 22CV never came to pass. After his death, the new masters of the Quai de Javel soon put a stop to the ambitious project. All the prototypes and demonstration cars were either destroyed or converted into 11CVs and sold off, leaving only the barest traces of its existence – to the point where today the '22' has an almost mythical status among Citroën enthusiasts.

From the fragments of reliable information that survive it is clear that the car was not without problems, especially in its braking, steering and handling – and there are stories of unfortunate accidents with prototype cars. Although the V8 engine appears to have performed well, it may well have been simply too powerful for its chassis, so that the 22CV was virtually undriveable because of a pronounced torque steer effect.

By 1937 the failings in the design and construction of the Traction Avant had largely been resolved. So in response to a demand for greater power and performance than was offered by the 11CV, the Michelin management turned its attention to a prestige model to occupy the top-of-the-range position previously intended for the 22CV.

There was no question of resurrecting the V8, or even of incorporating some of the 22CV's other special features such as its faired-in headlamps. Instead, to achieve the greatest possible commonality of parts, the engine chosen for the new large Traction Avant model, announced at the 1938 Paris *salon* as the 15-Six, was a 2,867cc straight-six based on the

11CV 'four' and having the same bore and stroke, allowing use of identical pistons and cylinder liners. This power plant developed 76bhp at 3,800rpm, just 3bhp less than the 22CV's V8, and enough to propel the car to an outright top speed of 78mph, only 11mph less than the maximum claimed for the 22CV. In fact, the 'six' packed a far more powerful punch than these figures suggest; its true performance can be gauged by its impressive torque of 141lb ft at 1,500rpm.

The 15-Six used a reinforced *Onze Normale* bodyshell, with a lengthened bonnet to accommodate the larger engine, making it a little over 4in longer overall. An entirely new three-speed gearbox and transmission were employed, together with a redesigned front cradle to accommodate the bigger engine and gearbox, while the driveshafts, swivels, suspension arms and torsion bars were also beefed up. In order to reduce the length of the gearbox, the compact layout adopted for its layshaft and differential required the engine to rotate in the opposite direction to normal, ie anti-clockwise from right to left when viewed from the front, so that the car was referred to as the 15-Six 'G' – for *gauche*, or 'left'.

From the exterior, the 15-Six could be distinguished from other Traction Avants by its radiator grille, which had the chevrons fixed behind rather than in front of the grille bars, and by having bonnet louvres rather than the adjustable vents then used on four-cylinder cars; additionally the horns were mounted on the front bumper irons, while the bumpers had small overriders. In its pre-war form the car was always painted black, with ivory Pilote wheels shod with 185x400 low-profile Pilote tyres. The headlamps were chromed, but otherwise there was a notable absence of brightwork. The 15-Six's interior was similarly subdued and restrained, with chestnut-brown velour seats and a painted dashboard identical to that of the four-cylinder cars but for two vertical brightwork bars in its centre.

Although a small pre-series was built

Traction Avant 15CV (post-war)
1947–1956

ENGINE:

Six-cylinder in-line, water-cooled

Capacity	2,867cc
Bore x stroke	78mm x 100mm
Valve actuation	Pushrod
Compression ratio	6.3:1
Carburettors	Single-choke Solex downdraught
Power output	76bhp SAE at 3,800rpm
Torque	138lb ft at 2,000rpm

TRANSMISSION:

Front-wheel drive

Three-speed, second and top synchronised

SUSPENSION:

Front: Independent, longitudinal torsion bars, upper and lower arms, telescopic dampers
Rear: Beam axle, transverse torsion bars, telescopic dampers; hydropneumatic suspension on 15H

STEERING:

Rack-and-pinion, unassisted
2½ turns lock-to-lock

BRAKES:

Drum, hydraulically operated

WHEELS/TYRES:

Michelin 'X' radial, 185x400

BODYWORK:

Four-door steel monocoque
Available post-war as saloon and (from 1953) six-light Familiale

DIMENSIONS ('Big Boot' Slough):

Length	15ft 11in
Wheelbase	10ft 1½in
Track	4ft 10½in
Width	5ft 10½in
Height	5ft 1½in

WEIGHT:

27.0cwt (with 5 galls fuel)

PERFORMANCE:

(Source: *The Autocar*)

Max speed	80mph
0–50mph	12.5sec
0–60mph	19.3sec

PRICE INCLUDING TAX WHEN NEW:

£1,333 (June1953)

NUMBERS BUILT: 50,602

The roadster version of the 3,822cc V8-engined 22CV, exhibited at the 1934 Paris Motor Show but never produced commercially. Note the faired-in headlights and double bumpers. (Citroën)

The 15-Six in pre-war limousine/Familiale form. The 15-Six had ventilation louvres in its bonnet from the outset, rather than the slats seen on the four-cylinder versions. Note also the Michelin Pilote wheels and painted radiator shell. (Citroën)

for members of the Michelin clan and other privileged customers in 1938, the first series-production 15-Six saloons did not appear until February 1939, priced at 36,500 francs – against 27,700 francs for an *Onze Normale*

saloon. The saloon was closely followed by long-wheelbase six-light limousine and Familiale models, in March and April 1939 respectively. A roadster was planned, but never introduced into regular production, although a handful

– perhaps five – were assembled, one of them after the war.

The *Reine de la Route* – or 'Queen of the Road' – as the 15-Six came to be called, soon won recognition as the foremost volume-production prestige

The two Presidential 15-Sixes

Early in 1955 the then President of France, René Coty (whose normal conveyance was a 15-Six saloon), commissioned from the coachbuilder Franay a closed state limousine based on the newly introduced 15-Six H. The styling of this car was actually the work of the well-known designer Philippe Charbonneaux. The limitations imposed by the restricted budget required that certain parts be bought off the shelf from elsewhere – the door handles, for example, came from a Bentley and the windscreen from a Ford Comète. The car was exhibited at the 1955 Paris *salon* and delivered to the Elysée palace shortly afterwards. Unfortunately, insufficient attention had been paid to upgrading the cooling system – essential for a ceremonial vehicle spending long periods on parade, moving at a walking pace. The result was that the car overheated and broke down when conveying HM the Queen during her state visit to Paris in 1957. Later, in 1963, the car was overhauled, modified and improved for the use of Coty's successor, President Charles de Gaulle.

In 1956 it was decided to add a new open-topped parade car to the Elysée fleet, once again based on the 15-Six H. This time the commission went to Henri Chapron. His styling of this second car was unabashedly American in its inspiration, with a kinked waistline at the 'C' pillar strongly reminiscent of the chrome moulding on the contemporary Chevrolet. The Traction Avant state cabriolet carried visiting royalty and heads of state for almost 20 years, serving throughout the presidencies of both General de Gaulle and Georges Pompidou, from 1956 to 1974.

These two coachbuilt ceremonial cars adapted from the 15-Six H for the President of France were used throughout the late 1950s and the 1960s. On the left is the limousine built by Franay in 1955, and on the right is the Chapron cabriolet of 1956. (Citroën)

car of France. A true *grande routière* in the tradition of such marques as Delage and Delahaye, it was a spacious, luxurious but relatively inexpensive high-performance tourer, capable of cruising the *routes nationales* with an unprecedented combination of speed and safety.

Following the resumption of Traction Avant production in June 1945, almost two years elapsed before the return of the 15-Six saloon in March 1947. At first the car was fitted with the pre-war six-cylinder engine which turned in an anti-clockwise direction, but, after only 240 examples had been built, the 15-Six G was superseded by the 15-Six D (for *droite*, or 'right'), equipped with

Chromed radiator shells were introduced on the 15-Six for 1949. (Citroën)

This 'small boot' 15-Six has the big-bladed 'cow-catcher' bumpers, introduced in June 1950. (Citroën)

a new three-speed gearbox that allowed the engine, which was also improved, to rotate in the normal clockwise direction.

Initially the external appearance of the post-war 15-Six was identical to that of the pre-war car, except that the headlamps were no longer chromed. In October 1947 the Pilote wheels were replaced by Michelin's new BM disc wheels, fitted with large dome-shaped chrome hubcaps from 1949, and in summer 1948 a new chromed grille was fitted – the headlamps remaining unchromed. During 1950 small opening air-scoops were fitted between the grille and the wings, to improve cooling, and the car was equipped with deeper straight-bar bumpers. It also received a revised dashboard, while interior trim was changed to chestnut, grey or aquamarine (bluish grey) velours.

Despite the popularity at that time of the American look, the 15-Six retained its sober, conservative appearance with an almost complete absence of brightwork: the only embellishments were the alloy wing spats and a broad polished-alloy decorative strip below the window line. The 15CV also retained its chromed horns on the front bumper, and had a '15 6 cyl' badge covering the starting-handle aperture, with another on the right-hand rear wing. In July 1952 the 15-Six was given the new 'big boot', together with other internal and external modifications including the repositioning of the windscreen wipers and the provision of direction indicators.

In July 1953 came the return of the long-wheelbase, six-light Familiale, which had been absent from the catalogue since 1940. As with its 11CV counterpart, it was a full nine-seater, thanks to the middle row of three folding occasional seats. At almost 16ft 4in in length, the 15-Six Familiale was the longest Traction Avant of all.

As with the 11CV, from October 1953 onwards a selection of new colours was introduced to supplement the habitual plain black finish that had been standard since the start of production. These new shades were pearl grey, iceland blue and

Special-bodied Traction Avants

Being a mass-produced and relatively cheap motor car of monocoque construction, it is hardly surprising that relatively few Traction Avants received specialist coachwork. It was really only post-war that a few examples were to be seen – primarily as a response to the fact that there was no longer a cabriolet in Citroën's catalogue – and as often as not these were based on the 15-Six.

It was the Swiss coachbuilders – talented in this field and with wealthy customers on their doorstep – who responded in the main to this gap in the market. Thus between 1948 and 1949 Worblaufen made 13-15 cabriolets, all on the 15-Six chassis, while Langenthal made a substantial 52

cabrios – 50 Onzes of both types and a pair of 15-Sixes. Graber also essayed a single 15-Six cabrio, while Beutler made just a single fixed-head 15-Six coupé.

Rather more common were roll-top saloons, with a full-length fabric hood. Pioneered pre-war by the Neuilly firm AEAT, this type of conversion was offered by various coachbuilders in France, Belgium, Holland, Switzerland and Germany – including, of course, AEAT itself. Plans were available for bodyshops who wished to do the work themselves, so it's perfectly feasible to come across a convertible-saloon of no obvious provenance.

One of the dropheads created by Swiss coachbuilder Langenthal. (Neill Bruce)

smoke grey. The following year the shade-card was further enhanced by the addition of midnight blue, airforce blue (or RAF blue), mist grey and heather grey. Even so, the traditional black remained the most popular choice.

In April 1954 the 15-Six underwent a major improvement when it became the first Citroën to be equipped with the company's unique independent, self-levelling hydropneumatic

suspension. This revolutionary technology was intended for the DS19, to be revealed at the 1955 Paris Motor Show. But to gain experience under normal service conditions, it was decided to fit this system to the series-production 15-Six – but on the rear wheels only, where it replaced the existing torsion bars and telescopic dampers.

Initially, the 15-Six H or *Hydraulique* was offered (in saloon form only) as an

Driving the 15-Six

Although the 15-Six Traction Avant is undoubtedly a large and heavy car with a poor steering lock, it is not a ponderous vehicle to drive, at least when parking manoeuvres, which require definite muscle power, are over and the car is on the move. On the contrary, the Citroën is remarkably agile in its handling and at speed it can always be positioned on the road with absolute precision.

The big 2.8-litre engine is lusty but refined, with massive torque at low revs – which helps overcome the disadvantage of the three-speed gearbox. Most of the time, in any case, only second and top are used, and changing between them using the 'mustard spoon' dashboard lever is easy work, provided that the action is not hurried.

The 15-Six is not a particularly fast car by modern standards, but once wound up to its natural cruising gait of 65–70mph its exceptional roadholding (allied to a characteristically firm ride) allows high average speeds to be maintained. Indeed, its excellent balance and exceedingly direct rack-and-pinion steering make it possible for its driver to change direction, swerve or take avoiding action rapidly with little risk of losing control: doubtless it was these very qualities that in its hey-day made it the chosen getaway car of French crooks.

From July 1952 the 15-Six was equipped with the big boot. But until October 1953 it was still only available in black, with ivory wheels teamed with the large chromed hubcaps that had been introduced for 1950. (Ludvigsen)

optional alternative to the conventionally sprung 15-Six 'D' saloon. However, the greatly improved comfort, stability and security afforded by the new suspension system was quickly recognised by motoring press and public alike, and so despite its considerably higher price (940,000 francs as opposed to 870,000 francs) the 'H' very soon began to outsell its sister saloon, which was withdrawn early the following year – though the 15-Six 'D' Familiale continued in production until August 1955.

When parked with its suspension system de-pressurised, the 15-Six 'H' could easily be distinguished from its conventionally-sprung sister car by its low-slung attitude at the rear, but with the engine running and the car on the move there were few visual clues to mark the two vehicles apart. A giveaway was that to provide a softer ride, in phase with the rear, the front suspension had elongated, more flexible torsion bars which protruded

The final incarnation of the Traction Avant was the 15-Six H, or Hydraulique, introduced in May 1954. On this model, the torsion bar springs of the rear wheels only were replaced by the fluid-and-gas springs of Citroën's hydropneumatic suspension system, soon to be employed on all four wheels of the DS19. (Citroën)

well beyond the leading edge of the front wings; there was also a '15H 6 cyl' badge on the boot lid.

The last 15-Six H saloon was built in July 1956. Just 3,079 examples had been produced, in contrast to 42,168 conventionally sprung 15CVs. Thus a grand total of 47,671 examples of the six-cylinder Traction Avant were constructed – 2,424 pre-war and 45,247 post war.

Buying Hints

1. In general, the advice given for the four-cylinder cars applies equally to the 15-Six – although you should note that engine overhauls will, logically enough, be at least half as much again more expensive.

2. Only two surviving 15-Six roadsters are known to have an absolutely genuine provenance.

3. Judder when taking up power, accompanied by a smell of burnt rubber, is a sign that the rubber-and-metal driveshaft dampers used on the 15-Six are in a state of disintegration. Replacements are available, on exchange.

4. Top wishbone inner bushes are of silentbloc type on the 15-Six, and do not wear in the same fashion as do the metal bushes on four-cylinder cars; the tests mentioned in the previous chapter do not therefore apply.

5. You are unlikely to come across many 15-H 'sixes'. Should you set your heart on one, check that the rear suspension rises up quickly, that the pump does not click at intervals shorter than 20 seconds when the car is idling, and that when the ignition is turned off the rear of the car does not slump rapidly; check also for fluid leaks. Beware that parts specific to the 15-H hydraulics will be very difficult to source.

The Type H van

In the characteristic metallic grey in which most were supplied, this 'H' dates from the 1964–69 model-year period, as it has a single-piece windscreen but the original style of rounded rear wheelarches. (Citroën)

The Traction Avant and the 2CV were not the only Citroëns to shape the motoring landscape of post-war France. At the 1947 Paris Motor Show a strange, angular, corrugated-panelled tin-box-on-wheels was launched – the unmistakeable Type H van, a symbol of all that was inventive and original about the output of the Quai de Javel.

More than just a national institution, the 'H' was the first commercial vehicle to combine front-wheel drive, rack-and-pinion steering and all-independent torsion-bar suspension. It was also among the first to adopt the layout now standard practice on modern-day vans: forward-control, a walk-through cab with no separation of front compartment from rear cargo

The TUB

Type H van
1948–1981

The 'H' was a development of ideas first seen in Citroën's pre-war TUB van, produced in small numbers between 1939 and 1941. The TUB boasted such advanced features as torsion-bar independent front suspension, hydraulic brakes, and rack-and-pinion steering – and more particularly pioneered the forward-control configuration for European light commercials. It differed from the Type H, however, in that its body was supported on a conventional chassis frame. The TUB was constructed largely from flat panels, with roll-up canvas side-curtains – a feature found on the very first 'H' vans. Powered by the engine of the 7CV Traction Avant, it had a payload of 850kg – or 1,200kg in later TUC form, when it used the 11CV engine.

Progenitor of the 'H' was the pre-war TUB, based on Traction Avant mechanicals and built on a separate chassis. (Citroën)

area, a sliding side door to allow loading and unloading directly from the kerb, and a very low load-floor. This last feature was emphasised by a versatile three-part tailgate, formed by a top-hinged upper section and two side-hinged lower doors, permitting walk-in access.

This layout was made possible by the adoption of unitary construction, the body being built on a flat platform instead of the traditional ladder frame chassis. Another useful feature of the design was its ease of maintenance, as the engine, transmission and front axle could simply be detached and withdrawn forward as one single unit.

The most striking feature of the Type H, though, was its corrugated panelling. Drawing on the same principle used on the Junkers JU52 aircraft, this gave stiffness to flat thin-gauge panelwork, thereby enabling smaller quantities of scarce sheet steel to be used. The whole design was arranged to allow for simple yet strong construction using only the most basic metal-forming techniques, avoiding the necessity of expensive tools and presses.

The floorpan itself was a punt-type platform structure, strengthened by substantial longerons or side-members running beneath it. Along its lower flanks ran two hollow chambers providing additional stiffness; these

ENGINE:
Four-cylinder in-line, water-cooled
Capacity — 1,628cc/1,911cc (petrol)
Bore x stroke — 72mm x 100mm / 78mm x 100mm
Valve actuation — Pushrod
Compression ratio — 7.5:1
Carburettors — Single-choke Zenith downdraught
Power output — 43bhp SAE at 4,000rpm (9CV) / 56bhp SAE at 4,100rpm (11CV)
Torque — n/a

TRANSMISSION:
Front-wheel drive
Three-speed, second and top synchronised

SUSPENSION:
Front: Independent, longitudinal torsion bars, upper and lower arms, telescopic dampers
Rear: Independent, transverse torsion bars, telescopic dampers

STEERING:
Rack-and-pinion, unassisted

BRAKES:
Drum, hydraulically operated

WHEELS/TYRES:
Michelin radial, 400x17in

BODYWORK:
Steel monocoque
Available as van, pick-up, chassis/cab

DIMENSIONS (normal wheelbase):
Length — 14ft 0½in
Wheelbase — 8ft 3in
Track, front — 5ft 3½in
Track, rear — 5ft 5in
Width — 6ft 5in
Height — 7ft 8in

WEIGHT:
N/A

PERFORMANCE:
(Source: Citroën)
Max speed — 56mph/63mph

PRICE INCLUDING TAX WHEN NEW:
Not available in UK

NUMBER BUILT: 473,289

H vans around the world

Although its principal home was France, the 'H' was also assembled in Belgium (1952–63), Holland (1963–70), and in Portugal. From 1968, Dutch-built examples had front-hinged doors, to meet legal requirements, and after assembly had ceased in Holland those vans for the Dutch, Belgian and Swiss markets were supplied from France with forward-hinged doors. The 'H' was never sold in Britain, although in the late 1950s the Slough works proposed adding the van to its catalogue, and took the trouble to convert three H-types to right-hand drive as prototypes.

contained on the right-hand side the petrol tank and on the left the spare wheel. Moreover, as the rear wheelarches intruded only minimally, the load capacity in relation to overall dimensions was particularly impressive – the 'H' was in effect a cube on wheels.

No other contemporary vehicle was so flexible or adaptable, and indeed the Type H offered operators an unparalleled degree of practicality, versatility, safety and comfort for the

The farmers of France found plenty of uses for the Type H van. (Citroën)

time. Its small wide wheels were located at its corners for optimum handling and roadholding, while its low, wide platform floor ensured maximum stability, thanks to its low centre of gravity even when fully loaded to its initial 1,200kg (1.2 ton) payload. So for over 30 years it acted as the standard delivery van of urban and rural France, serving in a hundred different guises: mini-bus, ambulance, fire-appliance, police 'paddy-wagon', horse-box, cattle-truck, car-transporter, tipper-wagon, furniture pantechnicon, workshop-on-wheels, mobile post-office – and of course

Driving an H van

If the idea of piloting a medium-sized van is something new for you, rest assured: the 'H' is no chore to drive. Indeed, it's actually quite fun. So long as you accept that speed is not on the agenda, even with the 1,911cc petrol-engined version, and providing you can live with very high noise levels, you'll find that the 'H' will churn along happily, corner with stability, and ride with surprising comfort thanks to its relatively long-travel suspension and soft damping. The three-speed gearbox, one cause of the noise and the limited performance, is easy to manipulate, the steering heavy only when manoeuvring, and the brakes perfectly adequate. As a fun workhorse for a small business you could do a lot worse, although you should not expect anything other than mediocre fuel consumption.

The rear bumper bars were designed so ramps could be hooked to them, as here. Note that this is a pre-1953 example with the fabric side curtains. (Citroën)

Its low flat floor and walk-in rear doors made the 'H' ideal for use as a mobile shop. Clearly visible is the roll-up left-hand side-curtain fitted to the earliest examples. (Citroën)

motorised shop or café, in which role it was a familiar sight at markets across the country.

Entering production in June 1948, the Type H was powered by a detuned version of the 11CV Traction Avant engine, a 1,911cc unit developing a modest 35bhp at 3,500rpm. This engine was coupled to a three-speed gearbox, the powertrain being reversed so that the engine sat forward of the transmission and ahead of the driven front wheels. Speed was never a strong point; nevertheless, the torque available at low revs made for adequately brisk and tractable progress around town. Even when fully loaded the van could be driven about in second gear all the time, with scarcely a need to change up or down.

In October 1948, a second version, the HZ, was announced, also painted in the same metallic grey that was to remain standard on the 'H' for many years. Although its engine and overall dimensions were identical to those of its sister vehicle, its payload was reduced to 850kg (0.84 ton) and its top speed raised from 49mph to 55mph, thanks to different gearbox ratios. October 1949, finally, saw a third version, the 1,500kg (1.5 ton) HY; notwithstanding its increased payload it was no larger, and used the same powertrain. In September 1958 the original 1,200kg payload H van was discontinued and the 1,500kg capacity HY upgraded to offer a total permissible kerb weight of 2,925kg (57.6cwt), up from the previous 2,600kg (51.2cwt).

Throughout its long career, the technical evolution of the 'H' was slow but steady. Most notable were the changes made under the bonnet, which commenced in May 1955 when the improved 11D version of the

1,911cc engine was fitted, in detuned form. Then, from January 1960, a British 1,621cc Perkins 4/99 diesel engine was offered as an option, initially only on the HY but a year later also on the HZ. Next, in September 1963, a new 1,628cc petrol engine – a version of the DS unit with alloy cross-flow head – was introduced on both the HY and the HZ, raising the top speed of the former to 57mph and of the latter to 55mph; from 1967 this engine was also available in 1,911cc form. Finally, in February 1964, a new French diesel was announced. This was an 1,810cc unit developing 50bhp at 4,000rpm, and was built by the Indenor company (Industrie de Nord SA) co-owned by Citroën and Peugeot; from 1970 it wholly replaced the Perkins power unit.

During its 34-year life the appearance of the 'H' barely changed. In February 1964 a one-piece windscreen replaced the archaic split screen, and later that year the full-width double chevrons on the grille gave way to a smaller badge, mounted centrally. At the same time, the metallic grey which had been the

only colour ever available on the 'H' was joined by off-white, pale blue and pale yellow. The only other modification of importance came in November 1969, when the rear wheelarches were changed from a semi-circular pressing to one that was rectangular. Thus from first to last, all vehicles in the Type H range had forward-opening suicide doors – with the exception of the last Dutch-assembled vehicles of 1968-70 and vehicles made for certain export markets.

Throughout its production lifespan the Type H series was also available as a low-sided pick-up truck and as an unfinished chassis-with-cab, for fitting with specialist coachwork. Firms such as AEAT, Currus and Heuliez adapted the kits supplied by Citroën to meet the individual requirements of their customers – sometimes going the whole way and devising entirely fresh bodywork bearing no resemblance to the original. By the time that production ceased in December 1981, over 473,000 examples of the 'H' had been constructed.

Not least among the H-type's virtues was its versatility and adaptability, which allowed it to perform a wide variety of public-service duties. This fire appliance has an extended rear body. (Citroën)

Right: For more than 30 years, the Type H van was an essential part of the French rural scene, serving as a motorised market stall. (Citroën)

Buying Hints

1. The chassis resists rust well, but check the main chassis rails and the front and rear crossmembers for corrosion; the smaller crossbracing members are less vulnerable. The traverse at the very rear is notably decay-prone, especially if the vehicle has been used to transport livestock – you can probably work out why . . .

2. The body doesn't stand up well to the elements – and for some reason the Netherlands-built versions are less rust-resistant than French examples. Check for corrosion along the bottom of the body, especially around the jacking points: this area is often bodged with filler. Rust also breaks through by the headlamps, and to the top and bottom of the rectangular pressing behind the driver's door, as well as along the guttering.

3. The doors can develop cracks along their rear edge, and the steps up into the cab can break away. Check all the moving panels for rust and free operation.

4. Some play in the steering is not unusual. Check also for play in the rear swinging arms. The front suspension is basically as the 15-Six Traction Avant, so the same checks apply.

5. Mechanicals are unburstable, so long as regular maintenance has been carried out – which is why you're laughing if you manage to locate a low-mileage former fire-service 'H' with full service record…and these do still come onto the market in France, albeit rarely these days. On petrol engines rattles from the tappets and/or timing chain aren't unusual, and there are often leaks from the sump area – hardly serious problems.

6. The petrol engines take about 2-3 miles to warm up, and the gearchange should not be rushed. If the gears 'snick' when the car is warm, despite gentle handling, the synchromesh is likely to be fading.

7. The 'H' makes an excellent camper-van. If this tempts you, the best method is to find an old two-berth trailer caravan from the 1960s and use its furnishings for the Citroën.

8. Parts supply is less good than it used to be, but mechanical parts are obtainable without too much difficulty. Having contacts in France helps – and there's a good French club. Most French scrapyards have the odd 'H' quietly mouldering away, and this is your best source for secondhand bits – especially body panels.

The 2CV

Once the Traction Avant had been refined and re-engineered into a reliable and profitable product, Pierre Boulanger and Citroën's new Michelin management turned to a new challenge: the creation of a small and cheap motor car for rural use. As defined by Boulanger, the *Toute Petite Voiture* ('Very Small Car') – or TPV – was to be a motorised pony-cart, for people with no previous experience of motor cars, or indeed of owning machinery of any kind. As pre-war France was predominantly an agrarian nation of farmers, smallholders and winegrowers living in widely-scattered villages and small market towns, what was needed was a lightweight, all-purpose, go-anywhere car that even a farmer's wife could drive, to replace the bicycle, pony-trap or horse-drawn wagon for bringing produce to market.

No more than 'four wheels under an umbrella', it was to be capable of carrying two peasants, plus 50kg (110lb) of potatoes or a small cask of wine, in the greatest comfort over the poorest roads – so that even when transporting a basket of eggs over a ploughed field, not one single egg would be broken. Economy, practicality and versatility were what mattered: the appearance of the finished vehicle would be unimportant but the highest priority was attached to reliability and durability.

Tasked with the job, André Lefèbvre

During the late 1950s Citroën began to advertise the Deux Chevaux with glamour photos like this. Up till then it had sold well enough by word of mouth alone; in fact the waiting list accounted for several years of production. (Citroën)

tackled a specifically French transportation problem in an idiomatically French way, with radical, inventive and original ideas that were at the same time entirely logical: typically, thanks to his aeronautical background, he approached the priorities of automobile design from a different perspective.

For maximum stability and ease of control in inexperienced hands the car would have front-wheel drive, with its engine and gearbox ahead of the front wheels. Secondly, it would be equipped with rack-and-pinion steering, geared to give just 2.3 turns lock-to-lock and set up to offer very pure steering geometry, free of bump-steer and fight-back effects. Thirdly, to give a comfortable ride, a fully independent torsion-bar suspension would be adopted, with generous wheel travel to cope with rough terrain. Finally, for maximum fuel economy, the TPV would be made as light as possible – 300kg (5.9cwt) at the most – through using aluminium

Pre-war TPVs

Shortly after the outbreak of war, P-J Boulanger ordered that those of the first batch of 250 TPVs that had been completed should be hidden for the duration. In 1949 he decreed that all the remaining examples of the TPV should be destroyed. One, however, had already escaped: used as a pick-up truck by Michelin at Clermont-Ferrand during the war, it had been thrown out as scrap in 1946 but was saved from destruction and is today exhibited at the Musée Henri Malartre, in Rochetaillée-sur-Saône. For two decades this appeared to be the only survivor, but in 1968 a complete car was discovered at la Ferté-Vidame and restored by Citroën for publicity purposes. Later, in 1994, the old-car world was amazed to learn that three more complete examples had been uncovered at la Ferté-

2CV

1949–1990

ENGINE:
Two-cylinder horizontally-opposed, air-cooled
Capacity
 375cc/425cc/435cc/602cc
Bore x stroke
 62mm x 62mm/66mm x 62mm
 68.5mm x 59mm/74mm x 70mm
Valve actuation
 Pushrod
Compression ratio
 6.2:1 (375cc); 8.5:1 (late 602cc)
Carburettor
 Single-choke Solex downdraught
Power output
 9bhp SAE at 3,500rpm (375cc)
 29bhp DIN at 5,750rpm (late 602cc)
Torque
 16.6lb ft at 1,800rpm (375cc)
 29lb ft at 3,500rpm (late 602cc)

TRANSMISSION:
Front-wheel drive
Four-speed, all synchronised

SUSPENSION:
Front: Independent, by leading arm, with horizontal coil springs interlinked to rear suspension; inertia and friction dampers (latterly telescopic dampers)
Rear: Independent, by trailing arm, with horizontal springs interlinked to front suspension; inertia and friction dampers (latterly telescopic dampers)

STEERING:
Rack-and-pinion, unassisted 2½ turns lock-to-lock

BRAKES:
Drum, hydraulically operated; inboard at front. Disc front brakes from 1981

WHEELS/TYRES:
Michelin 'X' radial, 125x400

BODYWORK:
Platform chassis; steel body with fabric roof Available as four-door saloon, van, (UK-built) pick-up

DIMENSIONS:
Length	12ft 6¾in (late cars)
Wheelbase	7ft 9¼in
Track	4ft 1½in
Width	4ft 10¼in
Height	5ft 3in

WEIGHT:
13.5cwt (375cc, with 5 galls fuel)
15.5cwt (602cc, as tested – *Autocar* figure)

PERFORMANCE (375cc/602cc):
(Source: *The Autocar*)
Max speed	39.3mph/69mph
0-30mph	22.7sec/6.5sec
0-60mph	unobtainable/32.7sec

PRICE INCLUDING TAX WHEN NEW:
£565 (Dec 1953);
£2,285 (2CV6 Special, Jan 1982)

NUMBERS BUILT:
3,868,634 saloons, 1,246,335 vans

Vidame, having been hidden in a barn on a remote part of the estate. Thus a total of five pre-war TPVs exist today.

Constructed from light alloy and canvas to save weight, the pre-war TPV had only one headlight as two were not then required by legislation. (Citroën)

Pierre-Jules Boulanger

Although Pierre-Jules Boulanger was undoubtedly the father of the 2CV, he was not its designer in the accepted sense of the word. He was an administrator and industrialist, and not an engineer. Even so, as a man who had a genuine love of cars and an enthusiasm for driving, he played a vital, active part in its creation, in particular by personally testing prototypes throughout all stages of the 2CV's development. Indeed, he was so closely identified with the creation of this spartan, quasi-monastic, utilitarian vehicle that it seemed to reflect not just his philosophy but also his very personality and physique: tall and lean and wearing a trilby hat rather than the Frenchman's traditional beret, he fathered a car with notably generous headroom and legroom.

Pierre-Jules Auguste Vital Boulanger was born in 1885 at Sin-le-Noble, on the outskirts of Douai in northern France. At the age of 23 he emigrated to the US, arriving on the west coast in 1908. After working as a ranch-hand in the Rockies and a tram-driver in San Francisco, he was employed as a draftsman with a firm of Seattle architects, and by 1911, at the age of 25, he was his own boss, having founded a construction firm in British Columbia.

On the outbreak of the First World War, as a reservist Boulanger returned to France to rejoin the unit in which he had completed his national service in 1906–8. Eventually he became a specialist in aerial photographic reconnaissance, flying behind enemy lines in spotter aircraft to observe German troop movements and artillery positions. In 1917, he was shot down, suffering injuries that confined him to hospital for six months. For this exploit he was awarded the Légion d'Honneur. Ultimately he was decorated eight times for bravery and meritorious service, winning amongst other

Pierre-Jules Boulanger, 1885–1950, the architect-turned-industrialist who ran Citroën from 1935 until 1950. Although he did not actually design the 2CV, it was created under his direction and its character undoubtedly reflected his austere personality. (Citroën)

medals the Belgian Croix de Guerre, the American Distinguished Service Medal and the British OBE.

During the war, Boulanger renewed his friendship with Marcel Michelin (whom he had met during his national service) and with the Michelin family at Clermont-Ferrand, making such a favourable impression that Marcel's uncle, Edouard Michelin, head of the Michelin organisation, invited him to join the tyre firm when the conflict was over. Boulanger accepted and by 1922, now aged 37, he had worked his way up to its upper management echelons.

When Michelin took over Citroën, he became joint managing director, reporting to Edouard Michelin and his son Pierre. Unfortunately in December 1937 Pierre Michelin was killed when driving from Paris to Clermont-Ferrand. Boulanger was immediately appointed as chairman of Citroën and later, in 1938, as a co-director of Michelin.

Boulanger was a most unlikely person to replace the ebulliently optimistic *bon viveur* André Citroën.

Completely contrasting in both personality and physique, he was a dour introspective man who disliked flamboyant self-promotion and always avoided the free-wheeling socialising and junketing that so appealed to his predecessor. A tall, austere-looking figure with close-cropped grey hair and a trim grey moustache, he always dressed in a quasi-uniform of grey suit, grey shirt and grey tie, completed by a grey felt hat and an enormous, crumpled grey raincoat, and was never seen without a Gitane cigarette dangling from his mouth. Some observers said that he was more of a Michelin than any of the family themselves.

Boulanger established at Citroën a research department which at the time was unrivalled by any other automotive company in the world. By encouraging its staff to avoid imitation and reject dogma and convention, he fostered a remarkable esprit de corps. But despite his commitment to progress, his approach was always practical and pragmatic. Being self-taught, he preferred to employ similar *autodidactes* and people who had studied at the Arts and Métiers technical colleges, believing that engineers trained at the universities and the *Grandes Ecoles* were blinkered by their formal education and incapable of truly original thought.

Reserved and austere in demeanour, he deplored egotism and self-promotion and was completely uninterested in the material rewards of achievement that normally motivate motor industry bosses, preferring to work in a sparse office devoid of the normal trappings of executive power and prestige. In Boulanger's scale of values, simplicity was never to be equated with poverty, or frugality with deprivation, and his abhorrence of ostentation, frivolity and self-indulgence was reflected in the car that he created.

alloys instead of steel. Built on a separate platform chassis of welded aluminium, the bodywork would have no structural function other than to protect occupants, cargo and mechanical components from the elements. To save weight and expense, the roof would be in fabric and the side windows in plastic rather than glass.

Eventually, in December 1938, after having personally tested scores of prototypes, Boulanger authorised series production for the following May, so that a stock of around 250 cars would be ready for launch at the Paris Motor Show in October 1939. Had this happened, it would surely have been a commercial disaster: the TPV would almost certainly have proved problematic to manufacture in quantity, and would have been severely criticised for its exaggerated crudeness. But fortunately for

Boulanger and his staff, the outbreak of war prevented the car's debut, and during the occupation Citroën had time to begin a complete redesign.

The expensive and complicated torsion bar arrangement was replaced by horizontally mounted coil springs, interlinked between front and rear to prevent pitching and give the car a very comfortable ride. Damping was achieved by both integral friction units and the unusual feature of inertia dampers – quite literally lead weights that moved up and down in cylinders attached to each wheel.

The original water-cooled engine was replaced by an all-new air-cooled light alloy flat-twin. A marvel of compact, weight-saving design and high-quality precision engineering, it was capable of running flat-out for 100 hours non-stop, the equivalent of travelling 50,000 miles at maximum revs without a break. Reputedly

Exaggerated roll when cornering is typical 2CV. This particular car was built before June 1953, as shown by the oval-ringed double-chevron badge on its grille. (LAT)

The original 2CV dashboard was spartan in the extreme, and featured a separate speedo that also drove the wipers; the only other instrument was an ammeter, petrol level being determined by a dipstick. (LAT)

The 2CV Engine

Citroën's engines have often been unfairly dismissed as a disappointment, with performance unworthy of the cars which they powered and being less refined and sophisticated than the rest of the vehicle in question. But there can be no such criticism of the power plant that propelled the 2CV.

Designed by Walter Becchia, who joined Citroën from Talbot in 1941, it must surely rank as a high point in the evolution of the internal-combustion engine and one of the very greatest achievements of automotive design. It was certainly among the most enduring; of its contemporaries, VW Beetle flat-four excepted, only the Jaguar XK engine lasted anywhere near as long – for 38 years compared with the 2CV unit's unbeaten record of 42 years in continuous production, between 1948 and 1990.

Brilliantly simple, utterly logical, Becchia's lightweight, air-cooled design eliminated almost all the normal electrical and cooling-system trouble spots of conventional engines of its era. With no radiator to leak, no hoses to burst, no fan belt to break, no pump to seize up and no coolant to freeze or cause corrosion, there was precious little to go wrong. By attaching the fan to the end of the crankshaft, and locating an oil-cooler in the resulting airflow, optimum working

temperature was guaranteed for as long as the engine continued turning.

Moreover, by dispensing with the normal distributor and placing the contact-breaker on the end of the camshaft, working in conjunction with a double-ended coil to provide a spark at both plugs for every revolution of the crankshaft, enduringly accurate ignition timing was also assured, despite the waste of a spark – and since there was no high-tension current at the contact-breakers, the life of the points was also extended. To reduce moving parts, even the dynamo was designed to work integrally with the crankshaft, its armature forming the spigot to

which the fan was attached.

In short, the 2CV engine exhibited a sophistication and precision that completely belied its rustic sound. Manufactured and assembled to a tolerance of one micron, the fit between the principal components was so precise that gaskets could be dispensed with throughout. The integral crankcase and sump was an aluminium-alloy casting split vertically along the centre line and these two halves with their respective single cast-iron cylinder, finned for cooling, plus the alloy cylinder head with its hemispherical combustion chamber, were all bolted together in an exact, oil-tight and gas-tight fit

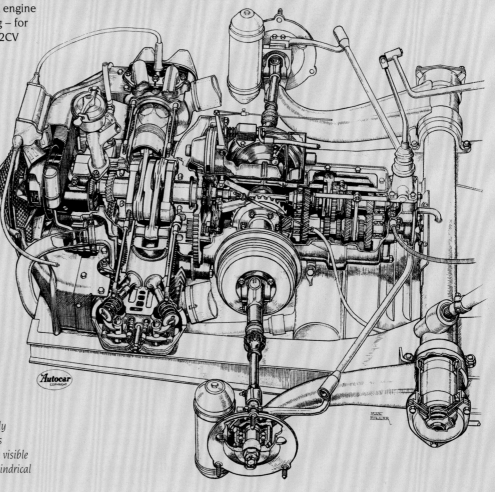

The 2CV's engine was a profoundly ingenious design, as shown by this cutaway from The Autocar. *Also visible are the inboard brakes and the cylindrical inertia dampers.* (LAT)

without the need for the usual seals.

But perhaps the most interesting and unusual feature of the 2CV engine lay in the ingenious crankshaft and con-rod assembly. For maximum strength and perfect balance, the normal practice of using split big-ends with two-piece bearings retained by bolted-on caps was rejected in favour of one-piece con-rods with sleeve bearings, fitted to the crankshaft at the assembly stage, the whole forming an extremely rigid and compact self-contained assembly. This integral five-piece crankshaft unit – comprising the crankpins, bearings, webs, con-rods and the front journal bearing – was pressed together hydraulically at the factory, the crankshaft having first been temporarily shrunk by immersion in liquid nitrogen.

As the various component parts could not be stripped down and replaced independently, main-bearing failure meant that the entire unit had to be exchanged. Yet thanks to the low thermal and mechanical stresses inherent in the design, this was rare. Provided that the sump contained the correct amount of clean oil at the start of the journey, and that the grille muff was removed when cruising fast, the 2CV engine could always be relied upon to run flat-out at maximum revs for hours and hours on end without missing a beat.

When production began, factory bench tests established the engine could withstand 100 hours at full throttle (5,000 rpm) without damage, the equivalent of travelling 50,000 miles flat-out, without a stop. It is hardly surprising, then, that under normal driving conditions, countless thousands of high-spirited 2CV drivers subsequently discovered that the harder it was pushed, the better Becchia's engine performed, and that vigorous use of the throttle had absolutely no effect on overall fuel consumption.

designed within the space of a week, to the same 375cc capacity and overall layout as the earlier design, it combined extreme simplicity and reliability of operation with excellent fuel economy, and could be depended upon to start first time, whatever the weather – although with no electric starter this could only be achieved by hand.

As for the body, this was no longer so crude, although it was still largely unstyled, and was fashioned from steel rather than aluminium – as was the platform chassis. Flat-panelled, to save on expensive presswork, it featured lift-off doors, front wings that could be removed by slackening four nuts, and simple flap-type opening windows at the front in conjunction with fixed windows in the rear doors. The suspended hammock seats of the pre-war cars, meanwhile, gave way to simple tubular-framed benches with rubber-strap springing, both front and rear seats being easily removable. Inevitably the car's weight had increased, as more and more extra but essential items were incorporated into the design, such as proper window glass, a second headlamp and a rudimentary heating system. Even so, Boulanger still drew the line at a conventional electric starter motor; his intention – only abandoned after the car's 1948 unveiling – was that the car would be equipped with a recoil starter device, operated by a cord pulled from the driver's seat, to avoid the weight and cost of a battery.

When the TPV made its memorable debut at the Paris Motor Show in October 1948, few visitors could have predicted that it was destined to stay in production for 41 years and to sell almost seven million examples. Indeed, the press panned the car. With one exception, not a single reviewer had the foresight to suggest that the 2CV would become a landmark in motoring history.

Even Citroën's own dealers thought that Boulanger had made a huge mistake, begging him to change his plans, or at least to do something to beautify the car. But the *patron* was adamant – the 2CV was not meant to

be a status symbol or object of prestige like other cars, and the launch would go ahead regardless. As he proudly presented the three first examples, the crowds surged onto the stand to get a closer look. Security guards had to prevent the public forcing open the sealed bonnets to inspect the mechanicals and to stop them bouncing the cars up and down to see the novel suspension in action. In fact, the bonnets were empty, as the engine specification had not been finalised. No matter: thousands of orders were taken on the first day alone and by the end of the proceedings over one and a quarter million visitors had flocked to the stand.

Sales began in July 1949, with only 924 cars made by the end of that year, all in a dark metallic grey. Since the 2CV's unveiling its price had climbed by some 25 per cent to 228,000 francs, but the waiting list lengthened by the day. The first examples went to customers claiming a particularly deserving need, especially those in rural occupations such as doctors, midwives, vets and priests. Also favoured were the country shopkeepers, tradesmen, smallholders, farmers and wine-growers for whom the car had always been intended. By February 1950, just 1,086 examples had been delivered, all of them to the kind of drivers who, in Boulanger's words, 'have to travel by car because of their work and for whom ordinary cars are too dear to buy'. By 1952 – when the sole colour changed to a non-metallic dark grey with ivory wheels – production was nudging 400 cars a week, but an 18-month wait was still unavoidable, no matter how prominent or influential the customer.

In October 1954 a new model, the AZ, joined the range, its principal feature being an enlarged engine of 425cc, developing 12bhp. This 33 per cent increase in power boosted top speed to almost 50mph. A centrifugal clutch, which disengaged automatically when the car was at a standstill, was also standard on the AZ, making town driving easier.

The archetypal 2CV, a 1957 model-year AZL: note the bigger rear window and the extra aluminium trim strips. Until 1959 the only colour available was grey. (Citroën)

In December 1960 the 2CV was given a new bonnet and grille, though little else was changed. Originally intended as transport for farmers and country folk, the 2CV continued to fulfil this role throughout the sixties and beyond. This car is finished in Panama Yellow. (Citroën)

The 2CV van

Although rarely seen in the UK, the 2CV van or *fourgonnette* played as important a part in the story as the more familiar saloon – ultimately, 1¼ million examples were built, accounting for nearly a third of total 2CV production.

First seen at the 1950 Paris show, sales of the Type AU van began in spring that year. The payload was of 250kg (roughly ¼ ton), and the saloon's 9bhp 375cc engine was used. From the 1955 model year the 425cc power unit was standardised, however, and the van given the AZU designation.

In this guise it continued largely unchanged until July 1961, when it received the new bonnet introduced on the 2CV saloons at the end of the previous year. The oval porthole-like windows in the rear doors continued until spring 1963, though, when the van's appearance was modernised with large rectangular windows for the rear doors and the introduction of square windows in the side panels – which lost their ribbing to facilitate sign-writing.

Originally painted in metallic dark grey, like the 2CV saloon, and then from October 1952 in dark non-metallic grey with matching wheels, for the 1961 model year the vans became a little more colourful: buyers were given the additional choice of cactus green or pastis yellow.

In May 1963 the 350kg payload (0.34 ton) AK 350 model joined the range. Powered by the 3CV 602cc Ami engine, the AK was immediately recognisable by its longer body overhanging the rear wheels by an extra 8in. With a full 22bhp at its disposal, the AK was good for a 53mph top speed.

This AKS, displaying the final style of grille, has a taller roof and the longer rear overhang introduced on the AK; as an AKS it has indentations rather than corrugations to strengthen the side panels. (Citroën)

The vans gained front-hinged doors at the same time – December 1964 – as the saloons, and in August 1967 the AZU gained a 21bhp engine; in May 1968 the AK saw its power boosted to 29bhp.

In July 1970 came a modernised and improved AK, christened the AKS 400. An enlarged high-roof body took payload to 400kg, and the rear panelwork had strengthening corrugations in the form of indentations rather than protruding ribs or ripples; in 1972, the smaller 250kg AZU received this new style of bodywork, and went on to receive the new 435cc power unit.

In these two forms the van continued to be listed until March 1978, with only one change of note: in January 1974 the side-windows were deleted

Just as important in the story of the 2CV is the fourgonnette or light van, introduced in March 1951. The oval rear windows lasted until 1963. (Citroën)

for taxation reasons . . . only to reappear in January 1977. There is however, a final twist to the story of the 2CV van: although displaced in March 1978 by the Dyane-based Acadiane, manufacture in fact continued quietly until 1981 to honour fleet orders from the French post office and the state-owned EDF electricity company.

Between 1965 and 1974 the 2CV featured this third type of grille; also new for 1966 was the six-light body configuration. This photo was taken in 1972, and shows the round winkers on the front wings introduced in 1970. (Citroën)

In 1956, the 2CV catalogue was further expanded by the introduction, in November, of the AZL. Costing 392,000 old francs as opposed to the 352,000 francs of the basic 2CVA, this de-luxe model boasted a demister – for the driver's side only – and seats covered in blue or green striped plasticised cotton. To relieve the austerity of the exterior, aluminium strips appeared along the sills, on the rear bumper, along the waistline of the doors, and on the crest of the bonnet – while the trim strip for the front bumper was wider than on the A and AZ models. Finally, there was an enlarged rear window, rectangular in shape. This feature was extended to all variants for the 1958 model year, at which point a significant body modification took place: a metal boot lid was introduced, on a new model coded AZLP. In theory cars with the full-length canvas roof and roll-up boot-cover remained available until 1967, but in practice most people ordered cars with the security of a

Special-bodied 2CVs

The number of people over the years who have created their own body for the 2CV is enormous. But if one excludes one-offs, modern-day cabriolet conversions and the various kit cars on offer, relatively few have actually made it into series production.

One of the earliest was the Dagonet, an extraordinary lowered and tuned version of the 2CV available during the 1950s. Other than a kitsch mock-'30s roadster called the Jorgia, one of the only other projects of any consequence was the UMAP, an elegant glassfibre-

bodied coupé first seen at the 1957 Paris Motor Show. Built in a tailor-made factory at a rate of eight cars a month, it is not known how many were completed; what is certain, however, is that Citroën refused to supply rolling chassis, thereby ending the venture. Among the inevitable Jeep-like Méhari clones one can include the Belgian Van Clee and the German Fiberfab Sherpa. One-offs worthy of a mention are a smart coupé created by Philippe Charbonneaux and another, less sleek, by Italian coachbuilder Allemano.

proper lockable steel boot lid.

As a new decade approached, Citroën began to add some variety to the 2CV's colour chart, beginning in September 1959 with the option on

the AZL and AZLP of glacier blue (with a matching blue fabric roof) alongside the traditional pale grey. At the 1960 Paris Motor Show a pale green became available, and at the very end

The 2CV 4x4 'Sahara'

Some of the unique exterior features of the Sahara can be seen here, including the cutaway rear wings and the spare wheel mounted on the bonnet; however, this is a prototype, with less pronounced cutaways to the rear wings, no holes in the doors for the petrol filler-caps, and a bonnet without louvres. (Citroën)

Still not to final specification, this example lacks the exposed petrol filler-caps (Citroën)

Intended for mountain and desert use, particularly in French North Africa, the most extraordinary 2CV of all was the 2CV 4x4 – sometimes known as the Sahara. The world's one-and-only two-engined, four-wheel-drive production car, it had a second 2CV engine and gearbox mounted in the boot, and could run either with both engines or with just the front power unit.

With both engines running, it could reach a top speed of 62mph on flat ground, consuming petrol at a rate of 28–35mpg; 47mpg was claimed with only one engine running. Mounted on a specially strengthened chassis-platform, the body differed from that of the standard 2CV in a number of very noticeable ways. These included a spare wheel recessed into the bonnet, reinforced bumpers, fatter 155-section tyres, widened, cut-away rear wings, and of course the air-intake grilles for the second engine. The filler caps poking through both front doors were also unmistakable: there were twin fuel tanks, one for each engine, located under the front seats.

Because of its very light kerb weight of 14.5cwt, optimum 50/50 weight distribution, and excellent traction, the 4x4 possessed exceptional climbing ability, and could easily outperform most conventional heavy-duty 4wd vehicles; indeed, it came to be regarded as one of the best-performing off-roaders ever developed. However, only 693 examples were built, between 1960 and 1966 – plus a further 'rogue' car in 1971 – and no more than 25 are believed to remain in existence today.

A key user was the Guardia Civil in Spain, which ordered 80 examples.

High cost had a great deal to do with the 4x4's limited diffusion. When the prototype was revealed in October 1958 it was listed at 815,000 old francs, more than twice the price of the standard 2CVA saloon, but when the 4x4 was finally deleted in September 1966, its price tag had risen to 10,259 new francs – not far short of the 11,905 francs being asked for a basic ID19 Luxe.

The British 2CV

Slough 2CV (right) displays its unique bumper design, wider-spaced Butler headlamps, standard-fit hubcaps, and its unique bonnet badge. The French-built 1952 car, (left), demonstrates its roll-up canvas boot cover. (LAT)

The 2CV is such a quintessentially French car that it is hard to believe that examples could ever have been sold bearing the label 'Made in England'. Yet from 1953 to 1960 a right-hand-drive version of the *Deuche* was actually built in the UK by Citroën Cars Limited, for sale in the British Isles and the Commonwealth. Indeed, it had been intended from the start that the Slough factory should build a rhd 2CV. But then it was discovered that British regulations prohibited vehicles with inboard brakes. Therefore it was not until these rules were relaxed in 1953 that manufacture could begin.

The Slough-built 2CV was something of a hybrid, with French-sourced mechanicals and body panels, but seats, trim, glass, lighting, and tyres made in England. The result was a car that differed from its Continental equivalent in a number of ways, most noticeable being the wide choice of colours available, including black, white, cream, green and maroon as well as grey. Beyond this, the cars had a Slough-fabricated steel boot lid, Butler headlamps set further apart, Lucas trafficators forward of the front doors, opening (but still flap-type) rear windows, and unique bumpers. Inside, there were separate front seats; the speedo was re-positioned in the centre of the dashboard; there was a separate switch panel incorporating an ashtray, and on the cant rail there was an interior light, which also illuminated the speedometer. Other unique features included a circular bonnet badge bearing the words 'Citroën Front Drive', and a Citroën script insignia on the boot lid.

In all a total of 673 'Slough' saloons were made, in 375cc (1953–55) and 425cc forms, with a substantial 340 of this number being exported. The Slough factory also produced two commercial variants, the AZU van and the AZP pick-up, of which a grand total of 363 were made, 147 going abroad. None of the 72 pick-ups made were exported, but 65 went overseas all the same – in service with the Royal Marine Commandos on board the aircraft carriers HMS *Bulwark* and HMS *Albion*.

Surprisingly, the 2CV enjoyed a very good press in the UK, being generously praised by many motoring journals. 'A vehicle with almost every virtue except speed, silence and good looks', reported *The Motor*, sentiments echoed by its rival *The Autocar*, which avowed that 'Comment other than praise is confined to criticism of the position of the rear-view mirror'. Even Bill Boddy, editor of *Motor Sport*, was impressed. In April 1954, after covering some 2000 miles in 18 days, he declared the 2CV 'a splendid, fascinating little car. Its designer, who must be a brilliant engineer indeed, has approached fearlessly the problem of providing a modern people's car. From now on I shall refuse to regard as an economy car any vehicle which does not give a genuine 60 miles per gallon.' Unfortunately, the great British motoring public declined to agree with the experts, and refused to buy the car. Part of the reason was the price: when launched in 1953, the 2CV cost just on £565, of which no less than a third was purchase tax, compared with £511 for a Ford Anglia and £529 for a Morris Minor. Yet, viewed superficially, the 2CV appeared spartan and unrefined and sounded worse; it was hardly the kind of neat and nippy second car that would be regarded as a desirable asset by the suburban housewives who represented its most likely market.

Admitting failure, Slough attempted to save the situation by transforming the 2CV into the Bijou (see next chapter), and Slough's last 2CV saloon left the works at the end of 1959. Following the Energy Crisis of 1974, however, Citroën decided to begin importing the Paris-built 602cc 2CV6 to offer alongside the Dyane which had been on sale in the UK since 1968. It was a decision that ultimately paid off, with the 2CV reaching the height of its popularity in 1986, when UK imports of 7,520 cars were recorded. Sales in the 1968–90 period totalled 68,254 2CV saloons and 39,408 Dyanes – an all-in figure of more than 108,000 vehicles.

of that year a bold Panama Yellow (with maroon roof and upholstery) arrived – just ahead of the 2CV's first real facelift.

This took place in December 1960 when the original one-piece corrugated bonnet was replaced by an entirely new design featuring five slender strengthening ribs and a smaller pressed-aluminium grille. The side panels were incorporated in the body rather than being integral with the bonnet and ventilation of the engine bay was now achieved through recessed longitudinal slots rather than louvres. Mechanically the 2CV was unchanged, as was the interior, but in October 1961 the 425cc engine was uprated to 13.5bhp, taking top speed up to 53mph. As for the 375cc engine,

this had soon ceased to sell in more than trifling numbers after the arrival of the larger unit, and was deleted from the catalogues in 1959; it was in theory available to special order, however, until early 1961.

After serious competition arrived in the shape of the Renault 4, Citroën improved the 2CV's interior furnishings and fittings in September 1962 by installing a completely new dashboard with a proper instrument binnacle boasting a conventional speedo and fuel gauge, plus electric windscreen wipers.

March 1963 saw power output raised to 18bhp – sufficient to propel the *Deuche* at up to 59mph. At the same time a luxury 2CV, the AZAM (see box), was introduced. The next step in

the gradual process of improvement took place in December 1964 when the 2CV received forward hinged doors, along with lap-type seat-belt mountings to comply with EEC regulations. During 1964 also, the 2CV made motoring history by becoming the first vehicle to be fitted with Michelin X tubeless radial tyres as standard.

At the next Paris Motor Show, in October 1965, the 2CV received its second – and last – facelift of any consequence when all saloons gained six-light bodies with a glazed rear quarter panel. At the same time a new three-bar alloy grille was introduced. On the technical side, on the AZAM (and optionally on the AZL and AZLP) fully constant-velocity driveshafts

AZAM – the luxury 2CV

Those who regard the Charleston as the most elaborately equipped of 2CVs should think again: the title of 'super 2CV' is more correctly awarded to the now near-extinct AZAM, in particular in its final Export form. The AZAM – for AZ AM*éliorée* or improved – was announced in March 1963, at the same time as the uprated 18bhp engine was introduced. Externally the AZAM was distinguished by stainless-steel hubcaps, tubular over-riders front and rear (with rubber buffers incorporated in the rear assemblies), and sundry items of brightwork: a strip down the centre of the bonnet, inserts in the windscreen and rear side-window rubbers, stainless-steel front window frames, chrome headlamp rims, and chrome wiper arms. There was also a specific design of door handle, slightly more substantial than the normal 2CV fitting. Inside, the AZAM boasted fully upholstered velour seating similar to that of the Ami 6 and with the front bench mounted on sliders, plus a grey two-spoke Quillery steering wheel. Other details included a rear parcel shelf 'hammock', plastic-covered interior door handles, an

interior light, a passenger's sun visor with mirror, and – later standardised on other 2CVs – an indicator switch mounted on the steering column.

With the arrival of the six-light body and the new radiator grille for 1966, the AZAM also gained constant-velocity joints, these becoming optional on lesser models. In April 1967 the AZAM was replaced by the AZAM Export, a short-lived and today ultra-rare variant, as it

The AZAM in its original form, with 'suicide' doors, as introduced in 1963. Clearly visible are the tubular overriders front and rear, and the standard-fit hubcaps. (Citroën)

lasted only until August that same year. The new model had white plastic trim rings for the wheels, and rectangular flashers on the front wings, while inside there was a new dashboard featuring the Ami 6 instrument cluster.

The limited-edition cars

To boost sales of the latter-day 2CV, Citroën embarked on another marketing innovation, at least in France – the limited-run special edition. The first of these was the 2CV Spot of April 1976, of which 1,800 were made, all painted orange over white, with an orange and white striped roof. The Spot, powered by the 435cc engine (or the 602cc unit for Britain and some other markets), was followed in October 1980 by 1,000 examples of the 2CV6-based 2CV-007. Painted in brilliant mimosa yellow, and offered with bullet-hole decals for the owner to apply, this celebrated the 2CV's starring role in the then-current James Bond film *For Your Eyes Only*; alas it didn't feature the 1,015cc GS engine used in the four specially-prepared cars featured in the film. Next, in April 1983, came the 2CV France 3, known as the Beachcomber in the UK and based on the 2CV6. Limited to just 2,000 examples, this was painted in the blue and white livery of the successful French challenger in the Americas Cup yacht race that year. Then in 1984 the UK-only 2CV6 Bamboo arrived, painted appropriately in a vivid shade of jungle green. As for the Dolly of 1985, this was so successful that three batches were made, two in 1985

The art-deco 2CV6 Charleston was so successful that it became a standard model, available until the end of production in 1990. (Citroën)

To celebrate the 2CV's appearance in the James Bond film For Your Eyes Only, *in October 1981 Citroën introduced the 2CV6 007 special edition. Only 1,000 were built, all bright yellow and decorated with stick-them-on-yourself bullet hole decals. (Citroën)*

and a further run in 1986, totalling 5,000 cars in all. Introduced in recognition of the 2CV's loyal following of lady drivers, over 40 per cent of latter-day buyers being women, the Dolly was effectively a

Charleston (see below) with a different set of duotone colour schemes. Finally, in 1986, came 1,000 examples of the jokey France-only 2CV6 Cocorico, finished in white with red and blue sides and with its seats covered with a blue-jeans fabric.

But the most successful special edition of all was the art-deco 2CV6 Charleston launched in October 1980. It was so well received, indeed, that it became a standard model, remaining in the catalogue for a whole ten years until the end of production It was available initially in two-tone burgundy and black, then later also in canary yellow and black, and finally also in a dark and light grey combination. It was always fitted with round headlamps, initially painted but chromed from September 1981 onwards, when the Charleston became a regular catalogued model. Interestingly, two thirds of Charleston customers were under 35 years old.

The next special edition was the Dolly, produced in three series, all available in three colour schemes. The first, introduced in March 1985, came in grey/red, grey/cream and white/grey. The second, in October 1985, came in white/green, white/red and cream/maroon. The third, in March 1986, came in blue/cream, cream/maroon and white/red. (Citroën)

replaced the simple Hooke joints formerly used. Finally, conventional telescopic units superseded the old friction dampers, but at the rear only.

With a total of 168,357 saloons being assembled, 1966 was the year when 2CV production peaked. The following year saw the introduction of the new Dyane sister model, described in the next chapter. The 2CV was not left to wither on the vine, though, and indeed its appeal was expanded in February 1970 when a new 2CV6 model was introduced, powered by the 602cc engine of the Dyane 6, developing 33bhp SAE (or 28.5bhp DIN, as is sometimes quoted). At the same time the 425cc 2CV gained the 435cc Dyane 4 power unit, pushing output up to 26bhp (24bhp DIN); in this guise the car became known as the 2CV4. At this stage proper front and rear indicators replaced the lamps on the rear quarters that had served for many years as winkers for both front and rear. At the rear Ami 6 light clusters incorporating flashers were fitted and the front wings gained rectangular indicators, replaced in the course of the year by neater circular

units. Inside, the 2CV received the Ami 6 instrument binnacle seen earlier on the short-lived AZAM Export, plus the AZAM's smarter steering wheel. It was only in January 1972, though, that a

The 2CV Special was introduced in September 1975 as a 'back to basics' low-cost model, and marked the brief return of the four-light body. (Jon Pressnell collection)

Citroneta: the 2CV from Chile

One of the oddest versions of the 2CV was the Chilean Citroneta, an ungainly three-box design made between 1959 and 1969 by Citroën's outpost in Chile. Based on a French sourced AZU chassis-cab unit, the first Citronetas had a two-door body (initially only in black) and an open pick-up style of boot with an exposed spare wheel. Later versions gained rear doors and a boot lid. The Chileans also made their own 2CV van, the *Furgon Comercial*; this had flat rather than corrugated rear panels and in its original form featured a horizontally split rear door arrangement. A pick-up version was also available. In 1970 the Citroneta was replaced

by the AX330, which had a regular six-light 2CV body but a unique design of rear tailgate hinged conventionally from above the rear window. Citroën ended production in Chile in 1976.

A battered Citroneta in later four-door form. (Julian Nowill)

12-volt electrical system was adopted, along with an alternator.

Although by then the 2CV had been on the roads for more than 20 years, and more than 1,716,000 examples had been built, it was still only just approaching adulthood, let alone middle age. For just when its retirement seemed due, the 2CV received a formidable boost from the 1973–74 oil crisis – a resurgence of interest that helped keep the little Citroën alive for another two decades, as a new generation of drivers discovered its frugal, rustic virtues. As proof of this, in 1974 production of the 2CV and its derivatives reached an all-time high of over 370,000 vehicles. For the first time since 1960, too, the 2CV was offered in the UK: it was re-

introduced on the British market at the 1974 motor show – in 2CV6 form only.

One by-product of the economic stringencies of the time was the return of the four-light body on a back-to-basics, bargain-basement model introduced in September 1975 – and never, incidentally, sold in the UK. Available solely in primrose with a dark grey roof, the new 2CV Special – 435cc only, of course – was stripped of all superfluous internal and external trim, and used the old instrument nacelle abandoned in 1970; it also reverted to round headlamps, in contrast to the rectangular units which the 2CV4 and 2CV6 had gained a year earlier, when they had also been given a new style of grille made of plastic.

Mechanically, the 2CV received few

modifications in these later years. For 1976 the steering was given a lower ratio to reduce effort, and orthodox telescopic dampers replaced the inertia and friction dampers on the front wheels of all 2CVs, while the following year a twin-circuit braking system was adopted as a prelude to the July 1981 standardisation of front disc brakes. This was indeed a sensible improvement, for it was now possible to attain 75mph, twice the top speed possible in 1949.

By this time the frugally equipped 2CV Special had gained better trim, a choice of colours and a six-light body for the 1979 model year – at which time the 2CV4 was deleted and the 2CV6 given a twin-choke carburettor, raising power to 29bhp (DIN) from the

In September 1979 the saloon range was reduced to just two models, the 2CV6 Club (left, with rectangular headlamps) and the 2CV6 Special (right, with round headlights). Both now had the same 602cc engine. (Citroën)

The 2CV in Belgium – and around the world

Thanks to its platform-chassis construction and simple body, the 2CV was a natural for CKD assembly in other countries. Leading the way was Citroën's plant in Belgium, which accounted for a substantial 712,421 2CVs and Dyanes over the 1952–78 period.

The Belgian 2CVs are of particular interest in that they differ in several respects from the French cars. The first real departure was in January 1954 when a Luxe model was introduced: this had a steel boot lid extending down to the rear bumper, a trapezoidal rear window, thicker alloy-bladed bumpers, hubcaps, and front and rear stoneguards. Additionally aluminium trim was fitted to the sills, the centre of the bonnet, the window frames, the guttering and the waistline, while the long boot lid necessitated the fitment of horizontal light units on the rear wing, in conjunction with an aluminium embellisher strip. In April 1956 a rectangular instrument panel and a smarter two-spoke steering wheel were added, along with front door pockets.

With the arrival of the steel boot lid on French cars, the long boot, wing-mounted lights and trapezoidal rear window all disappeared in February 1958, but in October that year this revised Luxe, tagged AZL2, was displaced by the AZL3, which boasted a six-light body seven years before Paris-built cars. The result was a seemingly odd hybrid with the ripple bonnet and suicide doors of the first-generation 2CV but the six-light body of third-generation cars; adding to the mix, in 1959–60 the cars had cutaway rear wings. Re-named AZL and then AZM3, this luxury 2CV was joined in January 1965 by the AZAM6, which had the 602cc Ami 6 engine – this 1965–67 model again putting Belgium ahead of the game.

In addition to these models, from 1955 until 1961 the Forest plant offered an AZC *Commerciale*, in which the rear seat was replaced by a two-piece floor and the fabric boot lid was rearranged so that it hinged upwards from the top of the window. The model was not a great success, customers preferring the Belgian-assembled vans. These had bigger windows in the rear doors and were also available in an estate version coded AZUL and known as the Weekend. Big side windows and two-tone paint were features of these smart vehicles, which in 1963 gave way to AK-derived versions; these were known as the AKL or AK Luxe and were current until 1966.

Besides being manufactured in Britain, Belgium, Portugal and Chile, the 2CV (and/or derivatives) was also officially assembled in Spain, Cambodia (van-based estates and a pick-up), Yugoslavia, Argentina, Madagascar, Iran, Tunisia, Côte d'Ivoire, Dahomey, Ecuador, Greece, Guinea-Bissau, Indonesia, Paraguay, the Central African Republic, Senegal, and Uruguay.

The Belgian-assembled 'Weekend' version of the 2CV van had rear seats, generous rear side windows, hubcaps and bigger bumpers. (LAT)

26bhp (DIN) to which emissions-tuning had reduced it in 1975. For 1980 the Special gained the 602cc engine, to become the 2CV6 Special, while the 2CV6, which had earlier acquired the appellation 2CV6 Confort, was renamed the 2CV6 Club – with no change in specification.

In June 1981, a special economy saloon version, the 2CV Special E was introduced, though it lasted for two seasons only, being phased out in February 1983. Intended principally for urban use, it was equipped with the centrifugal clutch last available in the early seventies. Thanks also to its modified second gear ratio the Special E returned a 17 per cent better urban-cycle fuel consumption figure than the standard 2CV6.

While the 2CV still sold well in Germany, Belgium and the UK, by now registrations in France had tumbled. So the unavoidable decision was made to close down the antiquated Levallois plant and concentrate production – now of just the Special and the Charleston – at Citroën's facility at Mangualde in Portugal, where labour costs were lower. Thus, on 25 February

Driving the 2CV

As you might expect, a 2CV does not drive like any other car. Whether you find this a good thing or a bad thing depends on your attitude of mind, and on how well you take to one of the two driving methods best suited to the Citroën.

Although power progressively increased over the years, any 2CV will seem underpowered. An early car with a mere 9bhp under the bonnet is – in all frankness – too slow for modern conditions: the car needs to be thrashed to within an inch of its life to maintain forward motion on anything but a perfectly flat road. Later cars with the 425cc or 435cc engines are more usable, but require something of the same approach.

The engine must be kept on the boil, and speed not allowed to fade away through hanging on too long in a higher gear; at the same time the road needs to be read for inclines that you would ignore in even the most modest of orthodox small cars. Observe these disciplines, and you'll soon understand that working the flat-twin hard will not abuse it. It can take endless punishment, and you'll be surprised at how rapidly you cover ground: an 18bhp '425' will swoop along at a happy 40mph in top on the open road – especially with even a slight downhill slope – and at lesser speeds, aided by good low-down torque delivery, the car pulls well in third. But you notice the difference if the wind is against you, or you are carrying any extra passengers. With the 602cc cars the same principles and observations apply, but there is much less of a struggle involved.

To muster the maximum power you need to master the 2CV's gearchange, which puts second and third conveniently in the same plane – ideal for hill-work – but has fourth on a limb, requiring a deliberate twist-and-push movement that a novice is likely to make too slowly, thereby losing speed. You will soon learn, too, that you don't need to slow for corners. The 2CV will not come unstuck, despite the alarming angles of roll it will assume, so you can keep your foot firmly on the accelerator – so long as your passenger has got used to the mistaken impression that the car is about to topple over.

Allied to the roll is the extraordinary ship-in-a-swell under-damped ride – even (although to a slightly lesser degree) on cars with all-round telescopic dampers. It really is the complete opposite to the choppy ride of a rubber-suspended Mini: sporty it isn't, but on bad country roads the 2CV is in its element. Indeed, there's something seductively soothing about rolling along in a *Deuche*, roof back, sun (hopefully) shining, the car bobbing up and down gently on its suspension.

Other characteristics are steering that is quick, not over-light, and which loads up quite markedly as you put on lock. Cars without constant-velocity joints suffer from unpleasant snatch if you pull away with the wheel turned, and if you have a car with the centrifugal clutch as well you need to master its wiles to avoid a desperately jerky take-off in such situations. The flip-side is that the centrifugal clutch gives you the fun of clutchless manoeuvring and allows you to trickle along in traffic without touching the clutch pedal. Whether drum or disc, the brakes are effective, with a firm short-travel pedal.

In short, there are two ways to drive a 2CV. Either you take a Zen approach, and just sit back and enjoy the relaxing virtues of slow travel and the challenge of reading the road, or else you adopt the technique of flogging the life out of that unburstable little flat-twin, pushing it along flat out with foot on the floor. Either way, you'll have fun.

1988, nearly half a century after the very first pre-war TPVs had been built there, the last French-built Deux Chevaux left the Levallois assembly line, the 3,418,347th car to have been assembled there.

Although the death sentence seemed at first to have been commuted, the end of the road was in sight. After a mere 30 months at Mangualde, during which another 42,000 or so cars were made, manufacture finally ceased. This time there could be no escaping the inevitable. By the end of 1989 the 2CV had been withdrawn from sale in Austria, Switzerland, Spain, Holland, Italy and Scandinavia, as the car no longer complied with regulations in those countries. That left only France, Belgium, Germany and the UK where the car was legal, and similar legislation was pending in those markets too. Thus on 27 July 1990, after 41 years of production, the very last Deux Chevaux, a grey Charleston, left the Portuguese lines. The final score was a staggering 6,956,895 vehicles – 5,114,966 2CV saloons and vans plus 1,443,583 Dyane saloons, 253,393 Acadiane vans and 144,953 Méharis and other assorted derivatives.

The 2CV had exceeded the normal life expectancy of a motor car many times over, finding itself in circumstances very different from those for which it had been created. Designed in an age before motorways, when average traffic speeds and densities were such that it was a rare occurrence for two cars to meet and overtake each other on a country road in France, it was out of place in a faster-moving society. Not only that, but in a modern consumerist world, austerity and self-denial were no longer appropriate, and to its makers this survivor from a bygone era had become not just an expensive-to-produce anomaly but also, perhaps, an outright embarrassment.

Buying Hints

1. First check the chassis, as it rusts badly. Replacements – even galvanised – are surprisingly inexpensive and many cars have had them fitted, thereby removing one source of worry. Citroën can still supply new chassis, rustproofed but not galvanised. Build quality of later cars – particularly those made in Portugal – was poor.

2. Floors corrode at the sides and at the front of the footwells; repair panels are available as complete sides or short floors, and are easy to fit. The lower bulkhead also rusts, and 2CVGB's Spare Parts Organisation makes a triangular box-section that can be let in – part of the club's increasing range of parts manufactured to replace items no longer available from specialists (see www.2cvgb.co.uk on the web for more details). Rear seatbelt mounts can fail on later cars. Also check the integrity of inner wing suspension bump stops, as these can rot: there's no box-section but there is a double skin. Also check front and rear valances for corrosion.

3. The top of the rear wheelarch seams suffer from rust, where they are welded to the lip of the outer bodyshell – this is particularly so on post-1980 cars. The external seam isn't sealed and, juxtaposed with the aluminium trim and the lip at the top of the rear wing, it forms a trap for moisture, muck and salt. First signs are little rust marks along the bodyshell 'sweeps'. Three-piece repair sections are available, but it's a fiddly (and thus costly) repair.

4. The bonnet hinge panel, where it slots into the top of the scuttle, always rots – all cars had mastic along the two seams, intended to inhibit rust, but this falls out over time. Repair sections can be let in easily, though, and electrical tape forms an excellent

gutter over the mastic for winter protection. While you're examining in this area, check the windscreen surround and vent flap, which are also notoriously rust-prone.

5. The A-post and the door bottoms are also vulnerable to corrosion. All external body panels are available, though be warned that the doors and bonnet are much dearer than wings – cataphoretically-treated 'pattern' wings won't make too big a hole in your budget. There is a good supply of second-hand panels available from clubs and specialists.

6. The engine feels unburstable, and can do up to 200,000 miles without major work as long as the oil has been changed every 3,000 miles, and the filter every 6,000 miles. Check that the filter is the correct Purflux type, and inspect the oil cooler, which should also be cleaned every 6,000 miles; beware notably oil-caked engines. Don't worry if the oil is a few millimetres over maximum on the dipstick as this is advisable for extra cooling with today's fuels. Tappet noise is not a worry, unless it is excessive – indeed, it is desirable to have a degree of noise.

7. Relining inboard front drum brakes is a complex if infrequent job – they can last 40,000 miles – but the handbrake is much better than on later ('81-on) front discs, which are a lot easier to service. Disc-brake cars use green LHM fluid. While you're under the bonnet, also check the state of the heater ducting, which can be the cause of fires.

8. Look for indications of regular maintenance. A groan from the suspension is usually indicative of general neglect: it is cured by squirting castor oil into the suspension cylinder and turning it upside down. Squeaks and clicks may

be caused by dry knife edges – where the suspension-actuating rods meet the suspension arms – and creaks or knocks can be a result of loose axle mounting bolts.

9. Kingpins need regular greasing (some say every 1,000 miles): heavy steering can be a result of their having seized. Check for wear by trying to move a jacked-up wheel back and forth. Judder on full lock indicates worn track-rod ends – the type used on late-model cars will take two adjustments and then need to be replaced. Still on steering, the pinion-shaft bearing can wear: check for play by grasping the bottom of the steering column and trying to move it.

10. A clink-clunk from the driveshafts indicates worn splines. With the bonnet open and the handbrake on, try to move the car back and forth by hand: if there is play in the shafts this should be visible. A final check is to jack the car up at the front and rotate each front wheel, handbrake still on: there should be no more than an inch of movement at the wheel. More likely is a worn CV joint (or joints), if a rubber bellow has cracked and allowed road-dirt to enter; a clacking on full lock will be a giveaway.

11. When correctly adjusted, there should be about 20mm (a little less than an inch) of free play in the clutch pedal. If there is a whistle in neutral that disappears when the clutch pedal is depressed, this is a worn thrust bearing. There is precious little synchromesh on bottom gear and synchro on third is often weak; howling from the gearbox indicates a worn mainshaft rear bearing. If the gearchange action is stiff, the lever has probably been greased, which ruins its bushes. It should be lubricated with talcum powder.

The Dyane, Méhari
and Bijou

In August 1967, the 2CV gained a new sister, with the announcement of the Dyane. Although it was not stated at the time, the newcomer was clearly intended as a replacement for the 2CV – whose basic mechanicals and platform chassis it shared.

The body, developed from a design by Panhard stylist Louis Bionier, was much the same size as that of the 2CV, in order to permit assembly on the same tracks at the constricted Levallois factory, and featured scooped-out sides in order to add rigidity and form to the panelwork. At the rear there was a hatchback door, but bizarrely the back seat did not fold – it remained removable, 2CV-style, although a folding seat was later made available. Still, at least the new model did away with the 2CV's flap front windows, in favour of less idiosyncratic sliding glass, while the full-length sunshine roof could now be opened from within the car and secured in a half-open position if desired.

Underneath the new body, now with the headlamps set into the front wings, was a 21bhp version of the 2CV's 425cc flat-twin. In January 1968, however, the new small Citroën was joined by a sibling, the Dyane 6, equipped with the Ami 6's 28bhp 602cc engine and its matching gearbox, plus larger drum brakes.

Two months later, in March 1968, the original Dyane – briefly referred to as the Dyane 4 – was given an uprated 435cc power unit developing 26bhp, a move that gave it a more clearly marked advantage over the 18bhp 2CV. The process continued at the 1968 Paris show, when the Dyane 6

Top: Intended as a replacement for the 2CV, the Dyane was launched in August 1967, but remained in the catalogue for only sixteen years. This is an early Dyane 6, with the four-light body. (LAT) Above: The full-length steel boot lid and roll-back roof are clearly visible in this shot. (LAT)

The Dyane's internal style was as individual as its exterior. (Citroën)

received the uprated 33bhp Ami engine. Finally, for 1970 the '6' gained the 35bhp Ami 8 unit. At this stage – in September 1969 – the body assumed a six-light configuration, gaining the rearmost side windows the 2CV had enjoyed since the 1966 model year.

Beyond this, the styling of the Dyane underwent only minor changes over the years. For example, in September 1974 the front grille changed from a mesh unit to one in plastic with horizontal bars, coloured grey at first but latterly black.

Further mechanical modifications were few: the 435cc Dyane was deleted in 1975, disc front brakes arrived for 1978 – four years ahead of their fitment to the 2CV – and the centrifugal clutch option disappeared in 1981.

As for special editions, there were only three. The first was the Caban of April 1977. This was a limited series of 1,500 vehicles, painted dark blue with white wheels and a white roof, together with white coachlining and some suitably nautical decals. The Capra of 1980–81, meanwhile, was intended solely for the Spanish and Italian markets, and featured yellow paint with black detailing, along with triple-spoked hubcaps of the type used on sports versions of the GS and GSA. Finally, the Côte d'Azur of

The Dyane gained windows in its rear quarters for the 1970 model year. (Citroën)

Dyane and Méhari

1967–1983/1968–1987

ENGINE:
Two-cylinder horizontally-opposed, air-cooled
Capacity
    425cc/435cc/602cc (Dyane)
    602cc (Méhari)
Bore x stroke
    66mm x 62mm/68.5mm x 59mm
    74mm x 70mm
Valve actuation
    Pushrod
Compression ratio
    8.5:1 (late 602cc)
Carburettor
    Single-choke Solex downdraught
Power output
    29bhp DIN at 5,750rpm (1969
    Dyane 6)
Torque
    29lb ft at 3,500rpm (idem)

TRANSMISSION:
Front-wheel drive; selectable four-wheel drive on Méhari 4x4 (1979-82)
Four-speed, all synchronised; reduction gearbox and differential lock on Méhari 4x4

SUSPENSION:
Front: Independent, by leading arm, with horizontal coil springs interlinked to rear suspension; friction and inertia dampers (later telescopic dampers)
Rear: Independent, by trailing arm, with horizontal springs interlinked to front suspension; inertia and telescopic dampers (later just telescopic dampers)

STEERING:
Rack-and-pinion, unassisted 2.6 turns lock-to-lock

BRAKES:
Drum, hydraulically operated; inboard at front. Disc front brakes from 1977 (Dyane) and 1978 (Méhari); rear discs on Méhari 4x4

WHEELS/TYRES:
Michelin radial, 125x15in; 135x15in on Méhari (145x14in optional on 4x4 from 1982)

BODYWORK:
Platform chassis; steel body with fabric roof (Dyane). Méhari has thermo-plastic body built on steel framework
Dyane available as four-door saloon and Acadiane van; Méhari as open Jeep-type leisure vehicle with various roof and door options

DIMENSIONS (Dyane/Méhari):
Length   12ft 9¾in/12ft 2½in
Wheelbase   7ft 10¼in
Track   4ft 1¾in (front)
    4ft 2in (rear)
Width   4ft 11in / 5ft 0¼in
Height   5ft 1¼in / 5ft 4½in

WEIGHT:
15.7cwt (Dyane 6, as tested – *Motor* figure)
11.3cwt (Méhari kerb weight, Citroën figure)

PERFORMANCE (1969 Dyane 6):
(Source: *Motor*)
Max speed   68.6mph
0-50mph   18.7sec
0-60mph   30.8sec

PRICE INCLUDING TAX WHEN NEW:
£648 (Dyane 6, July 1969)
Méhari not UK-available

NUMBERS BUILT:
1,443,583 Dyane, 144,953 Méhari

Ladybird – André Lefèbvre's ultimate Super 2CV

By the 1960s it had already become apparent that the 2CV was perhaps a little too rustic – and certainly unsuitable for fast long-distance travel. Accordingly, the *Bureau d'Etudes* began to study a vehicle no less avant-garde but suited to a wider role than merely carrying peasants and their baskets of eggs safely over a ploughed field.

For sheer ingenuity and vision, little could beat the resultant C1 prototype, constructed in the period 1955–56 by a small team under André Lefèbvre, shortly before ill-health forced him into retirement. In this, his penultimate design, Lefèbvre foresaw the motoring conditions of today and defined the car of tomorrow, fifty years ahead of his time – just as he had done with the original 2CV.

Nicknamed *Coccinelle* or Ladybird, this revolutionary Super 2CV followed Lefèbvre's principles to their logical conclusion. Ultra-light and aerodynamically-efficient, with a Cd of 0.258, its all-aluminium chassis and raindrop-shaped body allowed its tiny 12bhp 425cc air-cooled engine to propel four passengers and their luggage at 75mph while returning an average of over 70mpg. Measuring 12ft 7in overall, the C1 had a kerbweight of only 7.5cwt, distributed 75/25 front and rear. This arrangement enabled Lefèbvre to dispense with brakes on the rear axle, to eliminate all risks of skidding due to rear-wheel lock-up. The wheels, of magnesium alloy, were of a very small diameter (so as to intrude as little as possible into the passenger compartment) and were sprung by three hydropneumatic spheres, two in the front and one at the rear. The narrow trunnion-type rear axle was attached to the body at a single point and pivoted in two planes, with its twin wheels close together to give a

track of only 2ft, whereas the independent wishbone front end had a track of 4ft 8in. This reversed tricycle layout – coupled with the car's unusual steering geometry – gave the *Coccinelle* excellent stability, especially at speed.

The air-cooled twin-pot engine and transmission were placed ahead of the front axle, as on the 2CV, an arrangement that gave exceptionally generous passenger and luggage space for such a small and low-slung car. Access was by two huge double gull-wing doors, while the boot (which also featured two occasional children's seats) was reached by lifting the hatchback tail-door constructed entirely of plexiglas, the material from which the car's bubble-shaped roof was formed.

This extensive use of plexiglas led to the most amazing feature of all the novel highly advanced design features incorporated in this extraordinary car – no windscreen wipers or demisters were provided, nor even a conventional windscreen. Because of the optical problems inherent in the use of a curved plexiglas front panel, to allow clear, distortion-free forward vision, Lefèbvre cut a large slot in the nose, level with the driver's line of sight. The aerodynamic purity of his

The last of the Coccinelles, the C10, which lacked Lefèbvre's innovative windscreen arrangement. There is a single gullwing upper door on either side. An impressive 0.23 Cd was recorded. (Citroën)

design was such that at speeds of over 30mph the airflow was completely deflected over the roof of the car, preventing no more than just a gentle breeze from entering the slot to ventilate the interior. When travelling in rain or snow below this speed, however, a hinged flat screen could be swung into place to keep out the weather. Driving the *Coccinelle* must have been like piloting a plane that never left the ground.

The C1 was followed by a series of prototypes, culminating in the C10, produced in 1957. With half-doors and gullwing upper quarters, and rear brakes this time, the car was built around a bonded aluminium structure and had a less exaggerated frontward weight bias. With better stability under braking, and impressive performance from an uprated 2CV engine, the C10 is remembered with fondness by the engineers responsible; but the project was soon sidelined, although echoes of it may be found in the 1984 Eco 2000 prototype.

When equipped with a folding rear seat the Dyane had full hatchback versatility thanks to its full-length flat rear floor. (Citroën)

1982–83 was white with blue striping – and was available in the UK.

Although in many ways a better, more practical – and more powerful! – vehicle than the 2CV, the Dyane failed to equal that car's long-term popularity. Indeed many enthusiasts regarded it as an interloper in the 2CV family, lacking the character of the authentic *Deux Chevaux*. Squeezed on one side by the rejuvenated 2CV and on the other – from 1978 – by the more contemporary Visa, it outsold the 2CV only in 1968 and 1969, and began to lose ground fast after 1978. Until then Dyane sales were never hugely far adrift from those of the 2CV – so Citroën evidently succeeded in

wringing some useful extra profit out of the basic 'A Series' design. Production finally ceased in 1983, by which time 1,443,583 Dyanes had been built during the car's 16-year life span – which turned out to be a full 25 years shorter than that of the venerable vehicle it was originally intended to replace.

The Méhari, introduced in May 1968, was a very different device; indeed it was not, strictly speaking, a Citroën design at all, but was created by an outside enterprise specialising in plastics. Impressed by its originality and sales potential, Citroën subsequently decided to

commercialise the vehicle itself. Named after the dromedary favoured by Berber tribesmen for long-distance travel in the desert, the Méhari was the first series production vehicle in the world to feature a lightweight body made of flexible, self-coloured non-corroding ABS thermoplastic – this being assembled around a tubular steel frame.

Built on a Dyane 6 chassis, strengthened to allow a 400kg (0.39 ton) payload to be carried, the Méhari was more pick-up truck than car and – as with its British equivalent the Mini-Moke – was intended for agricultural and forestry work, light construction-

The Méhari in two-seat form, with optional ABS doors in place of standard security chains. (Citroën)

The full hood varied in format – side windows could be large or small. Later cars lost the housing at the rear originally intended for 2CV-type side flashers. (Citroën)

Dyane around the world

The Dyane was another international Citroën, being made not only in France but also in Spain, Portugal, Yugoslavia . . . and, until 1981, in Iran. In these latter two countries van and pick-up versions were also offered, the vans not to be confused with the 'factory' Acadiane.

site and public service duties, and as a practical, economical fun-car in the newly emerging leisure-vehicle market. As a consequence, it was initially fitted with two seats only, so as to qualify as a commercial vehicle for taxation purposes.

Normally, the Méhari had no doors or windows, so that its occupants were shielded by no more than a fold-flat windscreen, and a simple canvas folding roof with transparent plastic sidescreens. Various options were available over the years, however, from ABS doors to pick-up and full-length van/estate hardtops.

Throughout production, the design of the Méhari was modified only once, in 1978, when the grille was revised – a move that coincided with the fitting of front disc brakes. For 1979 the old 2CV-style instrument cluster was replaced by a twin-dial set-up derived from that of the LN, while in June 1980 power rose from 28bhp DIN to 33bhp.

Meanwhile, in 1979 a four-wheel-drive version was added to the range. Using a conventional 4wd config-uration rather than the Sahara's twin engines, there was a reduction gear-box and selectable drive to the rear wheels, whose differential could be locked by a central lever; the trans-

The Acadiane van

Introduced in March 1978 to replace the 2CV van in both AZU and AKS forms, the Acadiane ('AK' plus 'Dyane') was a hybrid vehicle formed by grafting the Dyane front end onto a modified AKS rear section, and mounting the resultant body on a lengthened and strengthened AKS chassis.

Powered by the 35bhp 602cc engine and gearbox of the AKS, it had an increased payload of 480kg, and boasted winding front windows – a feature never extended to the

Dyane saloon. The Acadiane was discontinued in May 1987, following the arrival of the Visa-based C15 van. In all, 253,393 were made, the peak year being 1979, when 49,679 left the factory in Spain where all Acadianes were made. The model was never sold in the UK.

The Acadiane van, first seen in March 1978, was a combination of the Dyane's front and the chassis, engine and body of the AKS; payload was 480kg. (Citroën)

Different permutations of the Méhari soft-top. (Citroën)

mission, controlled by three push-pull levers on the dashboard offered a total of seven forward speeds – top not being selectable when 'low' was engaged. The engine in the Méhari 4x4 was unchanged, and indeed other than the 4wd system the only significant departure was in the fitting of rear disc brakes, inboard-mounted.

The Méhari 4x4 could be recognised by its cow-catcher bumpers and by the optional bonnet-mounted spare-wheel it generally carried. For 1982 its side-panels were reduced in depth to increase ground clearance, and the rear wheelarches modified to an unribbed rectangular form to allow fitment of wider wheels as an option.

Top: Méhari 4x4 – note bonnet-mounted spare and tubular 'nerf' bars. All 4x4s have the second style of grille. (Citroën)

Even with a new five-dial dashboard, this wasn't enough to make the all-drive Méhari a success, and it was withdrawn from production at the end of that year, after only 1,213 had been made.

Production of the standard Méhari continued for another five years until 1987, however, by which time no fewer

Above: Late Méhari dash, with round-dial LN instrument cluster; note glove box. (Citroën)

than 144,953 examples – including the 4x4s – had been assembled, most of them in Citroën's Belgian factory.

Amongst them was a special edition, the Azure, equipped with a white body, blue doors and hood plus blue and white striped seats. Introduced in 1983, it became a regular model for 1984.

The Méhari was never offered on the

UK market, because it did not comply with British regulations, but cars have been imported privately over the years. Today the Méhari remains a popular vehicle in France, especially in holiday areas, and good examples are much prized.

If the Méhari was an oddball French-designed plastic 2CV, then the Bijou was an oddball British-designed plastic 2CV. After five years of uphill struggle against all the odds, in 1958 Citroën Cars in Slough decided on one last desperate effort to win the *Deux Chevaux* a place on the roads of Britain.

To make the 2CV socially acceptable to suburban Anglo-Saxon tastes, its engine and chassis would have to be hidden by sleek new bodywork, styled to give it housewife appeal and offering a proper boot for the shopping. And because the Slough factory had neither the facilities nor the funds for producing steel pressings, this body would have to be made from glass-fibre-reinforced polyester resin (grp) – giving the car the added advantage of freedom from corrosion. The resultant Bijou was the only European Citroën ever designed outside France – and, indeed, one of the most unusual cars ever made in Britain.

Styled by Peter Kirwan-Taylor, responsible for the lines of the original

The FAF

The FAF was intended to be an easy-to-make vehicle for the Third World. (Citroën)

So-called because it was intended to be *Facile à Fabriquer* ('Easy to Build') and *Facile à Financer*, the FAF was a Dyane-based Jeep-like vehicle intended for developing countries – hence its simple folded-steel bodywork, proposed in a variety of open and closed forms. Of authentic Citroën design, the first cars were built at the Mangualde plant in Portugal and the car unveiled at the 1978 International Fair in Dakar. Attempts to put it into production in Senegal, and in the Central African Republic and Côte d'Ivoire, came to nothing, however, and only Guinea-Bissau among African countries took up the project – making a paltry 500 cars in the 1979-81 period.

Indonesia also assembled the FAF, the last being made up from parts in stock as late as 1990. There were plans to replace the French army's Méhari fleet with a 4x4 version of the FAF, powered by the LN/Visa 652cc flat-twin, but the 5,000-car order was cancelled at the last moment. In the end only 2,295 FAFs were made.

Lotus Elite, its two-door body made it 1cwt heavier than a 2CV – equivalent to an extra adult passenger and holding speed down to a maximum of 45–50mph. Even so, with identical mechanicals to the 425cc 2CV it superseded, it achieved up to 10 per

Below: The unique glass-fibre Bijou, of which 211 were built at Slough between 1960 and 1964. (LAT) Right: Styled by Peter Kirwan-Taylor, the Bijou shared many design details (and trim components) with the DS19. (LAT)

Baby-Brousse, Dalat and Pony: sisters under the skin?

The first attempt to produce a basic 2CV-derived vehicle for the developing world dated back to the 1960s, when a Frenchman living in Côte d'Ivoire conceived a Jeep-like vehicle made of simple folded steel sections, called the Baby-Brousse. In 1969 Citroën took an interest in the project, and supported the setting up of manufacturing facilities in Côte d'Ivoire, where the car was built until 1979, by which time 31,305 examples had been made. Several thousand were also made in Iran, in the 1970–79 period, and a further 651 cars in Chile, between 1972 and 1976, under the name Yagan.

From the Baby Brousse's basic design sprang the better-known Pony, a slightly more civilised interpretation offered in the 1976–83 period by the Greek Citroën importer Namco; 17,000-odd were made, in all.

Meanwhile a similar vehicle – but apparently not directly related – was being manufactured in South Vietnam, under the name Dalat.

Manufacture effectively ceased with the fall of Saigon in 1975, but some cars built from parts in stock trickled out after the communist takeover.

The Greek-built Pony was related to the Baby-Brousse and the Dalat. (Jon Pressnell collection)

Son of Méhari: the Teilhol Tangara

Irony of ironies, the attempt to market a modernised 2CV-based leisure vehicle to replace the Méhari was the work of the company that had formerly made the Citroën's principal rival, the Renault Rodéo. With the Rodéo discontinued and the Méhari's days numbered, at the 1987 Geneva show the Auvergnat firm Teilhol revealed its Tangara, a grp-bodied pick-up characterised by notably crisp lines and built on the 2CV chassis. The body was self-coloured and featured a lift-off hardtop for the cab and the option of a glass-fibre rear section with or without side windows. Citroën approved the car and agreed to provide the running gear, and manufacture took off – with orders including 400 Tangaras for the French army. A 4x4 version became available, and in 1988 Teilhol changed over to Citroën AX mechanicals. The company ceased production in 1990, after approximately 1,400 2CV-based Tangaras had been produced, of which 47 were 4wd versions; additionally 151 AX-based models were built.

The Teilhol Tangara was a brave attempt to offer a modernised Méhari; the last cars were AX-based. (Jon Pressnell)

cent better fuel consumption due to its remarkably low drag coefficient of 0.37, as good as that of a late-model DS.

The prototype was shown at the 1959 Earls Court show and production began the following year. Alas, the arrival of the BMC Mini, launched in August 1959, put paid to the Bijou. Even given this elaborate disguise, there was now absolutely no chance of persuading British motorists to buy the car in sufficient quantities to make continued assembly worthwhile.

Not only that, but the car was exceedingly difficult to make; few of the panels fitted properly and extensive hand fettling was required, slowing down manufacture and increasing costs. Slough had the capacity to make up to 1,500 Bijoux a year, and the initial contract for body supply was for 1,000 shells, but with neither demand nor potential output at anything like the planned level, the plug was pulled in 1964 after only 211 cars had been made, of which a mere 34 are known to have survived.

Opposite: Interior of the Bijou retains 2CV hammock-style seats, but with more substantial upholstery. Wind-up windows and DS single-spoke wheel add a touch of class. (LAT)

Buying Hints

1. As the mechanicals and the platform chassis are shared with the 2CV, the relevant advice given in the 2CV chapter applies to the Dyane and 2wd Méhari.

2. 'It does everything that a 2CV can do, and it does it a little better, but it'll never be a 2CV,' says one specialist – so Dyane prices should be lower than those for a 2CV.

3. Dyane panels aren't as widely available as for 2CVs, and are getting scarcer – though 'pattern' steel or glass-fibre wings are available. The Deux Chevaux Club of Great Britain (2CVGB) has anticipated this problem and its Spare Parts Organisation has started to remanufacture repair panels: it currently offers sills and repair sections for the C-post and closing angle, the windscreen bottom/bonnet hinge, and the outer lower bulkhead.

4. Corrosion around the integral headlamps is a problem specific to the Dyane.

5. The Méhari's plastic body is prone to fading and cracking. All panels are available new, and the rivet-together construction makes replacement straightforward. The only long-term answer to fading is to paint the car.

6. The weak point of the Méhari is the tubular-steel framework around which the body is built. Check for rotten tubes at the rear, looking behind the light units and in the wheelarches; at the front, examine the jacking points and the metal adjacent to them. Repairs to the frame are not difficult, but dismantling the body to gain access is inevitably time-consuming and thus costly if you cannot do it yourself.

7. Should the chassis on a Méhari need replacement, that of a 2CV can be used with only very minor modifications.

The DS saloons

At the Paris Motor Show on 6 October 1955 Citroën detonated what the French motoring press described without exaggeration as a bombshell. The impact caused by the arrival of the DS19 – the long-awaited replacement for the Traction Avant – shook the motor industry to its core. Nothing like it had ever been seen before: virtually everything about it was completely new, so much so that it seemed as if a machine from another planet had landed in Paris and parked on the Citroën stand.

From the publicity viewpoint, the debut was a triumph, producing massive press coverage. In France, quite naturally, the journalists gave the car a wildly enthusiastic reception. 'The DS19 gives the impression of having jumped a generation in automobile history,' commented Paul Frère. Even the British were impressed. The technical editor of *The Motor*, Laurence Pomeroy, called the

This publicity shot from late 1959 shows the 'ash-tray' cooling vents in the wings, introduced in October that year. (Citroën)

Citroën DS saloons

1955–1975

The ultra-secret DS19, launched at the 1955 Paris show, had its first media exposure in Paris Match, with pictures featuring glamorous Italian movie star Gina Lollobrigida. Note the embossed aluminium front valance and red wheels used on early cars. (Author's collection)

ENGINE:
Four-cylinder in-line, water-cooled; alloy hemi head
Bore x stroke
　　78mm x 100mm (1,911cc DS19)
　　86mm x 85.5mm/90mm x 85.5mm (DS19/DS20/DS21)
　　93.5mm x 85.5mm (DS23)
Capacity
　　1,911cc (1955–65)
　　1,985cc/2,175cc (1965–75)
　　2,347cc (1972–75)
Valve actuation
　　Pushrod
Compression ratio
　　7.5:1/8.5:1
　　8.75:1/DS21 EFi 9.0:1
Fuel system
　　Double-choke Weber/Zenith
　　Bosch electronic injection (DS EFi)
Power
　　75bhp/83bhp at 4,500rpm (1,911cc DS19)
　　90bhp at 5,250rpm (DS19)
　　103bhp/108bhp at 5,500rpm (DS20)
　　109bhp/115bhp at 5,500rpm (DS21)
　　139bhp at 5,250rpm (DS21 EFi)
　　124bhp/141bhp at 5,500rpm (DS23/DS23 EFi)
Torque
　　101.3lb ft/104.7lb ft at 3,000rpm
　　109.9lb ft at 3,000rpm
　　107.8lb ft at 3,400rpm/112.1lb ft at 4,000rpm
　　128lb ft at 3,000rpm/125.9lb ft at 4,000rpm
　　144.7lb ft at 4,000rpm
　　138.2lb ft/148.3lb ft at 4,000rpm
　　(models as above)
Note: All power and torque figures are SAE

TRANSMISSION:
Front-wheel drive.
Four-speed gearbox, hydraulically operated; automatic actuation of clutch
Optional conventional gearbox and clutch, four-speed (from January 1963) or five-speed (from August 1970)
Borg-Warner three-speed Type 35 automatic available from November 1971

SUSPENSION:
Front: Independent, twin leading arms, anti-roll bar, self-levelling hydropneumatic units
Rear: Independent, trailing arms, anti-roll bar, self-levelling hydropneumatic units

STEERING:
Fully powered rack-and-pinion
Turns lock-to-lock: 2.9

BRAKES:
Fully-powered off high-pressure hydraulics
Front: hydraulic disc, inboard
Rear: hydraulic drum, outboard

WHEELS/TYRES:
Michelin disc, initially single-screw fixing; conventional five-stud system from 1966 model year
Michelin X/XA2/XAS radial
165 x 400 front, 155 x 400 rear (1955–65)
180 x 380 front, 155 x 380 rear (1966–75)
180 x 380 front, 165 x 380 rear (DS21)
185 x 380 front and rear (EFi models)

BODYWORK:
Four-door saloon; unstressed steel panels on steel body/chassis base unit; grp (sometimes aluminium) roof; aluminium bonnet and (until 1960) aluminium boot lid

DIMENSIONS:
Length	15ft 9in/15ft 11½in
Wheelbase	10ft 3in
Track – front	4ft 11in
– rear	4ft 3in
Width	5ft 10½in/5ft 11in
Height	4ft 10in

WEIGHT (kerb):
24.25cwt (1956 DS19)
26.4cwt (1970 DS21 EFi manual)

PERFORMANCE:
Source: The Motor/Motor
Models quoted: 1956 DS19/1970 DS21 EFi
Max speed	86.5mph/113.8mph
0–50mph	14.5sec/8.5sec
0–60mph	23.3sec/11.2sec

PRICE INCLUDING TAX WHEN NEW:
DS19, 1956: £1,726
DS21 Pallas EFi, 1970: £2,490

NUMBER BUILT (DS and ID combined, including estates; Citroën figure): 1,455,746

DS19 'one of the biggest advances in production car design in the whole history of motoring', while John Bolster of *Autosport* said that it was 'a startling machine which at once renders half the cars of the world out of date'.

As things turned out, these predictions were somewhat conservative, for when production ceased 20 years later the reputation of the DS as a motoring milestone had been strengthened rather than diluted by the passage of time. Today it has become a cult object, placed third in the 1999 'Car of the Century' competition as well as being voted 'Industrial Product of the Century' by a panel of design and engineering experts.

The new Citroën stunned spectators at the show with its extraordinary but aerodynamically efficient shape, the work of Flaminio Bertoni. Dispensing with the traditional radiator grille, the radiator received cooling air through a large aperture in the underskirt and openings in the bumper. Great attention was paid to the airflow under the car, in the interests not only of fuel economy but also of better handling and roadholding. The floorpan of the DS19 was smooth and flat with only the minimum of projections and cavities. Even the engine bay was shielded by an undertray, while the forward areas of the front wheelarches were enclosed by gussets.

The DS body was more than just a cleverly styled outer skin, however. In order to reduce tooling costs to the minimum, André Lefèbvre rejected the Traction Avant's monocoque body

Bertoni's trumpets

One of the boldest and most original styling features of the DS19 was its rear indicator housings, two flared conical tubes, made either from plastic or metal and resembling elongated ice-cream cornets, mounted at eye-level atop the C-pillars. These *cornets de frites*, as the French called them, were a rapid response to an urgent styling problem arising from the remodelling of the DS19's silhouette, resulting in the roofline being raised at the last moment. This left a pronounced step between the low-set rear screen and the roof, and the indicator housings were an ingenious way of masking this gap.

On most cars built before September 1959, the trumpets took the form of translucent red plastic mouldings that lit up along their entire length. These were teamed with C-pillar trims either in narrow-fluted anodised aluminium or painted in the

One of the most original styling features of the DS was its unique conical rear indicator housings. Positioned at eye-level on the roof, these trumpets were generally stainless steel or red or black plastic, according to the model and year of manufacture. (LAT)

body-colour. However, an alternative chrome-plated type of trumpet was sometimes fitted, specifically to cars with aubergine or black roofs. These extra-long indicator housings, which Bertoni called *trompettes de Jéricho*, merged smoothly into the guttering,

and were always combined with painted C-pillar trims. In February 1958 they were replaced by shorter stainless-steel housings. This treatment was soon standardised across the DS range, replacing the red plastic trumpets entirely; all-black cars, incidentally, continued to feature plain black-painted C-pillars, although alloy trim panels could be specified.

From the outset, ID saloons (see next chapter) were fitted with plastic trumpets; first brown and then later black, these were teamed until 1959 with painted C-pillars. For 1969, however, the plastic trumpets were replaced by the stainless steel type on the new ID20 model (subsequently renamed D Super), and latterly also on the export version of the D Special. However, the French home-market version of this base-level variant retained plastic trumpets through to the end of production.

shell design and chose the constructional principles of the 2CV. But where the 2CV used a lightweight platform-chassis to which the mechanical elements and superstructure were secured, the structure of the DS19 involved a complex welded pontoon which when joined to the superstructure formed a load-bearing skeleton of enormous strength. This was then clad with fully detachable panels, bolted rather than welded in place, for easier assembly, maintenance and repairs. Notably few in number, the external panels had no structural function, the roof and wings being unstressed.

The doors and wings were steel, but the roof panel was normally of glass-reinforced polyester. The bonnet was aluminium, as was, initially, the boot-lid, though from August 1960 onwards a steel lid was fitted. The doors had no surrounding frame to hold the window glass in place; wind and water tightness was achieved simply by the

pressure of the closed doors against rubber seals. The use of these novel frameless windows made it possible to achieve a big reduction in the size of the pillars, so that the total glazed surface area of the DS19 was some 25 per cent greater than that of the Traction Avant, providing remarkable all-round visibility. Similarly the wraparound windscreen and the rear screen were held in place by rubber seals and screw fasteners and thus were also easily detachable.

The futuristic interior of the DS must have seemed no less amazing than its exterior. Crammed with original ideas, many of them involving the first commercial use of certain new plastics and other man-made materials, its luxurious appointments came in spectacular contrast to the austerity of previous Citroëns, and marked a great advance in comfort and refinement.

Dominating the décor was Bertoni's inspired thermoplastic dashboard, a landmark in industrial design using

materials and manufacturing technologies hitherto unseen. Finished in black and off-white, this asymmetrically shaped work of sculpture incorporated a sloping glovebox lid and a unique and justly famous single-spoke steering wheel. Located immediately behind the wheel was a hooded instrument binnacle in front of which was the gear-selector lever, while air entered through large adjustable louvres either side of the dashboard.

Although the engine intruded into the front footwell, the absence of a transmission tunnel allowed the two front seats to be located close together, so that six people could be carried comfortably on short journeys. The front seats were of an unusual design, with high squabs and low backs, which, thanks to their generous foam rubber cushioning, gave them the rounded contours of well-stuffed armchairs. Equipped with reclining backs, they could be lowered fully and,

One of the first colour publicity photos of the DS19, shot in 1958. The adventurous duotone colours of these early cars – champagne-yellow with an aubergine roof, apple green with white, or pinkish rose-grey with turquoise – electrified customers used to the drab black or grey cars of previous years. (Citroën)

with further adjustment, slid back to form full-length beds. Initially the seats were covered with a newly available smooth-faced jersey-knit nylon cloth, warm in winter and cool in summer. But perhaps the most adventurous and sophisticated aspect of the interior was the striking colours chosen. Royal blue, brick red, jade green and elephant grey were on the shade-card in 1956, to tone or contrast with the equally vivid exterior paintwork – apple green, champagne yellow, aubergine and black.

A striking body, unorthodox construction and a stylish interior were only part of the DS story. Where

the car really differed from all other vehicles was in its use of high-pressure hydraulics to power the brakes and steering, actuate the clutch and the gearbox, and also, of course, to activate Citroën's unique self-levelling, fully independent hydropneumatic suspension, introduced earlier on the rear axle of the 15-Six. Coupled with front-wheel drive and centre-point steering geometry, this gave the car unerring stability and comfort.

The key components of the system were four rising-rate gas springs, one per wheel, which took the form of spherical metal chambers containing compressible nitrogen gas held under pressure by a flexible diaphragm fastened to the circumference of the sphere. These spheres were linked to the wheels by pushrods connected to pistons moving in cylinders filled with hydraulic fluid under pressure, and which flowed in and out of the spheres through damper valves. Bearing on the

axle arms holding the wheels, the pistons and rods acted as rams or jacks to raise or lower the bodywork to maintain the correct ride-height when governed by the action of height-correcting devices, front and rear, which in turn were actuated by the anti-roll bars. The height-correctors varied the flow of pressurised hydraulic fluid (drawn from a constant supply provided by an engine-driven pump) to the cylinders and spheres.

Therefore, no matter how heavy the passengers and cargo being carried on board, perfect equilibrium was achieved on the move under all road and load conditions, to ensure a smooth and stable ride at speed, even when traversing the poorly surfaced, pot-holed or cobble-stoned French highways of that era. As a bonus, the system also made it possible for the driver to jack up the vehicle to change a wheel by moving a lever, linked to the height-corrector devices.

Another unique feature of the DS

'Et Dieu créa la Femme, mais Citroën créa La Déesse'. This shot from a mid-1959 catalogue borrows the imagery of the contemporary Nouvelle Vague cinema to give the DS19 movie-star status. The parallel was not unjustified. Never previously had a new car incorporated so many original and sophisticated ideas, and never since has a mass-produced vehicle achieved so great an advance in safety and comfort in one single step. (Citroën)

The sensational dashboard of the DS19, designed by Flaminio Bertoni. A greater visual contrast between its asymmetrical and highly sculptural shape and the bare flat metal fascia of the Traction Avant could hardly be imagined. (Citroën)

The DS Pallas

For the first ten years of its existence the DS saloon was available in one standard level of finish only – disregarding the Chapron-modified Prestige, which was little more than a DS with a central division. But in September 1964 Citroën introduced the DS19 Pallas – followed, for 1966, by the DS21 Pallas.

Although the Pallas was mechanically identical to the regular DS, Citroën claimed that it had no fewer than 41 interior and exterior improvements and embellishments, including quartz-iodine long-range driving lamps. The Pallas could easily be distinguished from the standard DS saloon by its stainless-steel rubbing-strips, the stainless beading on the top and bottom edges of the doors and wings, and the smooth anodised aluminium C-pillar trims. The wheel embellishers were also of a completely different design, with a flat, plate-like profile. Additionally the sill covers were stainless steel, and matched to stainless steel kick-plates rather than the glued-on aluminium-effect vinylised cloth used on standard cars.

Inside, the entire roof panel and cant-rail, together with the rear pillars, were trimmed with high-quality cloth, while the high-grade,

deep-pile carpet matched the seats – these being even more generous in shape than those on the standard cars, and upholstered in a more elaborate way, in either jersey-nylon cloth or optional black or tan leather.

Similarly, the engine bulkhead and the visible areas of the chassis side-members were also trimmed with the same colour-matched carpeting instead of being covered by vinylised fabric. The doors were fully trimmed, using a contrasting quilted leather-cloth material that covered the lower section of the door as well as the capping; this was painted on the standard DS. The recesses beneath the door handles were embellished with brightwork protective plates. Other interior refinements exclusive to Pallas cars were passenger grab-straps, elaborate interior lights with decorative glass lenses, and a sports-style accelerator pedal.

With one notable exception, there was no difference between Pallas and standard cars in the range of colours offered. When the Pallas was

introduced in 1964 a shade of metallic paint – Palladian Grey – became available for the first time. In due course, a number of other metallic shades were offered for the entire D series range, but Palladian Grey always remained a Pallas exclusive. By tradition, black Pallas cars were generally (though by no means exclusively) produced with either black leather or steel-grey jersey-cloth upholstery.

Above: A right-hand-drive DS21 Pallas, built in 1967 and painted in the metallic Palladian Grey shade exclusive to this model. (Paul Debois) Below: A typical leather-trimmed Pallas interior, here on a 1969 DS21. The alternative was jersey-cloth upholstery. (LAT)

was the design of its front half-axles, which took the form of alloy castings carrying two curved leading-arms located by four massive Timken bearings. To the arms were attached by ball-joints the hubs carrying the roadwheels and the driveshafts. The pivot-points of these swivels were placed exactly in the vertical axis of the wheel, an arrangement which had the effect of keeping them positioned in such a way that an imaginary line drawn downwards through them always bisected the front wheels and tyres through the centre of the tyre contact patch and hit precisely the point where rubber met road.

This unusual arrangement, known as *le pivot dans l'axe* or centrepoint steering, was a central tenet of André Lefèbvre's design philosophy, as besides ensuring uninterrupted contact between the tyres and the road it also conferred a positive self-centring action to the steering. By eliminating bump-steer, it kept the car from being deflected from its intended course. Even in the event of a high-speed blow-out, the DS could be

relied upon to steer straight and remain under the driver's full control during emergency braking.

The adoption of centrepoint steering was intended to exploit the characteristic vertical and lateral flexibility of the Michelin X radial tyres with which the car was fitted. The DS19 had been designed specifically to run on these tyres and they and their successors, the Michelin XAS, were mandatory equipment. Indeed, it was held that the use of any other type or make of tyre could seriously impair the car's handling, roadholding and braking.

The centrepoint steering also dictated, at least initially, the use of a unique roadwheel, manufactured specially by Michelin. Deeply dished to provide adequate space for the hubs and swivels, these wheels were attached to the hubs by an unusual quick-release centre-screw fixing designed by Lefèbvre. However, in October 1965, when the design of the original suspension arms, swivel hubs and driveshafts was changed, this was replaced by a conventional five-stud

fixing. Another peculiarity of the DS19's running gear was that, again in accordance with the theories espoused by Lefèbvre, to increase its directional stability the car had a narrower track at the rear – 4ft 3ins compared to 4ft 11ins at the front.

The DS steering was of classic rack-and-pinion type. The difference was that it was fully powered by the high-pressure hydraulic-fluid supply, and operated in a quite different way from conventional power-assisted steering, since no part of the effort exerted on the steering wheel was transmitted directly to the pinion all the while the unit was pressurised. The steering column operated a rotating distributor device located in the rack-and-pinion housing, which sent fluid under pressure to the appropriate face of a double-acting piston attached to the rack, pushing it to left or right according to the direction in which the wheel was turned.

When the steering wheel ceased to revolve, however, the distributor valve cut off the flow of fluid in and out of the piston cylinder, so that the

De Gaulle's Presidential DS21

In November 1968 President de Gaulle took delivery of the most special DS of all, an ultra-long four-light saloon built by Chapron. Finished in dark grey with a contrasting silver-grey roof, it measured 21ft 6in from stem to stern, 5in longer than the stretched Lincoln used by US presidents, this being a specific requirement of the commission. Another stipulation was that despite its great length the car should have a turning circle tight enough to allow it to enter the narrow courtyard of the Elysée Palace and pull up at the entrance steps in a single pass without reversing, a manoeuvre which no American car could perform.

This Super-Déesse was equipped with a standard DS21 engine, but its gearbox and cooling system were

modified to allow it to travel at walking pace for long periods, even in very hot weather, so that it was not at risk of suffering a breakdown through overheating while on parade.

The ceremonial DS21 built for Charles de Gaulle by Henri Chapron in 1968. By his command its overall length had to be greater than that of the stretched Lincoln Continental used by the American president. (Citroën)

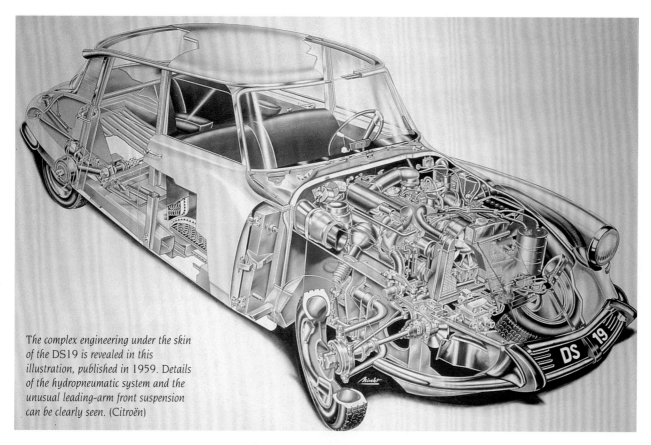

The complex engineering under the skin of the DS19 is revealed in this illustration, published in 1959. Details of the hydropneumatic system and the unusual leading-arm front suspension can be clearly seen. (Citroën)

resulting equilibrium of pressure held the road wheels at the required lock without deviation, whatever the cornering forces. The result was that no shock could be felt at the steering wheel, no matter if it were caused by a wheel hitting a pothole or other obstacle, or even by a puncture. Although there was normally no direct mechanical connection between the steering wheel and the front wheels, the system was designed so that in the event of a hydraulic pressure failure, a mechanical linkage between the steering column and the pinion was engaged, so that the car could be controlled manually in the conventional way. The action of the steering was extremely direct, movement of the road wheels from dead centre to full lock taking just 1.5 turns of the steering wheel.

The four-speed gearbox of the DS19 was entirely orthodox. Where it was unconventional was in its actuation, both it and the clutch being operated by hydraulic servo cylinders.

This relieved the driver of all manual effort when changing gear, and of the need to operate a clutch pedal, but not of the task of deciding exactly what ratio to select, and when. Constantly modified throughout the first years of production, the system reached its definitive form in September 1960 when a centrifugal regulator was introduced. By governing the disengagement and re-engagement of the clutch at a pre-set engine speed, this allowed the car to stop in gear without stalling when the brakes were applied, or to creep forward at a walking pace when they were released, as with a true automatic transmission. Although extremely complex and expensive to manufacture and install, the whole arrangement was a most intelligent compromise between the two conventional alternatives.

The DS19 and its successors were fitted with inboard front disc brakes and conventional drum brakes at the rear. Actuated by two independent

hydraulic circuits, front and rear, both containing fluid tapped from the vehicle's high-pressure hydraulic system, the design ensured that the braking effort was never limited by the amount of force that could be applied by the driver's foot on the pedal, or indeed by the travel of the pedal itself. In fact, the famous mushroom *pedalo* of the DS19 had little discernible travel at all – about half an inch instead of the 2in or more that was common on orthodox systems having a master cylinder. Clearly, the normal operating pressure of the hydraulic system – around 12,470psi – was much too great for progressive and sensitive braking, so a device was provided to step-down this pressure, in the manner of a transformer. This also served to create a balancing back-pressure, thus giving the driver the same 'feel' at the pedal. Therefore, as in any conventional system, the force applied to the brakes was related directly to the effort applied to the pedal. Yet on the DS19, this force was

Viewed from up high, the extraordinary form of the DS – this is a pre-1968 DS21 – is apparent. Notice how the bonnet runs right up to the base of the windscreen, and how there are no infill panels between it and the detachable front wings. (Citroën)

All this avant-garde engineering notwithstanding, it came as something of a disappointment to discover that under the DS 19s bonnet was an entirely conventional power-plant, longitudinally mounted with the gearbox in the nose. As late as 1952 it was envisaged that the DS would be powered by an entirely new all-alloy flat-six. But because of cooling and other problems this was abandoned in favour of a revised version of the four-cylinder 11CV 1,911cc engine of the Traction Avant, retaining its cast-iron block, three-bearing crankshaft, flat-topped pistons and 'wet' cylinder liners, but with a new alloy crossflow head which boosted output from 60bhp to 75bhp. This head incorporated the feature that had proved such a notable success on the 2CV engine: hemispherical combustion chambers with inclined valves. The spark plugs were located centrally, reached through long tubes in the rocker cover.

Production of the DS19 took time to get into its stride, with only a handful of cars being made in 1955 and fewer than 11,000 in 1956: the car suffered from severe teething-troubles that had to be cured before production could be increased. It was only really from spring 1957 that the car was a saleable proposition, and as a result the faithful old Traction Avant was not withdrawn until July of that year. Consequently, the evolution of the DS was, until 1967, largely a question of minor modifications – such as two grilles resembling ashtrays being incorporated in the front wings in September 1959, to counter overheating of the hydraulic system, and the arrival in August 1959 of longer rear wings.

In March 1961 an improved version of the 1,911cc engine, equipped with a crankshaft damper, was introduced. The bore and stroke were unchanged, but modified valves and porting and the use of higher-compression domed pistons together with a downdraught dual-choke compound Weber carburettor, yielded an extra 8bhp.

In time for the 1962 model year, the dashboard was restyled into a more

twice that provided by a conventional servo-assisted system – and thanks to the advantages of the mushroom pedal, it could be applied both instantly and effortlessly, allowing the driver to save vital seconds in an emergency.

On all DS models with 'hydraulic' transmission the parking brake was applied by a foot pedal. Spring-loaded, it was released by a knob located under the dashboard. On the later manual transmission versions of the DS a hand lever identical to that of the ID was used, mounted under the dashboard.

solid and easier-to-make vinyl-clad steel structure with a much-reduced plastic content. This was a prelude to the car's first exterior re-modelling, when in September 1962 a completely new front end was introduced. This featured an improved design of underskirt with revised cooling ducts for the engine and disc brakes, slots under the headlamps to collect fresh air for the heating and ventilation, and a revised vee-shaped bumper. The much-improved aerodynamic efficiency of this new front end increased top speed by 7 per cent. An important mechanical enhancement occurred when a column-shift manual transmission became available as an option, from January 1963.

In July 1965, a completely new series of engines was introduced. Although they shared numerous features with the old 1911cc long-stroke power unit, they had oversquare – ie shorter stroke and larger-bore – dimensions and the smoothness of a five-bearing crankshaft. In 1,985cc form, as used in

In September 1961, the original dashboard was revised, again by Bertoni. Now there was a place for a radio – albeit out of the driver's reach. The gear selector can be seen behind the steering wheel. (Ludvigsen) A year later, the

front of all D-series models was redesigned, with a new underskirt with revised air intakes, plus improved front bumpers with rubber over-riders. The ventilation grilles in the wings disappeared at the same time. (Citroën)

Driving the DS

The DS not only looks completely different from all other cars – it drives quite differently too. Firstly, the driving position is unlike that of a normal saloon – the driver sits higher up and closer to the wheel, in a softly cushioned seat that resembles an armchair.

No matter if the car is semi-automatic or manual, gearchanging must be undertaken in a gentle and unhurried manner, with finger-tip action on the selector lever if it is a 'hydraulic' car. As the clutch is operated automatically in tandem with the action of the selector mechanism, no footwork is involved when changing gear at cruising speeds on these versions: the driver has only to increase or decrease engine speed by use of the accelerator and then select the appropriate ratio by moving the

small change-speed lever located behind the steering wheel. Even at high speed, or under hard acceleration, a flick of the finger-tip is all that is required for a smooth, instantaneous gearchange, because the speed of clutch re-engagement is related directly to the setting of the throttle. As for the manual column-change, while its firm action and longish throw demand that it not be rushed, it is accurate and pleasant to use.

Braking with the mushroom pedal also demands the utmost delicacy: no force at all is required to slow the car down safely and progressively, even from very high speeds, and stamping on the pedal in panic will have disastrous consequences. Similarly, the steering action is quite effortless, and the car can be positioned with absolute precision and predictability

even though there is no mechanical connection between the steering wheel and the tyres.

No DS or ID will ever reward you with spectacular acceleration, but once wound up to its normal cruising gait – 75mph at 3,000rpm is the usual gearing for the DS21 and DS23 – progress is swift and sure.

The ride, of course, is far softer and more compliant than is considered desirable today, though it is not as spongy or sloppy as is often claimed by detractors. In fact, the whole experience is utterly restful and relaxing, so much so that very long journeys can be undertaken without fatigue. But if you are the kind of driver who thrives on excitement and likes to burn off energy and nervous tension behind the wheel, then be warned – the DS is not for you.

---

the DS19, the new engine produced 90bhp, but there was additionally a 2,175cc variant delivering 109bhp and used in the new DS21 model. At the same time the driveshafts were improved, the single-screw wheel fixing abandoned, and the gearbox of hydraulic-change cars given first-gear synchromesh and an improved clutch. Specific to the DS21 was an innovation that was typically Citroën: automatic height-adjustment for the headlamps, in response to changes in attitude prompted by braking or acceleration.

Throughout the sixties Citroën continued to refine the DS hydraulic system. Perhaps the most important change occurred in September 1966 when the last and most notorious weak-point was eliminated. Originally it had used red castor-oil based fluid, but this had the undesirable quality of absorbing moisture, leading to corrosion of steel components. In 1964 a synthetic fluid, at first clear but latterly red, was introduced, but for 1967 the switch

was made to an altogether more satisfactory green mineral-based ('LHM') fluid. At a stroke, Citroën's self-lubricating hydropneumatics became totally reliable and virtually maintenance-free.

The D-series received its second major facelift in September 1967, when it was given the so-called 'cat's eye' front, with twin headlamps mounted behind glass panels in reshaped front wings. This was not just a question of a restyle and an improvement in aerodynamics: in an industry-leading 'first' the inner long-range driving lamps – on the Pallas, Prestige and cabriolet, and optionally on the regular DS – were not fixed, but pivoted through a linkage to the steering so that they could swivel to follow curves in the road.

A year later the entire dashboard ensemble, including the steering column, was coloured black and the front seats were given higher, squarer backs for greater support. This was a prelude to the last major internal change, the arrival of an entirely new

dashboard for the 1970 model year. Flat and rectangular in aspect and sprayed with a charcoal-grey vinyl coating, its predominant feature was its three circular dials, one of which comprised a comprehensive warning display with a large red hydraulic-pressure warning light.

During this time the mechanicals of the DS had remained unchanged except in detail: for 1969 the 1,985cc engine had been uprated to 103bhp and the DS19 renamed the DS20, and the DS21 had seen power rise to 115bhp. For 1970, however, the DS21 was given Bosch electronic injection, significantly improving smoothness and pushing power output up to 139bhp SAE. After a further increase to 108bhp for the 1972 DS20, the final power-unit change took place for 1973, the DS21 being replaced by the 2,347cc DS23 that developed 124bhp in carb form and 141bhp when injected. As for the transmission, for 1970 the manual-shift DS20 was deleted, for 1971 the manual gearbox gained a fifth speed, and for 1972 a

For 1968 the new front was introduced, along with a revised design of bumper. The outer, fixed, pair of lamps are self-levelling and move vertically according to changes in the attitude of the car, while the inner pair of long-range lamps swivel horizontally, their beams scanning to left or right in phase with the steering. (Citroën)

For 1969 the dashboard was given a black lower section with rectangular push-button switchgear. This is a Pallas with leather trim. (LAT)

Borg-Warner automatic became optional on the DS21 – this being subsequently offered on the DS23.

In 1970, production had peaked with no fewer than 103,633 D-series cars being made; that demand was still strong is reflected in 1973 output of an impressive 96,990 vehicles. But the D's replacement, the CX, entered production in 1974, and April 1975 saw the inevitable ending of D-series production at the Quai de Javel and the final closure of the great car factory that André Citroën had created. Over almost twenty years of production, a grand total of 1,456,746 examples of all D Series types had been made, according to Citroën figures.

Buying Hints – all D-series cars

1. Relatively few pre-1968 cars have survived, so if your heart is set on one of these, be prepared for a long hunt. Additionally, a sizeable proportion of surviving D-series cars are left-hand-drive models imported relatively recently from France.

2. Beware fake Pallas models – it's not unusual for non-Pallas cars to have been fitted with Pallas leather trim. Avoid cars re-upholstered in non-original materials, and be wary of buying a car with a poor interior, as the correct fabrics to refurbish everything are not obtainable.

3. The 'D' rusts badly. Non-structural corrosion afflicts the door bottoms, the lower sections of the wings, and the bottom of the boot lid; this last panel is also prone to developing cracks. Rust beneath the headlamps on 'cat's eye' cars can be difficult – and thus expensive – to repair.

4. The closing panel of the boot corrodes, as does the boot floor and the rear corners of the boot by the bumper supports. Suspect a water-logged and/or rusted boot floor, or one that has been patched, as this may be an indication of worse but less visible maladies: water tends to run to the front of the boot and penetrate the rear box-section of the chassis, which is hidden by a closing plate. Repairs are complex and expensive. Rear bumper mountings also rot, on both saloons and estates.

5. Unbolt the rear wings – each is secured with a single exposed bolt – and check that the panels below the C-posts, or below the side window on estates, have not rotted through; at the same time you can inspect the closing panels at the front of the wheelarches. The steel 'epaulettes' at the rear of the inner wings also rust, but this is not serious, as welding in replacements is straightforward.

6. On estates, water trapped under the rubber seals of the upper tailgate can cause perforation.

7. There should be no bulges in the sills: if they don't run flat they are corroded. Beware patched sills, and inspect closely for rot where the A-post and B-post meet the sill, and where floor and sill come together. Sill repairs are not cheap.

8. Examine the scuttle area carefully, paying particular attention to the area around the screen pillars and to the points where the bonnet hinges mount; check, too, that there is no rot behind the screen rubbers.

9. A stainless steel roof moulding that is lifting above the windscreen suggests rust in the roof frame. Suspect a car with a heavy application of mastic around the roof joint – this is a sign that the cant rail underneath may be rotten, which is an indication that the car is likely to be badly corroded elsewhere.

10. The front apron and the area adjoining it – apron-to-wing brackets, the front crossmember, and the closing panels for the wheelarch –

A DS20 of 1972, equipped with the 1,985cc engine and semi-automatic transmission. The recessed door handles were introduced for the 1972 model year, at which stage all DS20 and DS21 models were given the directional and self-levelling lights as standard. (Citroën)

can rot out. Look beneath the spare wheel to check the state of the crossmember.

11. Properly maintained, the hydraulics should not cause serious problems. If you can, verify that the fluid has been changed regularly; a bad sign is dirty fluid and/or fine particles of rubber in the reservoir's filter. Remove the dust shield, inspect the main pipe loom for the rear hydraulic brake and suspension pipe circuits, where it emerges into the nearside rear wheelarch. Corroded, muck-encrusted pipes are a bad sign, shiny cupro-nickel lines a good sign. Start the car, and it should rise up without hesitation; a clicking from the pump (as it cuts in and out) at intervals of no less than 20 seconds is correct. A pump that does not cut out indicates a defective main accumulator.

12. A rupture of a pipe or hose in the high-pressure circuit will be detectable immediately by the very large quantity of fluid that escapes.

The source of minor leaks from the low-pressure circuit is usually found to be perforation in the rubber boots of the suspension cylinders.

13. A harsh ride suggests the suspension spheres need replacement, something that can be confirmed by a 'bounce test' – pushing the car downwards at each corner to check suspension compliance. If the vendor says the spheres have been 're-gassed', be cautious: it is better to replace the spheres or have them fully reconditioned with new diaphragms.

14. Heavy steering on power-steered cars suggests a problem – as does a high-pressure pump that is operating continuously on a car with a sound suspension system. If the steering fails to find a happy centre point, specialist adjustment of the mechanism will be required.

15. On 'hydraulic' cars, a snatchy gearchange – or a clutch that slips badly – suggests poor adjustment. Be

warned that clutch replacement is time-consuming and thus expensive.

16. If there is a clacking on full lock, the outer driveshaft joints are worn. Check for wear in the front balljoint swivels and in the front hub bearings – and note that replacing the latter is expensive.

17. Powered brakes should respond instantly and with minimal effort; if they don't, suspect problems. Repairing an ineffective parking brake could involve a lot of work, so be wary if this seems ineffective.

18. All the engines are durable, and their only weakness is that in old age they can blow their head gasket if the wet liners have sunk from their correct position. Be advised that the early three-bearing engines can seem rough by modern standards.

19. Michelin XAS tyres are essential from the viewpoints of both safety and authenticity, but are not likely to be cheap.

For 1973 came the DS23, powered by a 2,347cc engine, either naturally aspirated or with electronic fuel injection. A choice of manual, 'hydraulic' or Borg-Warner automatic transmissions was available. This is the Pallas version. (Citroën)

The last evolution of the dashboard occurred in September 1969 when this design was introduced on both DS and ID models. This particular example belongs to a manual rhd D-Super and is the version first seen in 1971 when the foam-padded safety steering wheel was added. (LAT)

The ID saloons,
the D-series estates, and the cabriolets

The ID19 was a cheaper, much simplified, manual-transmission version of the DS19, lacking its fully-powered braking, steering and gear selection but retaining hydropneumatic suspension. This version has the revised frontal styling introduced on all D-series models in September 1962. (Citroën)

For many potential customers the DS19 was too big a step forward from the relative simplicity of the Traction Avant – and certainly much too much of a jump in price. To cater for these people, Citroën announced the ID19 at the 1956 Paris Motor Show. This was a much-simplified manual transmission alternative,

lacking the DS19's fully-powered steering, braking and gear-selection mechanisms. Its name continued the punning theme established by its sister car, the *Déesse* or 'Goddess', the letters ID signifying I*dée* – 'Idea' in French. When it entered production in May 1957, its price of 925,000 old francs (for the Luxe version) contrasted significantly with the 647,000 francs that had been charged for the 11BL Traction Avant in its final season; but this was still appreciably cheaper than the DS19, which during the 18 months since its introduction had already escalated to over a million old francs.

That this was what the market wanted is proved by the sales figures. In 1958, the first full year of assembly, 28,654 ID19s were made, compared to 20,419 DS19s. The following year, 43,131 IDs were made as opposed to only 13,853 of the DS. By 1964, the split had settled down to around 60/40 in favour of the cheaper car – 45,218 IDs compared to 31,809 DSs – and this approximate balance continued to the end of production. Ultimately, about 750,000 IDs were made, as opposed to slightly less than 500,000 DS saloons.

It has to be said, though, that over the years the status of the ID19 gradually increased, as its specification was progressively improved; in particular, fully-powered brakes were soon standardised, in September 1961, and fully-powered DS steering was made optional from October 1962 onwards, eventually becoming standard on some models. Indeed, by the 1970s, with engines being shared between the two branches of the D-series family, it was often hard to tell the DS and ID versions apart at first glance. However, one fundamental distinction between the two types was permanently observed: no ID saloon was ever fitted with the same braking and semi-automatic transmission systems of its sister vehicle and therefore its hydraulic circuitry always followed a simplified layout compared to that of the DS saloon, with a brake pedal (on lhd cars) always of the conventional type rather than a mushroom button.

The ID19 range as generally sold comprised two versions, the Luxe and the Confort – there was a third model, an ultra-stark Normale powered by the 11D 1,911cc engine of the Traction Avant, but this was only current from 1957 until 1959 and a mere 393 were made. Both Luxe and Confort were

Citroën ID

1957–1975

ENGINE:
Four-cylinder in-line, water-cooled; alloy hemi head
Bore x stroke
   78mm x 100mm (1,911cc ID19)
   86mm x 85.5mm (ID19/ID20/
   D Special/D Super)
   90mm x 85.5mm (D Super 5)
Capacity
   1,911cc (1955-66)
   1,985cc/2,175cc (1966-75)
Valve actuation
   Pushrod
Compression ratio
   7.5:1/8.5:1/8.0:1
   8.75:1 (1,985cc/2,175cc)
Fuel system
   Single-choke Solex/Weber; dual-choke Solex/Weber (depending on model)
Power
   66bhp75bhp/81bhp at 4,500rpm (1,911cc)
   84bhp at 5,250rpm
   91bhp/98bhp/103bhp/108bhp at 5,500rpm (1,985cc)
   115bhp at 5,500rpm (D Super 5)
Torque
   97.6lb ft/104lb ft at 3,000rpm
   104lb ft at 3,500rpm (1,911cc)
   101.3lb ft at 3,000rpm
   112.1lb ft at 4,000rpm (1,985cc depending on model)
   125.9lb ft at 4,000rpm (D Super 5)
Note: All power and torque figures are SAE

TRANSMISSION:
Front-wheel drive
Four-speed manual gearbox; five-speed manual gearbox (optional on D Super, 1971-72 model years; standard on D Super 5)

SUSPENSION:
Front: Independent, twin leading arms, anti-roll bar, self-levelling hydropneumatic units
Rear: Independent, trailing arms, anti-roll bar, self-levelling hydropneumatic units

STEERING:
Rack-and-pinion, optionally fully powered (standard on D Super and D Super 5 from 1973 model year)
Turns lock-to-lock: 4.1 (2.9 powered)

BRAKES:
Unassisted until 1962 model year; thereafter fully-powered off high-pressure hydraulics
Front: hydraulic disc, inboard
Rear: hydraulic drum, outboard

WHEELS/TYRES:
Michelin disc, initially single-screw fixing; conventional stud-and-nut system from 1966 model year
Michelin X/XA2/XAS radial
165 x 400 front, 155 x 400 rear (1955-65)
180 x 380 front, 155 x 380 rear (1966-75)

BODYWORK:
Four-door saloon; unstressed steel panels on steel body/chassis base unit; grp (sometimes aluminium) roof; aluminium bonnet and (until 1960) aluminium boot lid

DIMENSIONS:
Length	15ft 8in/15ft 11½in
Wheelbase	10ft 3in
Track – front	4ft 11in
– rear	4ft 3in
Width	5ft 10½in/5ft 11in
Height	4ft 10in

WEIGHT (kerb):
24.25cwt (1959 ID19)
25.1cwt (1970 D Special)

PERFORMANCE:
Source: *The Motor/Motor*
Models quoted: 1959 ID19/1970 D Special
Max speed	82.6mph/95.1mph
0–50mph	15.1sec/10.6sec
0–60mph	19.9sec/15.0sec

PRICE INCLUDING TAX WHEN NEW:
ID19, 1959: £1,498
D Special, 1970: £1,399

NUMBER BUILT (DS and ID combined, Citroën figure): 1,456,115

powered by the same 1,911cc engine fitted to the DS19 but with modified carburation and induction de-tuning dropping output to 66bhp and reducing top speed by 6mph. The first of the pair to be introduced, the ID19 Luxe displayed at the 1956 Paris *salon*, was a budget version, noticeably austere in its fittings.

The ID19 Confort, available from July 1957 onwards, was a more lavish affair, its equipment closer to that of the DS19. Clearly it was intended for drivers who preferred the ID's manual steering and gearbox, but who were unwilling to sacrifice many other of the DS19's virtues.

As with the DS19, there was no

The DS & ID in competition

When the DS19 first appeared in 1955, few commentators predicted that the model would enjoy a long and successful competition career: it was judged to be too complex and too delicate, even, to survive the rough-and-tumble of the rally circuit. In fact, the reverse was true. The construction of the DS was immensely robust, while the hydropneumatic suspension enabled it to survive conditions that wrecked the springing of conventional cars. Time after time, long-distance events showed that its astonishing ride-comfort over poor surfaces cushioned both car and crews from shocks and fatigue. Citroën rally drivers were never as tired as their competitors, even after very long runs over arduous terrain.

The first notable victory occurred in 1959 when a standard ID19, privately entered by a team comprising Paul Coltelloni, Pierre Alexandre and

Claude Desrosiers won the Monte Carlo Rally, gaining for Citroën the manufacturer's prize. This success caused the company to recruit the Coltelloni team's organiser, René Cotton, to manage a semi-official competitions department with Citroën preparing the cars and funding entry costs and expenses.

Several years of strong achievement followed, with both ID19 and DS19 participating in numerous international events, the latter usually being equipped with the manual transmission introduced early in 1963 and preferred by drivers such as Neyret, Terramorsi, Toivonen and Bianchi. From 1965 onwards the team competed formally under the Citroën banner, initially entering a batch of DS19Ms in the East African Safari, then regarded as being among the toughest challenges in the competition world. Five out of the seventeen finishers were Citroëns. In

A controversial 'victory': Citroën won the 1966 Monte Carlo after the Minis in the top three places were disqualified for an alleged lighting infringement. (Citroën)

1966 Citroën won the Monte again, but under controversial circumstances: the BMC Mini-Coopers which had finished first, second and third were disqualified for alleged lighting infringements, leaving the DS21 of Pauli Toivonen to claim the laurels. This decision generated outrage in the British press and soured Anglo-French relations for many years, at least within the motor industry.

Thereafter, firstly under the direction of René Cotton and then latterly his wife Marlène Cotton (who took over control following her husband's death in 1971) Citroën's competition department began to concentrate on off-road endurance events such as the Moroccan and

Portuguese rallies and long-distance marathons which better demonstrated the qualities of the cars – as was proven when a DS23 won the 1974 World Cup Rally.

None of these later rallies equalled the drama and excitement of the 1968 London–Sydney Marathon. In this event, the Citroën team was actually entered by Citroën Cars Ltd, the cars being prepared in the Slough workshops. Two works DS21 cars took part, crewed by Bianchi/Ogier and Neyret/Terramorsi, with a third DS21 entered privately.

The longest and toughest rally so far devised, the Marathon covered 10,000 miles through Europe, Asia and Australia, crossing 12 countries in over 250 hours of non-stop driving. In all, 98 cars set out, on 24 November, but on arrival at Bombay eight days later, after covering 6,800 miles through France, Italy, Yugoslavia, Bulgaria, Turkey, Iran, Afghanistan, Pakistan and India, only 72 were left, with Bianchi/Ogier third, an excellent result as not one DS21 had required the slightest repair since leaving London. Many other entrants needed a complete re-build in Bombay, however.

On the final three-day, 3,500-mile leg, run mostly on dirt roads, Bianchi took first place, mid-way across the Australian outback, consolidating his position with every following hour until it seemed that he had built up an unassailable lead. No other competing car could cover the rough ground as fast as the DS21, thanks to its hydropneumatic suspension: a Citroën victory was thought inevitable.

But suddenly, a mere 100 miles from Sydney and just an hour or so short of the finishing line, disaster struck the Citroën in the form of a Mini driven by two local youngsters. Somehow their car strayed into the DS21's path, on a road that was supposedly closed and entirely clear of oncoming traffic. For all his skill, Ogier (at the wheel while Bianchi snatched a little sleep) was unable to avoid a head-on high-speed collision. The Citroën was wrecked, though both driver and navigator escaped with only minor injuries. At the time of the crash the car was 11 minutes ahead of Andrew Cowan's Hillman Hunter (which went on to win), having accrued only 39 penalty points against Cowan's 50 points.

In 1965 Citroën contested the East African Safari for the first time, with the DS, and accounted for five of the 17 finishers, with this manual-shift DS19 coming in fourth overall. (Citroën)

identifying badge of any kind on the car, other than the two small chevrons on the boot lid, which on the ID were silver as opposed to gold on the DS19. Initially offered in a completely different range of colours, the ID lacked the DS19's alloy sill covers and large stainless-steel wheel embellishers, and had rear winker housings in black or brown plastic. At first the grp roof was entirely unpainted, its bare, translucent surface left exposed, inside and out. From September 1961, however, it was pigmented white and given a skimpy headlining; thus throughout the sixties the ID saloon always had a two-tone paint scheme, with a roof that never matched the bodywork except on all-white cars. From 1971 onwards, however, with certain colour combinations a toning roof was possible on the D Super (see below), but not on the D Special, which was restricted to a white top only.

Inside, until the 1970 model year, ID-series cars always had a different dashboard. In its original form this was of sheet metal rather than injection-moulded plastic, with black upper surfaces and ventilation louvres and the main section in off-white, with an inset square instrument binnacle. As for the upholstery, initially this was of a lower grade, but from the 1959 model year DS-style nylon-fabric seating was optional on the Confort.

Because the earliest examples of the ID lacked hydraulically powered steering and gear selection, the high-output seven-cylinder pump fitted to the DS was not required. Therefore it had a simpler single-cylinder reciprocating pump, driven by an eccentric on the camshaft. When power steering was later fitted to ID saloons – and estates – a greater output of hydraulic fluid was demanded, and so the belt-driven seven-cylinder pump of the DS was used instead.

Although all ID saloons were equipped with the same brakes as their DS counterparts, during the model's lifetime a succession of three quite different hydraulic systems were used to actuate them. Since the ID

Seen on this early ID19 are the unusual centre-fixing wheels, which were common to all D-series cars until 1965. The small hub plugs were replaced on the ID by proper hubcaps in mid-1958. (Citroën)

This 1960–61 ID19 has all the hallmarks of French home-market cars, including the characteristic small hubcaps, the plastic rear indicator trumpets, and the white glass-fibre roof. Originally, this was left in its natural translucent state but from the 1962 model year it was pigmented off-white. On the later ID20 and D Super it was painted white. (Citroën)

was not initially equipped with power braking, similarly it had no need for brake accumulators, so these were omitted. The first two systems, fitted during the first three years of production only, were entirely orthodox, save for the use of the same special hydraulic fluid as the suspension system. The master cylinder, linked to both front and rear circuits, was operated by a pendant foot pedal in the normal way.

In September 1961, however, a third method was announced. This was a genuine fully-powered system that at last made the benefit of high-pressure hydraulic brake operation available to the ID driver. However, the simplified system used was very different from the load-sensitive system employed on the sister vehicle, since there was no equivalent distributor valve to balance braking effort front to rear. Nor was there a means of varying the

The 1967 model-year cars, such as this ID19B, are considered the most desirable by many enthusiasts as they combine the rarity of the old 'frog-eye' bodywork with the performance of the new five-bearing 1,985cc engine and the easy maintenance of the green-fluid hydraulic system. (Citroën)

The ID received the new 'cat's eye' front simultaneously with the DS models in September 1967. This rhd D Super has the large DS-type hubcaps fitted to export ID models, and the painted white roof typical of all ID type cars. (LAT)

braking effect applied to the rear brakes in proportion to the load being carried by the rear axle. In the ID system, two sliding piston valves – one for each brake circuit, front and rear – were placed in tandem within a common cylinder, known as a *doseur de freinage* or brake control valve. This

was so designed that when the brake pedal was depressed, the front brakes were applied ahead of the rear ones, the response of which was briefly delayed by an ingenious interaction of the slide valves. Supplied by fluid tapped from the main accumulator (for the front brakes) and the rear

suspension circuit (for the rear brakes), the *doseur* was also actuated by an orthodox pendant foot pedal, rather than the mushroom pedal used on the DS. It's worth noting, finally, that for the greater part of the life of the ID-series the parking brake was applied by a hand lever located under the

First presented in prototype form at the 1958 Paris show, the range of ID19 breaks or estate cars comprised a seven-seater Familiale, a Commerciale and an ambulance as well as the 5/7-seater estate car itself. All were powered by the same 1,911cc engine as the saloon. (Citroën)

dashboard, rather than the foot lever employed on the DS19. In July 1970, however, a foot lever was introduced on lhd cars only, but with a different type of release catch from that seen on the DS.

In its original pre-1968 shape the ID generally followed the evolution of the DS, but with engine changes being slightly out of step. Thus – having received an all-synchro gearbox for 1963 – it was only for 1965 that the ID was given the uprated 'damper' 1,911cc engine, in de-tuned 75bhp form, while it had to wait a year before, for 1967, it received the new five-bearing 1,985cc power unit, in 84bhp tune, mated to the improved gearbox introduced on the manual DS

The ID ambulances

Two types of ambulance were produced. The first, the *Ambulance Mixte*, was fitted with individual front seats and a folding rear bench seat that split in two parts, an arrangement that was unheard of elsewhere then but which is now universal today. The second, the *Ambulance Aménagée*, was equipped with a bench front seat and a single rear seat located on the right, plus a full-length, removable stretcher on the left. This

configuration provided for a medical attendant to ride beside the patient. By virtue of its smooth, stable, shock-free ride and low centre of gravity, the ID19 Ambulance marked an enormous improvement in the transport of the sick and injured, particularly in the case of patients suffering from spinal injuries. It was also easily modified to allow extra headroom inside by means of the raised glass-fibre roofs made by specialists such as Currus.

19M the previous year. Earlier, the 1,911cc engine of 1966 model-year IDs was given a power-boost to 81bhp.

Inside, the biggest change took place in September 1964 when a new dashboard, more like that of the current DS19, was introduced; this

was formed mainly from steel pressings sprayed with a textured black vinyl coating, and as with the DS gained a black lower section and push-button switchgear for 1969 – at which stage upholstery on the Confort was standardised as either Targa vinyl or DS-type jersey velour.

Following the arrival of the 'cat's eye' front for 1968, an improved 91bhp version of the 1,985cc engine was standardised for 1969 and a new model, the ID20 Confort, was introduced, with a 103bhp engine. During 1969 a short-lived ID19 Export replaced the ID19 Luxe, though relatively few of these bargain-basement IDs were ever sold. This was a prelude to a complete range overhaul for 1970 – coinciding with the standardisation across the entire D-series range of the new three-dial 'safety' dashboard. For purely marketing reasons the ID name was dropped, along with the Export/Luxe and Confort tags, and the ID19 became the D Special and the ID20 the D Super. Mechanically the cars were unchanged, but for 1971 a five-speed gearbox became optional on the D Super and for 1972 output of the D Special rose to 98bhp and that of the D Super to 108bhp.

The process of bringing the DS and ID series closer together reached its conclusion with the 1973 range. In the first instance, a new 110mph model, the D Super 5, joined the range, equipped with the 115bhp 2,175cc engine (from the discontinued DS21) and the five-speed gearbox. The line-up was completed by the D Super (with power steering as standard) and the D Special fitted with the Super's 108bhp engine; to differentiate the Super from the Super 5, however, the former lost its optional five-speed gearbox. As for those famous self-levelling and directional headlamps, for 1972 the self-levelling had become standard on the D Super, but the full self-levelling and directional combination continued to be available only as an option – and on cars where power steering was standard or a chosen option.

Also part of the ID family were the *breaks* or estates first exhibited in October 1958 and eventually introduced one year later for the 1960 model year. The key models were an eight-seater Luxe or Confort estate,

With its ochre plastic upholstery, bench front seat and grey plastic door trims, this is a pre-1963 Luxe estate or a Commerciale; over the years various permutations of standard or optional front-seat configurations were offered, dependent on the model. The lower tailgate is in its raised position. (Citroën)

with two sideways-facing folding jump-seats set into the load-deck (and called the Safari in the UK), and a Luxe or Confort Familiale which had three forward-facing rows of seats, the central ones being folding jump-seats. Then came a Commerciale, which was trimmed to Luxe specification minus the rear jump seats, and lastly two ambulance versions.

Built on a DS punt structure of unchanged wheelbase, the newcomers brought the advantages of Citroën's hydropneumatic suspension and braking to the world of estate cars. The result was a vehicle that, even when loaded up to the roof with eight people and their baggage would ride and handle just as safely and securely

*A bird's eye view of a 1969 ID20 break,
showing the fixed roof-rack standard on all
estates, including the ambulance. Note, too,
that the roof was always painted grey.
Directional headlamps were optional on the
estates, which in France always wore ID
hubcaps; UK cars had the DS dish-type wheel
covers. (Citroën)*

long, projecting loads; it was fitted
with two numberplate holders, so that
the registration was always visible.

Longer by 7¾in, the estate was some
4.5cwt heavier than the equivalent
saloon, which resulted in an average
reduction of 7 per cent in performance
and a 4 per cent drop in its overall fuel
consumption. Although Citroën
installed the mechanical elements and
carried out final cladding and
trimming of the cars, the body sub-
structure was built up by specialist
coachbuilder Carrosserie de Levallois,
using a thicker inner face for the side
box-members, to provide additional
strength. The Levallois firm sprayed
the shell with a light-grey paint, rather
than the black employed on the
saloons, and the same shade was used
for the tailgate and the steel roof, so
that all the visible parts of the
superstructure were the same colour –
with the exception of the area under
the roof-rack, which was a slightly
darker grey. From the 1969 model year
this detail was abolished. The roof
featured an integral non-detachable
roof rack formed from aluminium rods,
capable of carrying a 175lb load.

To equip these vehicles for load-
carrying, reinforced trailing arms were
fitted, plus larger-diameter rear
suspension cylinders and rear spheres
pressurised to 526psi instead of the
369psi employed on the saloons; the
dampers were also specific to the
estates. To provide extra stopping
power, larger rear drums with cooling
fins were used, but the front discs
were unchanged from those of the ID
saloon of the time.

Where the estates differed was in
their brake systems. Instead of the
simplified twin-circuit version
employed on the ID, the estates were
equipped from the start with a more
elaborate set-up derived from the DS
saloons, similarly controlled by a load-
sensitive brake-pressure distribution
device and operated by a mushroom
pedalo rather than a pendant pedal.
An innovation incorporated from the
outset was a revised hydraulic circuit
for the rear brakes, as was later fitted
on the DS Saloon from May 1961. This
used a hydraulic fluid supply obtained

as if carrying only the driver. With all
but the front seats folded down, the
vehicle offered a completely flat and
unobstructed load platform 5ft 10in
long. For even greater versatility, a
novel two-part split tailgate was
provided featuring a short lower
section that could be left open for

The 1971 version of the ID20 break. Notice how the numberplate is visible when the lower tailgate is down; the hatches in the boot floor concealing the jump seats are clearly visible. (Citroën)

D-series models assembled at Slough 1956–1966

Saloons

DS19	hyd	1,911cc	75bhp	6/56–4/61
DS19	hyd	1,911cc	83bhp	4/61–9/65
DW19	man	1,911cc	83bhp	9/64–9/65
DS19 DL	man	1,985cc	90bhp	9/65–3/66
DS21 Pallas	hyd	2,175cc	109bhp	9/65–3/66
DS21 Pallas	man	2,175cc	109bhp	9/65–3/66
ID19	man	1,911cc	66bhp	3/58–9/64
ID19	man	1,911cc	75bhp	9/64–9/65
ID19 DE	man	1,911cc	81bhp	9/65–3/66
ID Super	man	1,911cc	75bhp	9/65–3/66

Estates

ID Safari	man	1,911cc	66bhp	9/59–10/63
ID Safari	man	1,911cc	83bhp	10/63–9/65
ID Tourmaster	man	1,911cc	83bhp	9/64–9/65
ID Safari S2	man	2,175cc	109bhp	9/65–3/66

not from a separate brake accumulator but directly from the rear suspension spheres, so that the pressure available to operate the rear brakes was directly related to the loading of the rear suspension. The modification ensured that the braking effort on all four wheels was always related to the distribution of the load on board the vehicle, front and rear, so minimising the risk in an unladen car of the rear brakes locking up under emergency braking. From the outset the seven-piston rotary hydraulic pump from the DS was used, instead of the ID's normal single-cylinder type. To begin with, the steering of the

Revealed to the press in August 1960, the superb D-series cabriolet or décapotable was constructed under contract by the coachbuilder Henri Chapron. However, it was listed in the catalogues as a standard model available on special order from Citroën dealers. This is the first example to be constructed, photographed in July 1960. (Citroën)

estates was manual, but from September 1962 onwards power steering was offered as an option, and for 1973 was fitted as standard to the regular estate and the Familiale.

Just as the estates were in advance of the ID saloon in their braking system, so they led the range in their engine specification. Initially the engines and transmissions fitted to the estates were the same as those used on the equivalent ID saloons except for a lower final-drive ratio. However, in March 1963 the 83bhp DS engine and its all-synchro gearbox were introduced, while later, for the 1966 model year, the estates (but not the

saloons) got the new five-bearing 1,985cc unit of that year's DS. At the same time an ID21 estate with the DS21 2,175cc engine was introduced. For the 1969 model year, the ID19 estates were replaced by a more powerful ID20 version. Further to this, in February 1968 the estate was offered with the option of the semi-automatic DS gearbox and either the 1,985cc or 2,175cc power unit. Most of the limited numbers produced were exported, particularly to the United Kingdom.

Naturally enough, the estate range received the 'cat's eye' facelift for 1968, and when for 1970 the ID name was dropped from the saloons the

The Chapron 'specials'

In addition to the La Croisette four-seater cabriolet first seen in 1958 (of which 52 were made), that same year the specialist coachbuilder Henri Chapron also showed a four-seat coupé called the Le Paris, featuring the 'dog's leg' style of rear pillar seen on some of his other designs of the period. This was a short-lived model, only nine being made before it was replaced in 1960 by the Concorde, which had a square-cut roofline, and of which 38 were made. The La Croisette, meanwhile, continued until 1962, when it was replaced by the Palm Beach, which featured wind-down windows in the rear quarters and was made until 1972; a total of 30 was built. The final four-seater model was the 25-off Le Léman, which replaced the Concorde in 1966. This had an angular glasshouse with a more sharply sloping rear screen, and the last example, built in 1972, had the cut-off tail of Chapron's Lorraine saloon, described below.

Less numerous were Chapron's 2+2 cabriolets and coupés of 1960–68, which featured a longer rear deck and an upright 'occasional' bench seat at the back. The cabriolet was called the Le Caddy while the coupé was known as the Le Dandy. In all 34 of the former and 49 of the latter were made, with only two examples of each having the 1968-on restyled front. In common with all the Chapron DS 'specials', from the 1965 model year the rear wings were reshaped to incorporated vestigial fins.

These were first seen on the final Chapron variation on the DS, a four-door notchback saloon called the Majesty, which was announced at the

Chapron Le Dandy coupé in its second form, with finned rear wings. The chrome embellishments and Robergel wheel trims are typical of the Chapron 'specials'. (Max Stoop)

1964 Paris show. After 25 had been made this was replaced by the Lorraine, which had a higher and more square-cut roofline and a squared-off tail; the last example of the 19 built left the Chapron workshops in 1974.

The second version of Chapron's DS saloon, the Lorraine, had a taller and more square-cut glasshouse. (Max Stoop)

estates became known as Break 20 or Break 21 (the Safari 20 and Safari 21 – or latterly D20 Safari and D21 Safari in the UK). From the 1973 model year the estates carried 'DS' badging. Meanwhile, 1971 had seen the disappearance of the Luxe versions of the estate and Familiale.

For 1973 the 2,175cc engine was replaced by the 2,347cc carburettor unit, coupled to either a five-speed manual or four-speed 'hydraulic' gearbox; the result was a true high-performance estate car. Unique in its era, the DS23 Break – capable of cruising at over 100mph fully loaded and still returning 25mpg – was the forerunner of the high-speed sporting estates so popular today.

But from this point onwards, the extent of the range was gradually reduced. By January 1975, the line-up comprised the DS20 and DS23 Break, the DS20 Familiale and the DS20 and DS23 Ambulance. These remained in production beyond the cessation of DS saloon assembly in April 1975, but in June the DS23 variants were deleted and in September 1975 the DS20 Break and Familiale also disappeared. With the completion of the last ambulance in January 1976 the D Series had reached its end.

The last stage in its development had been the arrival of the *décapotable* or cabriolet. Known as the *Cabriolet Usine*, or 'Factory' cabriolet, the soft-top was included in the catalogue from February 1961, and continued in limited production for ten seasons, evolving technically with the rest of the DS and ID range.

Unveiled in August 1960, this superb two-door convertible was available in DS19 form (initially with 'hydraulic' transmission but from January 1964 with a manual option) and, from July 1961, in ID19 form (with manual transmission only plus the option of fully-powered steering and, later, fully-powered brakes as well). To begin with, the regular 75bhp DS and 66bhp ID 1,911cc engines were used, but for 1966 the ID cabrio was deleted, in favour of the 2,175cc DS21 engine, in either naturally aspirated or – later on – fuel-injected form.

Other special-bodied cars

Over the years various enterprises built re-bodied or substantially modified versions of the D-series. A fair number of these cars were short-wheelbase two-door conversions, while Swiss coachbuilders Langenthal and Beutler both essayed a drophead – and German outfit Reutter came up with a four-door cabriolet. Pick-ups and flat-bed transporters were not uncommon, but more often than not these were made by chopping up aged second-hand cars. Best known in the field of DS-based commercials was Pierre Tissier, who made a series of six-wheeled high-speed newspaper delivery vans. Perhaps the most elegant of all the special-bodied DS/ID cars, though, was the GT19 styled by Frua and marketed by tuner Hector Bossaert: in all 13 were built. Bossaert also came up with two convertibles, one on a notably shortened wheelbase.

One-off short-wheelbase cabrio by Bossaert; the handling was challenging. (Jon Pressnell collection)

The idea of a stylish and elegant DS cabriolet was first developed by the specialist coachbuilder Henri Chapron. His first design, the La Croisette, appeared in 1958, and was constructed and marketed as a private venture, never seen in Citroën's own showrooms. But then, in response to public demand, in 1960 Citroën commissioned Chapron to build an authorised cabriolet for sale through its network – albeit to special order rather than from stock.

The basis of the car was a standard saloon shell minus B-pillar and roof supporting structure, and with the sidemembers of the chassis strengthened and stiffened in the same way as on the ID Break. This was supplied to Chapron with its engine and other mechanical elements and controls already installed. On this platform, Chapron installed the bodywork, seating, hood and other trim elements hand-crafted in his Levallois-Perret workshops on the outskirts of Paris, or purchased from Citroën-approved suppliers. The body featured a new one-piece steel rear wing structure, a new glass-fibre boot lid, and two new front doors that were 18cm (approximately 7in) longer than the originals, produced by 'cutting and shutting' two standard steel doors. The cabriolet was less than an inch longer than the saloon, but in original DS19 form was no less than 0.9cwt heavier – a testament to the extra steelwork that went into strengthening the chassis and constructing the bodywork. Fully carpeted throughout – even the chassis side-members were covered with a deep Wilton pile – and normally upholstered in leather, the interior was trimmed to a very high standard, with features subsequently copied on the Pallas saloons. Having two individual seats at the front and a narrow bench occasional seat at the rear, the cabriolet represented the height of Parisian chic, with exterior detailing that bore the unmistakeable Chapron touch. Special features included a wide stainless-steel strip running down the full length of the car at the crease point of the doors, with a further strip fitted along the bottom

The décapotable in its ultimate post-1967 form, equipped with the 2,175cc DS21 engine. (Citroën)

The spirit of the Swinging Sixties exemplified – the model is actress and singer Jane Birkin. A total of 1,365 'factory' cabriolets was built between February 1961 and August 1971 – in all 770 of DS19 type, 112 of ID19 type and 483 of DS21 type. (Citroën)

The Slough-built DS and ID

As the Slough-assembled Traction Avant had proved to be a sound commercial success, Citroën entertained high hopes that this achievement would be repeated with the DS19 and ID19. But sadly this was not to be.

Although exhibited at the October 1955 London Motor Show, the DS19 did not enter production at Slough until June 1956, followed by the ID19 in March 1958, and manufacture lasted for scarcely a decade. In February 1966 – exactly 40 years to the day after it had been opened by André Citroën – the Slough works was closed, having assembled a mere 8,668 D-series vehicles (4,948 DS19 and DS21 saloons plus 4,948 assorted ID19 and ID21 saloons and estates). From then on all UK-market cars came from Paris fully-completed.

For the first nine years, a CKD system of assembly was followed, with bodyshells, panels, engines, transmissions and hydraulic systems supplied from France, but with the highest possible proportion of other components UK-sourced in order to qualify for import/export tariff relief. Due to the unorthodox design of the DS and ID, the British content was less than before, though it was still substantial and included items such as wheels, tyres, glass, radiators, exhausts, batteries, lamps, instruments, wiring harnesses, dynamos, starter motors and other electrical equipment.

These variations made for certain visible differences. The most

noticeable were the front bumper, which incorporated a rectangular plinth to mount the numberplate upright to satisfy British regulations, the black-painted front apron, and the 'Citroën' script badge on the bonnet. Slough also went its own way in matters of interior trim, made for the most part in its own workshops, and produced its dashboards to its own designs, including the famous wooden fascias fitted to the ID19 saloons and estates up to September 1964. The colour schemes offered were also peculiar to Slough.

Throughout the 1957–1964 period Slough averaged around 1,000 cars a year compared to the 2,000 or so that had been typical for the Traction Avant – with production peaking at over 2,100 units in 1960. But by 1964 annual output had dwindled to below 500, because

This 1960 Slough ID19 is wonderfully original. The front apron is painted black, and the pillars are in the main body colour; other features include DS hubcaps, the front bumper with its vertical plinth for the numberplate, and DS sill covers. The auxiliary lamps are a period extra. (Jon Pressnell)

Australia and South Africa had by then set up their own assembly operations. Accordingly, in September that year, for the final 17 months of operations the factory changed to an SKD (semi-knocked-down) system of assembly. Instead of constructing cars, Slough simply painted and trimmed fully-built cars delivered from Paris minus their lighting and electrical systems, but with their engines, transmissions and hydraulic systems already installed and their body panels fitted but not finished.

edge of the doors, both trims terminating in a splash-plate forward of the rear wheelarch. At first standard DS wheel embellishers were fitted, but after the introduction of the Pallas in 1964, Pallas wheel covers were used, as were Pallas-type sill closing plates. The tail-lamps, meanwhile, were round units, and as the famous roof-level indicators of the saloons could not be

fitted, unique boomerang-shaped winkers were sited on the rear deck, forming the corners at the base of the folding hood, where they were visible from both the side and back of the car.

The cabriolet was finally deleted from the catalogue at the end of the 1971 model year, production having fallen to only 40 units in 1970 compared with the 241 sold during

1963, the year of highest output. However, at least three more examples are known to have been subsequently constructed by Chapron. In total, 1,365 'factory' cabrios were made – 770 DS19, 483 DS21 and 112 ID19 – compared with a total 289 examples of Chapron's own private DS-based cabriolet, fixed-head coupé and limousine designs.

The cabriolet was deleted from the Citroën catalogue in 1971, but a few further cars were constructed by Chapron, as private orders, and this is one of them. In fact, this car is not just the last décapotable to have been built, but also the final DS. Constructed using a 1973 DS23 saloon, it was delivered to its owner in 1978, three years after D-series production had ended. (John Reynolds)

The Ami 6
and the Ami 8

Introduced in April 1961, the Ami 6 marked Citroën's belated entrance into the mid-sized family-car market. Based on the 2CV, it was powered by a 602cc version of the air-cooled flat-twin. (Citroën)

By the late fifties, the scarcities and rationing of the *les années grises* – the grey years – were a thing of the past and motoring had become a leisure activity for the French middle classes, as elsewhere throughout Western Europe. Just as André Citroën had predicted, the automobile was by now well established as an indispensable recreational accessory as well as a commercial and industrial tool, to be enjoyed as much for weekend and holiday excursions as for daily commuting or other work-related travel. Increasingly it was also becoming a possession aspired to equally by women as by men.

The design of the roof has the effect of lengthening the glasshouse; side swages add both form and rigidity to the Ami's thin panels. (Citroën)

But in attempting to respond to this pressing new demand, and satisfy the requirements of the large increase in lady drivers then taking to the roads of France, Citroën's dealers found themselves in a quandary. Although they had in their showrooms two of the nation's best-selling cars, the 2CV and DS19/ID19, there was nothing in between to match the attractions of rival designs such as the Renault Dauphine and Floride, which were deliberately styled and promoted to appeal to females. What was needed was a new medium-class car that would plug the gap in the range.

Billed as 'The world's most comfortable medium-class car', this new intermediate Citroën, the Ami 6, was announced in April 1961, although sales did not begin until September that year. It was the first model to be built at Citroën's brand-new factory at Rennes-La-Janais in Brittany, opened by General de Gaulle the previous year, and using the platform chassis and proven mechanical elements of the 2CV in conjunction with an all-new body of a very different design. In fact the Ami 6, together with successors and derivatives, shared so many components with their 2CV cousins that they were always classed as

Ami 6 and Ami 8

1961–1978

ENGINE:
Two-cylinder horizontally-opposed, air-cooled
Four-cylinder horizontally-opposed, air-cooled (Ami Super)
Capacity
    602cc/1,015cc
Bore x stroke
    74mm x 70mm/74mm x 59mm
Valve actuation
    Pushrod/ohc, belt-driven
Compression ratio
    7.2:1 (early Ami 6)/9.0:1 (Ami 8 and Super)
Carburettor
    Single-choke Solex downdraught/ Solex twin-choke
Power output
    22bhp DIN (Ami 6)/32bhp DIN (Ami 8)/53.5bhp DIN (Super)
Torque
    29.6lb ft at 2,800rpm (Ami 6)
    30lb ft at 4,000rpm (Ami 8)
    52lb ft at 3,500rpm (Ami Super)

TRANSMISSION:
Front-wheel drive.
Four-speed, all synchronised; floor change on Super

SUSPENSION:
Front: Independent, by leading arm, with horizontal coil springs interlinked (except Super) to rear suspension; inertia and friction dampers until May 1963, thereafter inertia and telescopic dampers
Rear: Independent, by trailing arm, with horizontal springs interlinked (except Super) to front suspension; inertia and friction dampers until May 1963, thereafter inertia and telescopic dampers

STEERING:
Rack-and-pinion, unassisted
2.6 turns lock-to-lock

BRAKES:
Drum, hydraulically operated; inboard at front. Disc front brakes from 1969.

WHEELS/TYRES:
Michelin radial, 125x15in/135x15in

BODYWORK:
Platform chassis; steel body
Available as four-door saloon, estate, van

DIMENSIONS (Ami 6/Ami 8):
Length	12ft 8in/13ft 1in
Wheelbase	7ft 10½in
Track, front	4ft 1½in
Track, rear	4ft 0in
Width	5ft 0in
Height	4ft 10½in/5ft 0in

WEIGHT:
(Source: *Autocar*)
12.75cwt (Ami 6, half-full tank)
14.6cwt (Ami 8, idem)
15.9cwt (Ami Super, idem)

PERFORMANCE (Ami 6/Ami 8/Super):
(Source: *Autocar*)
Max speed: 68.0mph/72mph/88mph
0-50mph: 24.7sec/19.4sec/12.0sec
0-60mph: 44.0sec/31.7sec/17.1sec

PRICE INCLUDING TAX WHEN NEW:
£824 (Ami 6, Feb 1962); £733 (Ami 8, July 1970); £995 (Ami Super, June 1973)

NUMBERS BUILT: 1,039,384 Ami 6; 755,925 Ami 8; 44,820 Ami Super

Flaminio Bertoni

Although he was responsible for the shape and style of four of the most individual and instantly recognisable cars ever produced, Flaminio Bertoni, the stylist of the Citroën Traction Avant, 2CV, DS19 and Ami 6, remains virtually unrecognised in the English speaking world, not least among those drivers who own and admire the cars that he designed.

Yet experts on automobile and industrial design now acknowledge that he deserves to be ranked among the most gifted and influential automobile stylists to have worked on either side of the Atlantic.

The son of a tailor, Bertoni was born on 10 January 1903 at Masnago, a suburb of Varese in Northern Italy. He began work in 1918, aged 14, as an apprentice sheet-metal worker at la Societa Anonima Fratelli Macchi, a *carrozzeria* at Varese. Here his outstanding talent as a draughtsman, painter and sculptor was recognised by his employers who transferred him to their design department and enabled him to study at the local art school. His first known design for a car body was produced in 1922.

In 1923, aged 20, he made his way to Paris where eventually he found work as a designer and model-maker with the coachbuilding firm of Manessius. Within two years he had

Flaminio Bertoni, 1903–1964, the Italian designer and sculptor responsible for the exterior styling of the Traction Avant, the 2CV, the DS19, the Ami 6 and many other prototypes. Some say the Ami was his favourite among all his automotive creations. (Leonardo Bertoni)

moved to the Citroën factory at the Quai de Javel, where he started work as a bodywork stylist and designer on 1 January 1925. Four months later, however, he was on the move again, having decided to return to Varese where, eventually, in 1929, he opened his own design consultancy, the *Studio Tecnico di Carrozzeria Flaminio Bertoni*. The next two years were spent designing car, bus and lorry bodies

for various client companies, work that was supported by his other freelance activities as a graphic artist, illustrator and book-jacket designer.

By October 1931 he had returned to France, where he found another job, this time with the SICAL company (*Société Industrielle de Carrosserie de Levallois-Perret*) which produced special bodies for Citroën. Through this work he was able to resume his contacts at Citroën's *Bureau d'Études*, with the result that on 8 July 1932, aged 29, he rejoined the company to work on the forthcoming Rosalie models and later the Traction Avant. Initially he was employed only as a maker of plaster styling models, but as his talents became apparent, he gradually assumed overall responsibility for all matters of exterior styling and interior design.

But because during the Michelin era research and development were conducted in total secrecy and an absolute ban on personal publicity for employees and their achievements was rigidly enforced, throughout his career Bertoni worked in virtual anonymity. Consequently, his contribution – indeed, his entire presence at Citroën – remained unknown to the outside world until many years after his death. So

members of the Type A family of vehicles, in Citroën parlance.

Although rarely seen outside France, the Ami range was destined to become another smash hit for Citroën, and, like the 2CV, lasted much longer than was originally planned. By 1965, the daily production rate had overtaken

Thanks to the absence of a transmission tunnel and central console, the interior of the Ami 6 had a big-car feel; this is an estate with the dashboard top, steering wheel, gearlever knob and switchgear in black, as introduced for the 1967 model year. (Citroën)

that of the 2CV, and altogether, between 1961 and 1971, 1,127,649 Ami 6 vehicles of all types found customers. At the height of its popularity in 1966, when 180,000 were sold, it ranked as France's best-selling car by far. Later, between 1969 and 1979, healthy sales of the more powerful Ami 8 and Ami Super confirmed the design's enduring strengths and virtues.

Derived directly from the 2CV, the Ami 6 shared its principal components: an unburstable air-cooled twin-cylinder boxer engine, a four-speed gearbox with front-wheel-

complete was this ignorance of his work, that until comparatively recently the lines of the DS19 were still being attributed to the Italian styling house Bertone, due to an elementary confusion of names.

Small, dark and extremely energetic, Bertoni was a workaholic who never stopped creating things, beavering away late into the night and throughout weekends. He certainly didn't confine himself to designing cars. While constantly chewing aspirin tablets to fend off the migraines caused by a motorbike accident that he had suffered during the war, he kept up an impressive output of highly accomplished works of art – architectural drawings, charcoal sketches, clay statuettes and busts of his family, friends and colleagues.

Colleagues described him as working like a demon, keeping them amused with a constant stream of witty remarks delivered in his Italian accent, which he never lost even after living so long in France. Blessed with a natural eye for shape and form, he could visualise the finished appearance of a car, from every angle and then sculpt it out of a solid mass of clay.

Following this accident, caused by a collision with a German armoured car late in 1940, Bertoni took a year's leave of absence from Citroën to convalesce. It was during this period that he began to study architecture at the École Nationale des Beaux Arts in Paris, eventually gaining a diploma in 1947. Later, in 1953, he was awarded the distinction of *Chevalier de l'Ordre des Arts et des Lettres* for his work as a sculptor.

Flaminio Bertoni died suddenly on 7 February 1964, struck down by a cerebral haemorrhage at the age of 61, having completed 32 years of service at Citroën. An exceptionally inventive and imaginative talent of the type that flourished under the Michelin regime, he was above all a practical hands-on craftsman with the gift of being able not merely to appreciate the problems and preoccupations of engineers but actually to assist them in their work.

The remarkable originality of his imagination is obvious; what seems all the more remarkable is his deep, practical understanding of the properties and capabilities of the materials at his disposal. As one of the very first designers to work with thermoplastics and glass-reinforced polyester resins as well as the traditional aluminium and steel, his grasp of the opportunities was total.

drive transmission, rack-and-pinion steering and interconnected all-independent suspension. Early versions, equipped with an enlarged and uprated 602cc version of the 2CV engine, produced 21bhp at 4,500rpm and had a top speed of 65mph, slightly greater than that of the 2CV, with no loss of fuel economy, which was claimed to exceed 50mpg. Output was increased to 25.5bhp in September 1964, to 28bhp in September 1967 and to 35bhp in May 1968, bringing the top speed to almost 70mph. This gave the Ami 6 a surprisingly fast yet economical long-distance cruising ability for a car endowed with so little outright performance.

Part of the secret was the Ami's lightness: its kerb weight was 12.75cwt, when a contemporary four-door Morris Minor weighed 15.25cwt. This was because it used notably light external panels and featured a lightweight unpainted translucent plastic roof, riveted in place. A further weight-saving measure was the use of aluminium for the bumpers, grille and trim strips.

Styled by Flaminio Bertoni, the Ami 6 also shared numerous trim and styling features with the D-Series range, such as its single-spoke steering wheel, door handles and switchgear. Yet its aesthetics had little in common with the DS's elegant shape and style, the car resembling a pop-eyed frog rather than a slinky shark! For some people, the Ami represented Citroën's attitude to design at its most unorthodox and original – the raw, uncompromising result of engineering logic and integrity. For others, the Ami 6 was quite simply the ugliest car ever made.

Just like the 2CV, the Ami 6 was far superior to most small family cars of its era in the high standards of comfort, roadholding and ride that it offered. Despite displaying an alarming degree of body roll when

The reverse-rake rear window was the Ami 6's most controversial feature. This is a very early car with fixed rear windows. (Citroën)

The C60 prototype

The efforts to produce a medium-sized intermediate-class vehicle that would be a halfway house between the D and A series cars began in the late 1950s with an ambitious research project code-named the C60. This prototype combined hydropneumatic suspension with a flat-four air-cooled engine, and featured radically innovative bodywork styled by Flaminio Bertoni. Eventually, however, the proposal was abandoned in favour of a much less sophisticated (and less expensive to manufacture) solution that reached production in 1961, as the Ami 6, and which included the unconventional reverse-rake rear window of the C60.

The C60 represented a stylistic bridge between the Ami 6 and the DS, but this flat-four saloon with hydropneumatic suspension was stillborn. (Jon Pressnell collection)

Ami around the world

Naturally the Ami 6 was assembled at Citroën's factory in Brussels; it was also built in Spain from 1966, under the name Dynam, and in Madagascar. The Ami 8, too, was made in Belgium and Spain, and was also assembled in Portugal (as the 'Citroën 8') and in Yugoslavia; a peculiarity of the Spanish Ami 8 was that it was called the Citroën C8 – or C8 Familiar in the case of the estate. Further afield, Argentina assembled the Ami 8, as did Ecuador, Paraguay, Uruguay, Tunisia, Dahomey and Madagascar. The Ami 6 was never made at the Slough works, although a small number of right-hand-drive examples were imported into the UK, and, later, far larger quantities of the Ami 8. Surprisingly, the Ami 6 was sold in the United States, in both saloon and estate form. The US cars were characterised by their twin round headlamps, below which sat a round indicator in a sculpted chrome housing; at the rear paired round lamps were used, in conjunction with twin rectangular numberplate lamps, while both front and rear bumpers were reinforced with tubular nudge bars. The Ami 8 was never officially imported into the United States.

cornering, its stability and handling were always entirely predictable and forgiving, whatever the conditions, while its tight 18ft turning circle made for outstanding manoeuvrability.

When it arrived in 1964, the Ami 6 *break* or estate version (accompanied by the Ami 6 *Commerciale*, which differed from the passenger version only in that it had no rear seats) proved to be an instant success. At a stroke, the estate eliminated all aesthetic objections to the lines of the saloon, as well as offering an unrivalled amount of load-carrying space – 53 cubic feet no less, with a load floor length of 5ft 5in if the rear seat were removed. One of the first inexpensive small estate cars offered to the French motoring public, the *break* turned out to be the ideal vehicle for small families, small businesses and small farmers alike, offering all the qualities of reliability, simplicity, versatility and economy provided by the 2CV, but with the bonus of a much greater load-carrying capacity. Sales of the saloon declined rapidly, to the point where in the 1967 model year a mere 34,344 were made, against 135,046 estates.

Meanwhile, the Ami 6 gradually evolved. For 1965 the 2CV's centrifugal clutch was offered as an option, during 1966 12-volt electrics were introduced, and for 1968 a further new up-market estate variant, the Club, arrived. Immediately distinguishable by its twin round headlamps, the new model was joined by a short-lived saloon version at the 1968 Paris show. Finally, May 1968 saw the arrival of a two-door van, the *Service*, with either glazed or panelled sides.

Relatively few of these vehicles were made, for in the spring of 1969 the Ami 6 was replaced by the Ami 8, launched in saloon form at the Geneva Motor Show that March. The large improvement in performance implied by its numerically greater new name was misleading, however, as the Ami's engine capacity and fiscal rating remained exactly the same as before. All that changed was the appearance of the car, which was given a major facelift. The grille and headlamp

Left: The Ami 6 estate was a huge success, and ended up taking the lion's share of Ami 6 sales. (Citroën)

Right: The Ami 8, which replaced the Ami 6 in April 1969: its frontal aspect was completely redesigned, but despite the change of name, its engine and other mechanical details were not altered. (Citroën)

Left: The Ami 8 estate had a deeper tailgate and the same rear lights as the saloon. (Citroën)

In profile the Ami 8 was less startling than its predecessor. Viewed from the rear, the Ami Super saloon looks virtually identical to the Ami 8 –

but for the side-stripes, which were absent from the first cars. Note that these saloons are not hatchbacks. (Citroën)

The M35 coupé

The most extraordinary off-shoot of the Ami range was a two-door coupé with a rotary engine and hydropneumatic suspension. This bizarre hybrid, known as the M35, was made between 1969 and 1971. Every bit as abnormal as the car itself was the way in which it was launched on the roads of France.

For the M35 was no ordinary production model, but rather a small run of essentially experimental cars, sold only to carefully-selected high-mileage Citroën customers. Their purpose was to test the Citroën-NSU rotary engine in 'real world' conditions, as opposed to the more controlled environment of the in-house test department. The original idea had been to do this in secret, with the selected customers being given an otherwise standard-looking car equipped with the Wankel power unit. However Citroën PR chief Jacques Wolgensinger persuaded the company that it would be better to make a big publicity splash out of the whole operation, presenting it as a demonstration of how Citroën was investing in new technology and, moreover, in direct consultation with its customers.

Consequently it was decided to commission Heuliez to build 500 coupé-bodied Ami 8s, employing hydropneumatic suspension all-round. The Wankel engine was a single-rotor unit of 995cc equivalent, delivering 49bhp DIN, and was mated to an orthodox four-speed gearbox with the regular Ami dashboard push-pull-twist change. All the cars except the first prototype were painted in metallic grey, and all carried on their front wings the legend 'Prototype Citroën M35', accompanied by the number of the car. In the end only 267 examples were made, between 1969 and 1971. The 1970 price-tag of 14,120 francs positioned the little fastback between the GS Club and the D Special, but unsurprisingly the M35

was still sold at a loss to the guinea-pig customers – who had the benefit of a two-year engine guarantee and 'fast-response' technical support.

Despite modest performance, poor low-down torque, a lack of engine durability, and fuel consumption that was unlikely to better 30mpg, the experiment was clearly judged worthwhile, as it was to lead, as we shall see, to Citroën's one and only production rotary model. Most of the 267 cars were bought back from their owners by Citroën, and ultimately scrapped, but a handful of M35s survive in private hands.

The M35 had a coupé body built by Heuliez, and used hydropneumatic suspension. (Citroën)

Buying Hints

1. On mechanical matters, the advice given in the 2CV chapter applies to the Ami, though all but the very earliest examples of the Ami 8 had front disc brakes.

2. The Ami is now one of the rarest of Citroën's flat-twin models – especially in Britain. You may still find the odd Ami 8 advertised for sale in French local papers, but in its country of birth the Ami 6 has migrated to the classic-car press, and many have been bought

by Dutch enthusiasts. The Super is particularly scarce in the UK, not least because some have been cannibalised to make 2CV 'Q-cars': this is essentially a body swap, as to cope with the extra performance you also need the Super's chassis and suspension.

3. There is a quite common trap for moisture/muck/rust on the rear wings, from which corrosion can work its way into the body. As with the Dyane, panels aren't widely

available, though 2CVGB's Spare Parts Organisation (at www.2cvgb.co.uk) offers a range of repair sections, including the floor, lower bulkhead, and inner and outer roofline sections – as well as the clutch cable for right-hand-drive Ami 8s. This range of parts will expand in the future, as less becomes available from the specialists.

4. For checkpoints on the Ami Super's engine, see the GS/GSA chapter.

Driving the Ami

Not surprisingly the Ami driving experience is equally as unusual as the engineering and appearance of the car itself. In comparison with an early-sixties 2CV, an Ami 6, of course, is much speedier and can reach almost 70mph, whereas a 425cc *Deuche* of the era will be hard-pushed to hit 50mph, the Ami 6's natural cruising gait.

Beyond this, you have the same highly flexible under-damped suspension, which gives a floating ride and a degree of body lean that the uninitiated are likely to find off-putting. You also have the same easy-acting push-pull-twist gearchange, relatively heavy steering and brakes, and tenacious roadholding – characterised by a fair degree of understeer that can be reduced by

lifting off mid-corner in typical front-wheel-drive style.

The Ami 8 does not feel hugely different, other than being marginally less quirky both inside and out. The big-car ride (helped by comfortable seats) is still a major feature, and the engine still makes a fair old din when made to work for its living. A bonus is the effective and effortless disc front brakes, so much better than the Ami 6's drums.

As for the Ami Super, this rarity really is something of a Q-car – as testers noted at the time. Putting the GS engine in the lightweight Ami body resulted in a 90mph car with appreciably stronger acceleration than a regular Ami 8. As with the flat-twin, you need to rev the engine to get the best out

of the car: with its poor low-end torque you'll find that it really only comes alive above 3,500rpm. With the GS floor change, uprated brakes and firmer suspension (although roll is still pronounced), the Super has more of a sporting flavour than a twin-pot Ami, and is bound to put a smile on the face of any lover of A-series Citroëns. Those less steeped in all things double-chevron might find the recipe less appealing: the crudeness of the trim and fittings, the notchy and vague gearchange, the relentless understeer and the high noise level are all very real minus points. But if you like your small-car motoring to have a dose of individuality, you may be prepared to overlook these failings.

---

treatment was tidied up, the overhanging bonnet line was smoothed out, and at the rear the reverse-rake window was replaced by a more modern sloping fastback, though this improvement did not extend to providing a hatchback. Inside, meanwhile, the dashboard was completely revised. In autumn 1969 the Ami 6 estate and van gave way to Ami 8 versions.

As with the Ami 6, two different trim specifications were offered for the Ami 8: an up-market Club (available as a saloon only) and a more spartan Confort. Although the first Ami 8 saloons retained drum brakes, from the time of the launch of the estate versions in September 1969 all models were fitted with inboard front disc brakes. A further refinement was the arrival in June 1970 of winding front windows.

Finally, in January 1973, the Ami family was enlarged by the arrival of the Ami Super. Available as a saloon, an estate and a *Service* van, the Super was powered by a 53.5bhp version of the GS 1,015cc flat-four – recently rendered largely redundant in the GS

by the arrival of the much-improved 1,220cc unit. With four times the capacity of the original 2CV engine, it was capable of pushing the Ami up to a top speed of 87 mph. With a floor change for the ex-GS gearbox, rather than the traditional push-pull dashboard lever, the Super also had bigger brakes front and rear, non-interconnected suspension, and a chassis made of thicker-gauge steel.

Although the Ami Super offered a much-improved performance, it was relatively thirsty; more to the point, it compared poorly with more modern vehicles such as the Peugeot 104 and 204 and the Renault 12, all of which

were barely more expensive. Not surprisingly, production was halted in early 1976 after just three years, and with only 44,820 having been built.

Meanwhile the 602cc Ami 8 saloon continued for another two years until it was replaced by the new Visa model, which arrived in early 1978; the estate survived until 1979. During its 17-year career the Citroën Ami had made friends with over 1,840,000 customers.

The trim of the Ami 8 was more up-market, though the dashboard was still somewhat eccentric in design. Winding front windows arrived in 1970. (Citroën)

The SM

The fully glassed-over nose cowling is perhaps the most arresting element of the SM's styling. This shot also brings out the car's tapering form. (Citroën)

By the coming of the 1960s, Citroën's post-war revival was complete. With production approaching 400,000 vehicles a year in 1962, its position as a leading automobile company had been re-established, and future prospects seemed bright. Consequently, its management (now led by Pierre Bercot) embarked on an optimistic policy of expansion, authorising several developments that would have been considered impossible hitherto. Amongst these projects was the building of a new factory at Aulnay-sous-Bois on the outskirts of Paris to replace the outdated facilities at the Quai de Javel and the opening of a new engineering research centre at Vélizy, to which the *Bureau d'Etudes* was relocated in 1965.

Also sanctioned was an ambitious scheme to take the marque into new territory with a luxurious high-performance GT embodying all the technical sophistication for which Citroën was renowned. This scheme for a front-wheel-drive supercar featuring Citroën's hydropneumatic self-levelling suspension and fully-powered high-pressure braking and steering would do more than celebrate the renaissance of the marque and demonstrate its world leadership in automotive design: it would also re-assert the technological prestige of France, reclaiming its supremacy in the *grande routière* class, lost since the demise of such exalted names as Delage, Delahaye, Talbot-Lago and Bugatti.

Doubtless, Bercot also hoped that the emergence of a true sports model from Citroën would help to revive its fortunes in the North American market, which it had entered in 1955 with a disappointing lack of success. The research project he initiated in 1964 – codenamed DS Sport – had the objective of producing a vehicle capable of motorway cruising at over 120mph for long periods with unprecedented comfort, safety and reliability.

The eventual outcome was the Citroën-Maserati SM. The offspring of a short-lived relationship with the illustrious Italian sports-car maker, which had come under Citroën's ownership early in 1968, it combined the qualities of a competition-bred sports-tourer and a luxury limousine, to offer a synthesis of performance, comfort and safety unprecedented then and perhaps still unmatched today. Revealed at the Geneva Motor Show in March 1970, the SM was well over twice the price of the DS21 Pallas.

The nature of the SM and its genesis was typical of the Citroën ethos, for it was a car built specifically to express the engineering values of the marque and to delight the fanatics among its clientele. Little attention was paid to the normal disciplines of marketing and product planning: instead of defining consumer needs and wishes through market research, Citroën built the SM to satisfy its own priorities – to prove that a fwd car could be equally as fast and sharp-handling as any rwd design – fully expecting that the results would be interesting enough to attract sufficient customers.

By 1965, the DS Sport project had produced two DS-based prototypes,

SM coupé

1970–1975

ENGINE:
Six cylinders in vee, water-cooled, all-alloy
Capacity
    2,670cc/2,965cc
Bore and stroke
    87 x 85mm/91.6mm x 75mm
Valve actuation
    Two overhead camshafts per bank
Compression ratio   9.0:1
Fuel system
    3 double-choke Weber carbs/Bosch
    electronic fuel injection
Power output
    170bhp DIN at 5,500rpm (carb)
    178bhp DIN at 5,500rpm (Efi)
    180bhp DIN at 5,500rpm (3-litre)
Torque
    164lb ft at 4,000rpm (2.7-litre)
TRANSMISSION:
Front-wheel drive
Five-speed manual or three-speed Borg-Warner auto
SUSPENSION:
Front: Independent, twin trailing arms, hydropneumatic springs
Rear: Independent, trailing arms, hydropneumatic springing, interconnected with front and self-levelling

STEERING:
Rack-and-pinion, fully powered, with variable-assistance and self-centring (Vari-Power/Diravi)
BRAKES:
Discs front and rear, fully powered
WHEELS/TYRES:
Michelin steel disc or carbon-fibre; Michelin VRX radials, 195/70x15
BODYWORK:
Two-door steel monocoque
DIMENSIONS:

Length	16ft 0½in
Wheelbase	9ft 8½in
Track, front	5ft 0½in
Track, rear	4ft 5in
Width	6ft 0½in
Height	4ft 3½in

WEIGHT:
Kerb weight 30.3cwt (2.7-litre Efi manual)
PERFORMANCE (2.7-litre Efi manual):
(Source: *Autocar*)

Max speed	139mph
0-60mph	9.3secs

PRICE INCLUDING TAX WHEN NEW:
£5,478 (2.7-litre Efi manual, August 1973)
NUMBER BUILT: 12,920

both convertibles. The first, powered by a mildly tuned version of the old three-bearing 1,911cc DS19 engine, was capable of 109mph, about 10mph faster than the standard DS19 saloon of the time. The second was powered by a twin-cam adaptation of the new 1,985cc four-cylinder five-bearing engine recently introduced on the DS19, producing 130bhp as opposed to the 90bhp of the standard car, enough to raise maximum speed to around 115mph. In 1966 came a third DS Sport prototype, the DXGT. This was a short-wheelbase two-door pillarless coupé version of the DS, powered by a twin-Weber conversion of the new 2,175cc five-bearing engine of the DS21 saloon (boosting output from 109bhp to 124bhp) that made it the first Citroën to exceed 120mph. The series-production power unit envisaged for the DS Sport, however, was to be yet another enlarged version of the classic Citroën four-cylinder, or

one of a family of V4, V6 and V8 engines then under development. But in the event the fourth DS Sport prototype, built in 1968, served to test the new Maserati V6 engine which had speedily resulted from the technical and commercial cooperation agreement signed with the Modena firm in September the previous year, as a prelude to the full take-over established in March 1968, the point at which the SM (Sport Maserati) project was initiated.

The acquisition of Maserati promised not only to confer a sporting reputation upon the marque, but also to remedy the perceived deficiencies of its engines. Other products, to be marketed purely as Maseratis, were also expected to materialise from the marriage and these eventually included two outright sports cars, the Bora and Merak. The latter shared the SM's V6 engine, mounted amidships to drive the rear wheels, and both

The chiselled rear features a lift-up rear window, giving access to a surprisingly small boot largely taken up with the spare wheel. (LAT)

employed Citroën's high-pressure hydraulic braking system.

Work on the SM engine began early in 1968, when Maserati chief engineer Giulio Alfieri was asked to produce a power plant specifically for the proposed new car. The major constraint was that its dimensions had to fall within the all-important tax rating of 15CV, which limited capacity to a maximum of 2.8 litres. It is claimed that the work was accomplished within three weeks, by the simple expedient of chopping two cylinders from Maserati's then-current 4,136cc 90-degree V8 and reducing the bore and stroke to 87mm x 75mm, giving a capacity of 2,670cc. This configuration made for an exceptional compact and lightweight engine (just

2.75cwt) thanks in part to its short crankshaft. When coupled to a Citroën-made five-speed gearbox, the Maserati V6 could easily be installed longitudinally in the nose of the car, behind the line of the front axle, as in the DS, but without intruding into the interior.

The quad-cam all-alloy engine comprised four main castings, two identical cylinder heads and an upper and lower block, split along the centre line of the four-bearing crankshaft, which was located sandwich fashion between them, an expensive solution used only in the finest competition engines but which made for an exceptionally rigid unit. The pistons ran in dry cast-iron liners, while the valves, operating in classic hemispherical combustion chambers, were opposed at 75 degrees; the compression ratio was 9:1. The camshafts were rotated by long secondary duplex chains driven by a central jackshaft running in plain

bearings and located in the vee of the engine. This jackshaft was driven in turn by the crankshaft through a short primary duplex chain. Unfortunately, this arrangement proved to be the engine's Achilles heel, for although the secondary chains had automatic tensioners, there was no adjustment for wear in the primary chain. As the jackshaft also acted as a power take-off for various engine accessories including the distributor, water pump, hydraulic pump and air-conditioning pump, wear was inevitable, and if the engine was over-revved the primary chain was prone to jump a tooth on its sprockets, with disastrous consequences. The engines of most examples running today have been modified by the fitting of an automatic tensioner to the primary chain.

In its earliest form, with three twin-choke Weber carburettors, the V6 engine produced 170bhp DIN at 5,500rpm. The majority of the 9,892 cars built in the first three years of

The aerodynamically efficient lines of the SM can be seen in this side view. This car wears the standard steel wheels with clip-on embellishers. (LAT)

The massive stainless steel bumper pressing encompassing the rear lights (as seen in this prototype car) was not liked by some critics; the rear end was lightly restyled at the last moment to allow for the square numberplates used in some countries. (Citroën)

The Presidential SM cabriolets

As the coachbuilder most closely associated with Citroën, Henri Chapron lost no time in bringing out a drophead version of the SM, called the Mylord, which he presented at the 1971 Paris *salon*. A relatively straightforward adaptation of the standard two-door car, the wheelbase and overall length of the Mylord were unchanged, and apart from the installation of a hydraulically-operated folding hood, alterations to its styling were confined to rear-end

Commissioned for President Pompidou in 1971, two SM cabriolets were built by Chapron on an extended-wheelbase platform. Powered by the standard 2.7-litre carburettor engine, they were inaugurated in 1972 during the state visit to Paris of the Queen and the Duke of Edinburgh. (Citroën)

revisions made necessary by the replacement of the glass hatchback by a conventional boot lid. By 1974 seven of these cabriolets had been built for private customers who were happy to pay the considerably elevated price for the exclusivity of owning one of these superbly elegant cars. At the following year's show, Chapron went a step further by exhibiting a four-door saloon version of the SM, the Opéra, built on a wheelbase 15½in longer than standard. Eventually, eight examples were constructed, selling at 165,400 FF including tax.

Meanwhile, in 1971 Chapron had received an order from the Elysée Palace for two four-door dropheads for the use of President Pompidou and his guests on ceremonial

occasions. Both of these presidential cars (which measured 18ft 4½in overall and weighed 35cwt – 14.5 per cent longer and 22.8 per cent heavier than the Mylord) were painted in metallic anthracite grey and trimmed in beige leather. Despite their great size, the engine fitted was the standard 2.7-litre carburettor V6, and apart from uprated brakes and suspension, mechanical modifications were limited to a change to the final-drive ratio to allow the cars to travel slowly in processions for long periods. This restricted their top speed to 112mph. The cars are still in service, and were used during the state visit to Paris of HM the Queen and the Duke of Edinburgh in April 2004.

production were to this specification, giving a claimed top speed of 136.8mph and a 0–60mph time of 8.2 seconds. In an attempt to curb the SM's prodigious thirst, in July 1972 Citroën announced the adoption of the computer-controlled Bosch Jetronic electronic fuel-injection system seen earlier on the DS21. This increased power output to 178bhp DIN, raising top speed by 5mph to just over 140mph, but the greatest benefit was that the quoted touring fuel consumption was improved from 22.6mpg to 25.2mpg.

That these impressive levels of performance were achieved by an engine of modest dimensions was surely a result of the SM's outstanding aerodynamics, which enabled this large and heavy car (kerbweight was 28.5cwt) to maintain high continuous cruising speeds (102mph at 5,000rpm in fifth gear, or 70mph at 3,000rpm) with perfect stability and composure. After all, it took engines over double the size of the Maserati V6 to propel rivals such as the Daimler Double-Six (5,343cc V12) and the Jensen Interceptor (6,276cc V8) to similar top speeds. Styled in-house under Robert Opron, the bodywork benefited from extensive wind tunnel testing. The reduction of drag was also assisted, of course, by the action of the SM's self-levelling suspension, which assured the optimum angle of attack under all circumstances. A Cd of 0.39 was claimed. Indeed, this aspect of the design showed beyond doubt that the influence of André Lefèbvre still held sway at the *Bureau d'Etudes*, some ten years after his retirement. The SM conformed not only to the 60:40 ratio of weight distribution fore and aft that he considered ideal, but also to the tapering tear-drop shape that he consistently advocated. The car was 16ft 0½in long, with a wheelbase of almost 10ft, but was widest at the nose, the cross-section of the body gradually reducing, resulting in a difference of nearly 8in between the front and rear tracks.

The bodyshell itself, built by specialist constructor Chausson, was a massively strong welded steel

Special-bodied SMs

Considering the SM's exotic character, special-bodied adapations were few and far between. Heuliez modified the SM, transforming it into a semi-open T-top, called the Espace, featuring aluminium-slatted

The Frua-bodied SM, here on display at the 1972 Geneva Motor Show, remained a one-off. (LAT)

roof panels that retracted electrically into the T-bar and fully retracting side windows. Two examples were built, the first with a Lamborghini-style slatted cover for the rear window. Another SM-based styling exercise was the coupé displayed by Frua at the 1972 Geneva Motor Show and built on an SM underpan with its wheelbase reduced by just over 1ft.

structure, as was subsequently demonstrated by the SM's brief rallying career. The shell was a true monocoque of which the roof formed an integral part, contributing to the rigidity of the central passenger section and forming a safety cage. It consisted of two main structural units, front and rear, linked by two large outer box-section longerons. The front unit, designed to deform in a collision, extended forward from the bulkhead to a crossmember located on the axis of the driveshafts and beyond that to the nose, so forming a collapsible cage within which the engine, gearbox, axle-arms and steering rack were mounted. Similarly, the rear unit formed a bulkhead dividing the passenger compartment from the boot, at the same time providing a means of locating the rear anti-roll bar and the rear trailing arms. Only the front headlamp panel and front wings were detachable.

Although visually unique, the SM preserved certain styling themes that had been established with the DS19, not least the faired-in rear wheels which by now had become an essential Citroën characteristic. But because the rear wings were welded in place, small detachable spats were used to cover the wheels.

Familiar styling themes continued inside the car where the heavily-padded single-spoke steering wheel and the curved, asymmetrical dashboard echoed Bertoni's original DS19 design, except that the three main dials on the instrument panel had unusual oval-shaped faces. Another novel feature – at least for Citroën – was the large centre console. Although not required for any engineering reason, the console created an impression of power by housing the gearlever and handbrake plus the radio and heating and ventilation systems. The steering

The SM's dashboard evokes the asymmetrical lines of Bertoni's original DS19 dash. The one-spoke wheel is fully adjustable for rake and reach. (LAT)

wheel could be adjusted for height and reach and the integral-headrest front seats (often criticised for lack of lateral support) were also fully adjustable. Considering the vast size of the car, the interior, though comfortable and well appointed, was not exactly spacious and the rear seats were suited only for occasional use by adults: the SM was really a two-plus-two rather than the claimed full four-seater. Upholstery was in jersey nylon cloth but leather was optional – as was tinted glass and air-conditioning.

Naturally, the SM featured front-wheel drive and centre-point steering geometry, both of which had become holy writ at Citroën. In fact the general design of its front and rear axle-arms, together with its front brakes, hubs and driveshafts, was identical to that

of the DS, except that the front arms were mounted in a trailing rather than a leading position. Similarly, the SM's self-levelling hydropneumatic suspension used the same componentry, but with modified damper-valve settings for a firmer ride. The fully-powered, load-sensitive braking system, actuated by a mushroom pedal, was also taken from the DS, except that discs were fitted on all four wheels. At the front, the discs were mounted inboard, as on the DS, with separate callipers for the parking brake which was operated by a conventional hand lever, rather than the foot-pedal employed on the DS. Many drivers new to the system found it over-sensitive, of course. The *Autocar* road test reported that only 40lb of effort on the pedal was enough to bring the 1.5 ton car to a rapid stop from 70mph, with over 1g retardation.

The fully-powered rack-and-pinion steering represented a major technical advance. Much thought had been devoted to creating a car capable of

responding precisely and rapidly to the finest movement of the driver's hands, as when making a rapid correction at high speed. At the same time, it was considered essential that this response should not be so sensitive as to amplify any small reactive or involuntary movements of the wheel, so throwing the car off course. Consequently, the SM boasted an important Citroën innovation – variable-assistance, fully-powered hydraulic rack-and-pinion steering, known as Diravi (*Direction à Rappel Asservi*) in France and Vari-Power in the UK. A development of the principle introduced on the DS19, this revolutionary servo device, tested in the DXGT prototype of 1966, was exceptionally high-geared, the steering ratio of the SM being 9:4.1 (compared to 14:7.1 on the DS) so that one turn of the steering wheel took the front wheels from straight-ahead to full lock.

As its name implied, the amount of assistance provided by the Diravi

The SM *has the gearshift and handbrake located in a central console as on a rear-wheel-drive car, even though there is no transmission tunnel. The seating is distinctively styled, with the reclining articulation set higher than normal; lateral support is poor.* (LAT)

Although presented as a full four-seater, the SM is really a two-plus-two. To make the interior look roomier than it was, Citroën used a particularly petite model in their launch-time publicity photos. (Citroën)

system varied with the car's speed. To eliminate physical effort from parking manoeuvres, when the vehicle was at a standstill no resistance could be felt at the steering wheel and the front wheels returned to the straight-ahead position automatically when the wheel was released, with no action required from the driver. But as speed increased, and the angle of the steering lock became greater, the amount of resistance felt at the wheel rose proportionately. This was achieved by the use of a centrifugal steering regulator driven from the gearbox so that its speed of rotation was related directly to road speed; thus, the effort required to turn the steering wheel was constantly adjusted according to circumstances. Automatic self-centring was also provided, ensuring absolute and effortless directional stability when cruising fast. As the system also eliminated all shocks and feedback from the front wheels, the end-result was to give the driver a feeling of maximum sensitivity and control when cornering, even though, as on the DS, there was no direct mechanical connection between steering wheel and tyres. These, incidentally, were Michelin's latest high-performance XWX tubeless radials as also used on the Ferrari Daytona, but in this case fitted on special 6J wide-rimmed Michelin steel wheels with five-stud

fastenings, manufactured specifically for the SM. Later Michelin produced unique lightweight carbon-fibre wheels for the SM, as an option from July 1971 onwards, these being less than half the weight of the steel wheels.

Lastly, the SM also boasted an extremely advanced lighting system featuring no fewer than six separate Cibié quartz halogen units, each bank consisting of a separate main beam, a dipped beam and a long-range beam. The latter innermost unit was directionally controlled, pivoting on a vertical axis in response to movements of the steering wheel, an innovation that had been introduced earlier on certain DS models. But whereas on the DS these swivelling beams were mechanically controlled by a system of rods and levers, on the SM the linkage was by means of two independent hydraulic circuits. As with the DS, these lights were set to turn at an angle slightly in advance of the steering lock angle to illuminate the curve of a bend. Similarly, the level of the beams of each group of lamps was stabilised and controlled by an automatic self-levelling device, also hydraulically actuated, which enabled them to pivot on a horizontal axis to compensate for any changes in the vehicle's attitude when accelerating or braking, independently of the self-levelling suspension system. The lamps and the numberplate were

housed behind a curved glass nose cowling to optimise aerodynamic efficiency. Unfortunately, this novel arrangement did not conform to US lighting regulations and the cars supplied for the North American market had a simplified system comprising four fixed circular headlamps.

By virtue of its short career – the shortest of any post-war Citroën model – the evolution of the SM was severely curtailed, and the range never gained the four-door version that admirers demanded. In fact, besides the change to fuel injection in 1972, its development was limited to the introduction, in October 1972, of a third, supplementary, 3-litre version, intended primarily for North America and fitted with automatic transmission. Citroën's experience with the DS had shown that a fully automatic gearbox was essential for North American customers and it had consequently tied up with Borg-Warner in England, to adapt B-W's Type 35 transmission, as used on the Rover P5 and Jaguar XJ6. A considerable amount of work was involved in re-engineering this box for installation in a front-

The SM in competition

With its substantial weight, size and complexity, the SM was not ideally suited to the role of rally car – especially in an era when rivals were becoming ever lighter and more specialised. Nevertheless, Citroën's competitions department made valiant efforts to campaign the car, and its endeavours were rewarded with some success. In particular, on its very first outing an SM won the 1971 Rallye du Maroc. Next, the competitions department concocted two lightweight short-wheelbase SMs during 1972, these cars having glass-fibre outer panels and 250bhp 3-litre engines. Competing in the coupé-prototype Group 5, one of the cars came third overall and first in class in the 1972 Portuguese TAP Rally, and the other was sixth in the Bandama Rally held in the Côte d'Ivoire.

For a car criticised as over-complicated, the SM was exceptionally strong and durable, as was proved in its short rallying career. On its competition debut in the 1971 Moroccan Rally, run under particularly demanding conditions, the single car entered won first prize and Citroën gained the manufacturers' cup. (Citroën)

wheel-drive car, since the drive had to be reversed through 180 degrees to return it to the differential, and this required a two-shaft arrangement, the first of its kind.

The Borg-Warner automatic box was initially fitted to a limited series of 2.7-litre carburetted SMs made available in the USA in October 1971. However, to provide the increased torque demanded by the automatic transmission, the original 2.7-litre engine was soon replaced on the SM auto model by the new 3-litre power unit, overbored to 91.6mm to give 2,965cc and a French fiscal rating of 17CV. Moreover, as the Bosch fuel injection used on the SM and DS had failed to satisfy US emissions regulations, the fuel-injected 2.7-litre

engine, introduced in July 1972, could not be sold in the USA, with or without automatic transmission. So when it appeared, just three months after the 2.7-litre EFi engine, the 3-litre engine reverted to the three twin-choke Weber carburettors of the original 2.7-litre engine. The power output achieved by this third and final power plant was 180bhp, only 2bhp more than the injected 2.7-litre, but torque was increased to 181lb ft at 4,000rpm, which was more the object of the exercise. Even so, top speed was reduced by 15mph to 127mph, and touring fuel consumption fell to just 21mpg. In September 1973, the 3-litre version was offered on the French market, with the option of five-speed manual transmission. The price was

63,900 FF as opposed to the 61,900 FF then being asked for the 2.7-litre manual version. Very few of the total 1,612 examples of the 3-litre SMs built were sold on this side of the Atlantic.

Throughout the early 1970s, the expansion of the automobile industry seemed unstoppable. Even large, thirsty and expensive prestige cars like the SM were in demand. By the end of 1972, almost two years after the SM's launch, a total of 9,892 cars had found owners, 868 in 1970, 4,988 in 1971 and 4,036 in 1972. It seemed as if Bercot's hunch had paid off and that Citroën would have no problem in selling the planned annual output of 4,000 vehicles. Initial reaction from both press and public alike had been extremely favourable. 'Is all the expense and complication worth it?', asked the normally sceptical *Autocar* magazine in its 1971 test, concluding that indeed it was: 'Getting back into other cars afterwards makes them, not the Citroën, seem odd and difficult, especially in regard to the steering. We feel that for a large and heavy car it sets new standards of handling and stability'.

But unfortunately the following year sales of the SM plummeted to almost half their previous levels. The reason, of course, was the onset, in the

autumn of 1973, of the first Energy Crisis. For Citroën this had dramatic consequences, forcing Michelin into selling out to its erstwhile rival, Peugeot. On arriving at the Quai de Javel in December 1974, the company's new masters lost no time in making major changes, although the only vehicle in Citroën's product portfolio to be affected by this clash of cultures was its flagship, the SM, which was declared to be an unnecessary and unprofitable extravagance, as was the entire

relationship with Maserati.

In May 1975, therefore, the Italian subsidiary was cast adrift by Peugeot and left to founder before eventually being rescued by de Tomaso. But, in truth, this decision came as no more than a confirmation of an established reality. French sales of the SM had already ended in December 1974, leaving the car available for export only; in fact, Citroën built just 273 examples throughout the whole of that year. Earlier, in April 1974, however, a statement had been issued by Citroën

The Hathaway SMs

The ultimate SM has to be the Bonneville speed-records car of Sylvia and Jerry Hathaway, proprietors of California's SM World. Boosted by two turbochargers, this extraordinary 530bhp creation has cracked the 200mph barrier, and there is the promises of more to come! In addition, the car is towed by a specially converted SM pick-up that served as the firm's daily 'hack' for over 15 years and 130,000 miles.

The Hathaways started record-breaking at the end of the seventies, achieving 154mph on the Bonneville salt flats with the car in 2.7-litre normally aspirated form. At the beginning of the eighties a 3-litre engine was fitted, equipped with two Air Research turbochargers and a water-to-air intercooler fed with iced water by twin electric water pumps from a tank in the boot. Fuelling was provided by two Holley racing pumps, and the electrics by two 12-volt batteries in the boot. The transmission used a Maserati Bora

clutch and a special Citroën-made experimental 3.88:1 differential supplied to Lotus for use on the Esprit, which used an SM gearbox. In 1986, a three-stage dry-sump oil system was adapted to the engine and a four-gallon oil tank installed.

The suspension spheres were charged at lower pressure, the front spheres at 100psi and the rears at 75psi, and there was no ride-height interconnection front-to-rear. The high-pressure pump and the LHM reservoir were inside the car; with the pump being run off an electric motor rather than off the engine; thus the hydraulics could function without the engine being started. As a failsafe measure in the event of the pump cutting out, three accumulators were lodged under the bonnet, so that sufficient pressure could be stored for five miles without need for the pump – thereby preserving power for the steering.

In this specification, and with largely standard bodywork, the car

exceeded 200mph in 1985. By 1987 the Hathaways had pushed its best speed up to 206.446mph. Experiments with raising the boost from 20psi to 25–28psi in 1988 brought an extra 100–150bhp, but problems with the oil-pump drive and the intercooler pumps meant this was not translated into any higher speeds than those attained in 1987.

Various circumstances saw a pause in the SM's campaigns, but its retirement has never been contemplated; indeed, a full rebuild and restoration was completed in 2002. The high-pressure pump and the fluid reservoir have moved from the interior to the boot, and the steering has been converted to manual operation, bringing with it a return to a single under-bonnet accumulator: at 200mph the powered steering had proved too sensitive!

The Hathaway record car and matching SM pick-up on the salt flats at Bonneville. (Stan Jennings)

Driving the SM

If you're new to big Citroëns, your first experience of the SM is likely to be intimidating: this is a car that demands a fair bit of acclimatisation before you are at ease with it. Its sheer bulk and left-hand driving position don't help, but the main hurdles are the powered brakes and the Diravi steering, both of which require a different and more delicate touch than on an orthodox car. Attempt to drive an SM as you might any other vehicle of the era and you'll make only jerky and erratic progress.

The trick with the steering is to make gentle caressing movements at low speed, when the assistance is at its strongest and the steering's responses feel at their sharpest. Once at speed, the assistance falls away, and you can revel in the steering's high gearing and the uncanny stability the self-centring confers on the car. Roadholding is superb, and the

steering effectively masks the SM's inherent understeer. The car rolls a fair amount, but less than a DS: the ride is still cossettingly comfortable, but without the magic-carpet insularity of the softer DS. What all this means is that the SM is happier on broad sweeping bends than on tight country lanes where speed must be varied constantly, and with it the steering assistance, and where the Citroën's size will work against it. As for those brakes, their effectiveness is not in doubt, but the mushroom pedal demands gentle footwork if you're not to stand the car on its nose; but this comes naturally after a while.

These lessons learnt, the SM's many virtues can be appreciated. The V6 lacks the ultimate smoothness of an in-line 'six' or the muscular low-rev 'grunt' of a V8, but the uneven low-speed firing impulses soften out with speed, the Maserati engine offering

turbine-like refinement when cruising; hang onto the gears, however, and push the engine to its 6,500rpm red line, and you'll be rewarded with that growling soundtrack only a thoroughbred Italian power unit can produce. Fortunately, too, this performance is achieved via an agreeable gearchange, positive if a little long-throw, and with an occasional metal-on-metal click if the lever hits the unusual gate surround; this is matched to a clutch which while not light has a well-judged length of travel.

In short, the SM is a car that is at its best in the Grand Touring environment for which it was intended. As a town car it is out of its element; as a relaxed cross-continental cruiser, on the other hand, whether on the autoroutes or across open country, it is at its most contented – and its most seductive.

announcing a last-ditch attempt to keep the SM project alive by moving assembly to Automobiles Ligier, a low-volume constructor of sports and racing cars located at Abrest near Vichy, whose JS2 model used an SM engine. Over 15 months a total of 135 cars was built by Ligier, 21 in 1974 and a further 114 in 1975. But following the abandonment of Maserati by Peugeot, there was simply no way that

Opposite: Paris by night, by SM: the ultimate in chic? This car wears the lightweight carbon-fibre wheels developed for the SM by Michelin. (LAT)

production of the SM could continue. It only remained to dispose of the remaining stock of bodyshells built by Chausson, rumoured to amount to several hundred. Despite pleas from Citroën that these shells should all be completed as cars, the order came back from Peugeot that they were to be sent to the crusher. The superb SM, the proud symbol of Citroën's aspirations, was dead. Just like the Concorde, it had proved to be simultaneously a technological triumph and a commercial disaster – and the only car of the Michelin era that had not achieved, or exceeded, expectations. In just five years,

between August 1970 and September 1975, exactly 12,920 examples were sold world-wide, 5,509 in France, 2,070 in Italy, 2,037 in the USA, 971 in Germany, 396 in Canada and 327 in the UK, with the remainder finding customers throughout the rest of the world.

All these cars were left-hand-drive, as at the start of the SM project it had been decided that no provision would be made for rhd; that said, several examples exist today; three cars in England and another five or six in Australia were converted to right-hand drive, those in England on a semi-official basis.

Buying Hints

1. Check for rust in the leading edge of the bonnet, the door bottoms, the tailgate and the rear wheelarches; the last-named are potentially the most serious (and costly) problem to repair because of their complex design – and replacement sections are not widely available.

2. The substantial chassis is strong; rust damage is fairly easy to repair. The smooth undertray helps if sections need to be let in. While looking underneath, check the five front subframe bolts: these can work loose.

3. Be wary of even minor front-end damage, because it can be expensive to rectify. Although the front wings are quite easy to repair, the complex headlamp units and stainless steel bumpers are notoriously expensive and hard to find. The plastic headlamp carriers are unavailable but the glass cover sections are obtainable, though they're not cheap. Avoid cars with lots of trim missing, as this is also scarce.

4. Don't be put off by the complex Maserati engine: it is reliable if it has been regularly and

correctly serviced. So look for a wad of bills, and ideally a complete history, revealing attention to the timing chain tensioners. These are not automatic and it is imperative they be checked every 10,000 miles – failure to do so can result in a huge repair bill; they can be reinforced for longevity. If the car has been abused, the original sodium-filled valves can break, again prompting massive expense. Stainless-steel replacement valves are available, and bronze valve guides. Also ask if the oil pump drive has been uprated (or look for a bill), as this is one of various later modifications intended to extend engine life.

5. Expect hisses and clicks from the hydropneumatics – but the engine should not make any odd noises. Rattles on later EFi models can be from the throttle butterflies.

6. Look for a switch to turn off the air conditioning, because there wasn't one fitted originally. The system is driven off the timing chain, causing stress and ultimately failure if the air-conditioning pump gives trouble. Fitment of a switch indicates a thoughtful previous owner.

7. The self-centring steering should always return to the straight-ahead position. The high-pressure pump can corrode, and leaking fluid can cause the hydropneumatic system to fail. If you check over the car where it normally lives, look for signs of green LHM fluid on the floor. When started, the car should rise promptly to its normal level: move the height control to all positions to check that it works – it won't happen instantly, but should be swift.

8. Rattling from the front suspension can be due to worn front balljoints.

9. Michelin tyres give the best ride and handling: original-pattern treads are still made by Michelin, but they cost around £250 each (equivalent modern types are about £90).

10. Other useful upgrades to look for include electronic ignition and uprated electrics including a modern alternator and voltage regulator – usually evidence that the car is in reasonably regular use. You're more likely to have problems on a car that's been standing idle for long periods.

The GS
and GSA

I n 1965 Citroën took 30.5 per cent of the French car market, going on the following year to claim 9.3 per cent of total European sales. Remarkably, this position was based on the outstanding success of just two designs, occupying opposing ends of the spectrum: the 2CV and its sister-vehicle the Ami 6, and the costly, complex, hydropneumatically-sprung DS and ID models.

Such a situation could not be permitted to continue, and as competition from Peugeot and Renault became ever stronger, Citroën began to take steps to fill the gap in its range with a true mid-market car, for which its faithful clientele had long been clamouring. The waiting was finally ended in October 1970 when the GS was unveiled at the Paris Motor Show.

The brief for the GS laid down in 1968 had specified a four-door, five-seater saloon, capable of 90mph.

The smooth lines of the GS compensated for the small size of the flat-four engine, which in its original form was barely more than 1,000cc in size. (Citroën)

Despite its short gestation period – a mere 24 months – the GS range was to remain in production for 16 years and become one of Citroën's very greatest successes, ultimately selling over 2,500,000 examples – second only to the 2CV. And yet, strangely, considering its many virtues, it has yet to achieve the classic status of its better-known sister vehicles, the DS and SM, at least in the Anglo-Saxon world.

Certainly, although it was aimed at middle-class, middle-income owner-drivers, the GS was most definitely not middle-of-the-road. It offered an astounding combination of advanced features, including an unburstable air-cooled flat-four engine, fully-powered disc brakes all-round, rack-and-pinion steering, all-independent self-levelling hydropneumatic suspension and, naturally, front-wheel drive. In short, the GS was a DS for the ordinary motorist, offering levels of comfort and security normally associated only with cars twice its size and price, which was just 12,100 FF at the outset. In 1971 it won the Car of the Year award: 'Without surrendering their aristocracy, Citroën have found the common touch, and motoring will never be quite the same again', commented LJK Setright in *Car* magazine.

Chief among the GS's novel features was its lightweight, all-alloy, flat-four ohc air-cooled engine, rated at 6CV in original 1,015cc form. Set low and ahead of the front axle, and with its four-speed gearbox positioned rearwards and downwards to lower the centre of gravity, in concept it was similar to the 2CV's power unit, and shared many details of construction. Its specific power output was 61bhp SAE at 6,750rpm with 52lb ft DIN of torque at 3,500rpm, enough to give the GS a top speed of 91mph, not much less than that of the then-current 1,985cc D Super. Petrol consumption of 35–40mpg at an average speed of 49mph was claimed, or 29mpg at a steady 68–70mph, although this was somewhat optimistic: independent tests revealed a disappointing average of only

GS and GSA

1970–1987

ENGINE:
Four cylinder, horizontally-opposed, air-cooled
Capacity
1,015cc/1,129cc/1,220cc/1,299cc
Bore and stroke
74mm x 59mm/74mm x 65.6mm
77mm x 65.6mm/79.4mm x 65.6mm
Valve actuation
ohc, one camshaft per bank, belt-driven
Compression ratio
9.0:1 (GS 1,015cc and 1200)/
8.7:1 (GSA 1,299cc)
Carburettors
Twin-choke Solex
Power output
55.5bhp DIN at 6,500rpm (GS 1,015cc)/60bhp DIN at 6,500rpm (GS 1220cc)/65bhp DIN at 5,500rpm (GSA 1,299cc)
Torque
52lb ft at 3,250rpm (GS 1,015cc)/72lb ft at 3,500rpm (GSA)

TRANSMISSION:
Front-wheel drive
manual gearbox, four-speed/five-speed;
C-Matic semi-auto optional 1972-83

SUSPENSION:
Front: Independent, double wishbones and hydropneumatic springing
Rear: Independent, trailing arms and hydropneumatic springing, interconnected to front and self-levelling

STEERING:
Rack-and-pinion, unassisted

BRAKES:
Discs, front and rear, fully powered

WHEELS/TYRES:
Steel disc or alloy wheels
Michelin radial 145x15

BODYWORK:
Steel monocoque
Styles available: four-door saloon (GS); five-door hatchback (GSA); five-door estate (GS/GSA); van (GS/GSA)

DIMENSIONS (GS/GSA saloon):
Length	12ft 6in/13ft 6¼in
Wheelbase	8ft 4½in
Track, front	4ft 5¼in/4ft 6¼in
Track, rear	4ft 4¼in
Width	5ft 3¼in
Height	4ft 6in/4ft 5in

WEIGHT:
Kerb weight 16.8cwt (GS 1,220cc)/19.5cwt (GSA 1,299cc)

PERFORMANCE:
(Source: *Autocar*)
Max speed:	90mph (GS 1,015cc)
	94mph (GS 1,220cc)
	95mph (GSA 1,299cc)
0–60mph	18.0sec (GS 1,015cc)
	14.9sec (GS 1,220cc)
	14.9sec (GSA 1,299cc)

PRICE INCLUDING TAX WHEN NEW:
£1,315 (GS 1200 Club, March 1973)
£4,399 (GSA Pallas, January 1980)

NUMBERS BUILT:
1,874,754 GS
565,009 GSA

23.3mpg overall, with 27.6mpg at motorway cruising speeds. At first sight, its 0–60mph acceleration time of 18 seconds was not particularly impressive either. But sloth at the traffic lights was compensated for by the ease with which the GS overcame drag and increased mid-range speed: when travelling at a constant 75mph just 30bhp of its engine's total potential power output of 50bhp was absorbed, leaving a reserve of 20bhp. Tests recorded that 60–80mph took just 24 seconds – a quite exceptional level of performance for a one-litre engine and an indication of the GS's remarkable aerodynamic efficiency.

At that time there was no other mass-produced small car in which a

family and its luggage could cruise all day at 80mph in such comfort and confidence. In theory, indeed, there was virtually nothing to go wrong, as just like the 2CV engine the GS power unit had no radiator, hoses, fan belt or water pump to fail, or coolant to boil or freeze, and with an oil cooler provided as standard overheating was virtually impossible.

The engineering of the GS was novel for an inexpensive car in that it utilised Citroën's unique high-pressure hydraulics not just for the suspension but also to power the brakes – though not the steering. Given that an hydraulic power supply was on tap, it is surprising that power steering was never offered on any GS variant.

The GS Birotor

The 1973 Paris Motor Show saw the launch of the GS Birotor, a modified version of the GS saloon powered by a Wankel rotary engine, coupled to the C-Matic semi-automatic three-speed gearbox. The engine was a two-rotor unit with a capacity equivalent to 1,990cc, and developed 107bhp DIN at 6,500rpm.

A feature unique to the Birotor was that the front discs were mounted outboard; as the engine and gearbox were mounted transversally, it was impossible to install the brakes inboard as on the standard GS. The Birotor could easily be distinguished from the standard GS by its exclusive metallic beige, dark brown, or metallic grey paint finish, by its special badges, and by its flared wheelarches which enclosed much larger wheels and tyres. It also had distinctive hubcaps, identical to those later fitted to the CX. The

Birotor had the shortest career of any Citroën model, its production ceasing after only 15 months, early in 1975, by which time only 847 examples had been built.

The sad story had begun back in the mid-sixties when Citroën decided that the rotary engine's inherent simplicity and silence would lead inevitably to it replacing the conventional reciprocating piston engine, and accordingly entered into a partnership with Wankel pioneer NSU. The jointly-owned manufacturing subsidiary Comotor built a dedicated factory at Alforweiler in the Saar province of Germany, and the plan was that Comotor rotary engines would ultimately power all Citroën's bigger models, including the forthcoming CX, a project that was already well underway. Unfortunately, the Wankel engine proved to be a huge disappointment for both partners,

In the autumn of 1973, Citroën announced the GS Birotor, powered by a Wankel rotary engine. The Birotor can be easily distinguished by its larger wheels and the flared wings needed to accommodate them. But only 847 units were made before the model was discontinued in 1975. (Ludvigsen)

displaying an alarmingly thirsty consumption of both fuel and oil – the latter being caused by premature wear of the rotor-tip seals. This could lead to engine failure after as little as 20,000 miles. With poor fuel consumption a less than attractive proposition now that petrol prices had doubled following the 1973–74 fuel crisis, and with the prospect of heavy warranty claims to boot, it was no wonder the plug was pulled on the Birotor. Citroën subsequently tried to buy back all the cars, stocking at La Ferté-Vidame those it had repurchased – before scrapping them as recently as 1986.

The clean, simple lines of the GS are evident in profile. Note the semi-enclosed rear wheels and the use of stainless steel for bumpers and window frame trims – typical Citroën styling themes of that era, developed by Robert Opron. (Citroën)

The sharply cut-off Kamm tail aided aerodynamics and allowed a cavernous boot – which incorporated the centre section of the bumper, thereby eliminating the loading sill. (Citroën)

Although a 30ft turning circle made for easy manoeuvrability, the steering was always on the heavy side at low speeds, though it became progressively lighter and more precise as speed increased.

A simplified version of the ID's system, the self-levelling suspension featured improved damping and re-positioned bump-stops, together resulting in a remarkable reduction in the roll, pitching and floating for which the 'D' had long been criticised. It also virtually eliminated the handling problems previously induced by any sudden change of attitude provoked by hump-backed bridges, changes in road camber, and the like, thus endowing the GS with leech-like cornering power.

In later years, Citroën's advertising made much of the GS's magic-carpet ride, and also the way it enabled its driver to maintain control under emergency braking, even in the event of a front-tyre blow-out at high speed. But this uncanny ability to run straight on three wheels was not just a consequence of the self-levelling hydropneumatic suspension, but was also a result of the clever design of the double-wishbone front links, which incorporated anti-dive geometry and at the same time followed the principles of centre-point steering found on the DS19. Unsurprisingly, the

Right: The dashboard was an original design featuring a revolving-drum speedo and a stylised tachometer. (Citroën)

Below right: The interior of a 1971 Club, with pleated fabric upholstery; note the stylised door furniture. (Citroën)

Below: For the British market this smart and more orthodox instrument panel was used, with its conservative white-on-black circular Jaeger dials; French GS owners were envious. (Citroën)

directional stability and general predictability of the GS's handling and roadholding at high speed were greatly praised by all commentators.

The GS's fully-powered braking system was also a modified version of the ID saloon set-up, with the front discs likewise mounted inboard, in order to reduce unsprung weight. The pressurised fluid in the two independent circuits was distributed by a *doseur* or brake control valve, actuated by a conventional pendant foot pedal rather than the DS's famous mushroom-head button. However, a load-sensitive, pressure-apportioning device was incorporated in the rear circuit to prevent the rear wheels from locking up under emergency braking when the vehicle was lightly loaded. The parking brake,

applied by a handle mounted on the dashboard, acted on the front discs through separate pads and callipers.

The monocoque body, styled under Robert Opron, who had succeeded Flaminio Bertoni in 1964, was exceptionally aerodynamic for its era, with a Cd of 0.36 – better than that of the DS, hitherto regarded as one of the world's most aerodynamically efficient cars. It has often been said that the shape was based on the *Berlina Aerodinamica* concept cars Pininfarina made for BMC in 1967, but naturally Citroën rejects this claim. A model of elegance and modernity, the GS was simply detailed and devoid of all unnecessary embellishment. Indeed, it established certain motifs that became Citroën trademarks. These included the pronounced kick-

up line running to the tail from the rear wheelarches and, of course, the partial shrouding of the rear wheels. With its sloping bonnet, rounded flanks, flowing, swept-back roofline and sharply cut-off fastback tail, the GS adopted a wheel-at each-corner stance, with very short overhangs. Apart from its aerodynamic advantages, the Kamm tail allowed for a completely rectangular, flat-sided boot, offering – thanks to the spare wheel being under the bonnet – no less than 16 cubic feet of unobstructed load space. Moreover, the rear bumper was integral with the boot lid and so there was no sill to hinder loading, the necessary torsional stiffness being provided by a fixed steel parcel shelf. Another notable feature was the trapezoidal headlamps; produced by Cibié exclusively for the GS, these lamps embodied the very latest in lighting technology, including halogen bulbs.

Inside was a futuristic dashboard which echoed the asymmetrical lines of Bertoni's original creation for the DS, and which featured one of the most talked-about points of the car, a 'magic eye' speedometer with a rotating drum under a magnifying lens, the whole display being permanently illuminated. Perhaps more controversial still, for dyed-in-the-wool Citroënistes at least, was the floor-mounted gearlever located in a central console. Apparently this concession to orthodoxy was adopted at the very last moment: originally a dash-mounted push-pull lever was intended, leaving room for an occasional third person to ride in the front seats. Instead, the space on the dashboard originally provided to house such a gearshift was occupied by an unusual pull-out handbrake.

Initially, the GS saloon came in two versions, Confort and Club. The base-level Confort had leathercloth upholstery and a rubber floor covering while the better-equipped Club offered a more luxurious interior with moquette carpets and a choice of red, bronze, blue or green jersey-nylon seat coverings or alternatively black or

brown vinyl, plus reclining front seats. British sales began in June 1971. To the envy of many French owners, the British-market GS came with a unique dashboard incorporating conventional Jaeger circular instruments.

In August 1971 Citroën announced three new variants, a four-door estate, a four-door *break commerciale* with no rear seat (deleted two years later), and a two-door Service van, available either with steel side panels or with two full-length fixed side windows. All three had the same tailgate, featuring a window that curved round to cut

A notable feature of the estate is the way that its tailgate opens down to floor level in the same way as the saloon's boot lid. The spare wheel is in the engine bay, of course. (Citroën)

into the roofline. As in the saloon, the tailgate opened right down to floor level, and in estate form the GS offered a total of 53.12 cu ft of load space with the rear seat folded.

Although the GS engine had been praised for its smooth turbine-like responses, low-speed torque and flexibility was poor – as indeed, in the

GS and GSA special editions

In March 1978 the first special-edition GS, the 1,800-off Basalte, was introduced. This was distinguished by its unusual colour scheme, of black overpainted with horizontal bands of red along its flanks. The Basalte also boasted Pallas wheel trims, headlamp wipers, long-range lamps, a sliding metal sunroof and a unique red and black interior. In December 1979 it was followed by the GS Quartz, limited to 50 left-hand-drive units only, all of them white with black interiors.

The first special-edition GSA appeared in March 1982, for the

French market only. This was the 1500-off Tuner, in black with a blue coachline and with a superior stereo radio-cassette system. In October 1983 came the Cottage, a well-specified version of the GSA estate; just 1,850 were built, but again none for the UK. Equipped to Pallas standards, this car was immediately recognisable by its alloy wheels, of the type available optionally on the Pallas.

During the 1983 and 1984 model years UK buyers were offered the GSA Pallas SE saloon. This featured such extras as alloy wheels, front fog

lights, a sunshine roof and tinted glass, and was available in a choice of either black or pearl-grey metallic paintwork, with a red coachline.

Finally, the last of the GSA special editions, announced in July 1984, was the Chic, again offered only in France. Based on the GSA Special, this car featured metallic pearl-grey paintwork teamed with black bumpers, black window-frames, and a band of black skirting on the lower part of the doors, plus tinted glass, alloy wheels and a rear spoiler; 1,200 examples only were constructed.

The frontal aspect of the GS is dominated by the large air-intake demanded by its air-cooled flat-four engine. This is the GSX2 version of 1977. (Ludvigsen)

early days, was reliability. Accordingly, in September 1972 Citroën introduced a 1,222cc engine, developing 60bhp DIN at 5,750rpm. The 1,015cc engine continued in the Confort versions of the saloon and estate and in the van. At the same time came the option of C-Matic semi-automatic clutchless transmission, this comprising a three-speed manual gearbox coupled to an electrically-operated torque converter which eliminated the need for a conventional clutch pedal.

For 1974 the 1,015cc engine was improved and the models using it re-baptised G-Special, while in the autumn of that year the range was strengthened by the arrival of the GSX and GSX2 sporting saloons, and a Pallas version. Recognisable by its large stainless-steel wheel covers and side rubbing strips, the Pallas, optionally equipped with C-Matic, offered detail refinements such as higher-quality upholstery and headlining, and deep pile carpeting on the floor and rear parcel shelf. Just like the DS Pallas, it came initially in an exclusive metallic pearl-grey paint finish, although all other colours were also available; a black vinyl roof covering could also be ordered as an option. The GSX and GSX2, on

the other hand, were aimed at a younger, more fashion-conscious driver – hence their sunflower-yellow paint, matt-black grille and window surrounds, and long-range driving lamps. Inside, the notorious revolving-drum speedometer and its accompanying instruments were replaced by round dials, and there were high-backed front seats. The GSX was identical to the GSX2 except that it was powered by the standard 55.5bhp 1,015cc engine; the GSX2, however, used a more potent 65bhp

version of the 1220 engine, married to a close-ratio four-speed gearbox. Its performance was decidedly lively, allowing the driver to exploit fully the GS's superb handling and roadholding. The GSX2 was capable of a claimed 96.3mph as opposed to the 93.8mph of the 1,222cc GS Club and returned 33.5mpg overall, against 31mpg for the standard car.

In 1977 the GS received its single facelift, the most notable feature being a new round-dial dashboard for all models. Outside, there were

GS around the world

The GS and GSA were assembled at various locations other than the principal facility at Rennes-La-Janais in France. Foremost was Vigo in Spain, which supplied the import-protected Spanish market, and from 1978 also sent cars to other European countries; from 1984 it was the sole source of GSAs. Portugal also built the G-series, but only to the tune of 2,940 GS models and 1,320 GSAs. This was well below the 15,600 cars

put together in Yugoslavia by Franco-Yugoslav venture Cimos, beginning in 1978. Assembly from CKD kits also took place in Indonesia, Thailand, South Africa, Mozambique, Zimbabwe and Chile, but the numbers were always on the small-to-insignificant end of the scale – a mere 105 cars in Zimbabwe, for example. The very last G-series vehicles to be made were 300 GSA Entreprise vans assembled in Jakarta, Indonesia, during 1987.

restyled rear lights and a new grille – with silvered horizontal bars for the Club and Pallas; additionally the bumpers of the GSX and GSX2 became matt black, to match the window frames, while the Service van was re-named the Entreprise.

A year later, in September 1977, the original 1,015cc engine, still used in the G Special, the GSX and the Entreprise, was replaced by an 1,129cc unit developing 56.5bhp. At the same time restyled wheels, less prominently vented than before, were adopted, and the GSX2 given a rear spoiler. For 1979 the GSX3 replaced the GSX2. Equipped with a new 1,229cc version of the flat-four, producing 65bhp DIN, it gave the X3 a claimed top speed of 98.2mph.

In September 1979, the 'G' range entered its second generation with the arrival of the GSA. The event was heralded by an award-winning

Top: In September 1975 came the GS1220 Pallas, a luxury saloon in miniature, featuring a much higher level of internal trim and refinement, including velour upholstery. Externally, the GS Pallas can be recognised by the rubbing strip along the doors and distinctive stainless-steel wheel embellishers. (Citroën) Above: By 1978, little had changed in the specification and appearance of the GS range, except the grille, the rear treatment (new lamps and broad alloy strip across the boot) and the design of the wheels. (Citroën)

The GSA was offered in Special, Club, X3 and Pallas saloon forms plus Special and Club estates. This is a 1980 Pallas. (Citroën)

In September 1979 the GS was relaunched as the GSA hatchback. All the characteristic external details of the GSA are visible here including the matt-black door handles and window surrounds, the side rubbing-strip and the grey thermoplastic bumpers that replaced the expensive stainless steel GS units. (Citroën)

Driving the GS

It is unfortunate that the modest dimensions of its engines have led to the GS being overlooked as a driver's car, in contrast to its contemporary rival the Alfasud, which is widely applauded as a sporting machine. Yet for those who are unafraid to push the accelerator to the floor and counter poor low-down torque by spinning the high-revving flat-four to the full, the Citroën's inherent sporting character and ability come as a revelation – and in 1,299cc form things are even better, especially in terms of mid-range power. The downside is relatively poor fuel consumption, and a rasping, obtrusive soundtrack when the engine is being worked hard.

Few small family cars have ever so effectively combined sharp handling, tenacious roadholding and such a superbly supple ride. True, the manual rack-and-pinion steering is heavy at low speeds, and quite low-geared, so that parking calls for a surprising amount of effort for such a small car. But on the move it lightens up, and the sure-footed poise and balance of the GS are a delight. On the straights, the unwavering directional stability is also impressive, while the positive action of the fully powered all-disc brakes give effortless and undramatic stopping ability in all circumstances, once you have adapted to the short travel of the pedal.

The one flaw is that the gearchange is vague and sloppy, discouraging the enthusiastic style of driving for which the car is otherwise so well suited. Even so, there is no other rival of its era that compares with the GS when it comes to fast, stable motorway cruising – especially in the case of the later GSAs with a five-speed gearbox.

The Bertone Camargue

Although special-bodied GS variants were rare, the mid-range Citroën spawned one of the more stunning styling exercises of the early 1970s – the Camargue coupé shown by Bertone at the 1972 Geneva Motor Show. Built on an unchanged wheelbase, the car offered adequate 2+2 accommodation and featured a substantially glazed rear section. The design never made it into series production.

The Camargue was a Bertone show car based on the GS. Its substantial glass area would have militated against its commercialisation. (Bertone)

The dashboard of the GSA had a large schematic drawing of the car as part of its warning-light display, and featured similar satellite-pod minor controls to those on the Visa. (Citroën)

advertising campaign demonstrating the model's unique safety features, its superb roadholding and its exceptionally comfortable ride. This, the advertisements claimed, was a motoring experience that could only be compared to travelling on a red carpet that was constantly unrolled before the car, smoothing out all the undulations in its path.

The principal novelty, as far as the saloon was concerned, was that it became a hatchback with a folding rear seat. The car was also substantially facelifted, with a new plastic grille, and bumpers of grey moulded polypropylene with black inserts. Attached to the underside of the front bumpers was a pair of small spoilers, projecting forwards into the airstream and serving to increase the flow of cooling air to the engine. Finally there were new rear lamps, while full-length rubbing-strips were fitted to all models and not merely to

the Pallas. Inside it was easy to overlook the new seats, when confronted with the GSA's radical new dashboard. This featured two cylindrical satellite pods, mounted either side of the single-spoke wheel, within reach of the driver's fingertips, and housing all the minor controls. The instrument panel itself was notable for the return of the revolving-drum speedometer but its display area was mainly devoted to an illuminated outline of the car, warning drivers of failures such as the loss of hydraulic or engine-oil pressure (necessitating an imperative stop), plus other minor conditions such as excessive front brake pad wear.

Powered by the 65bhp 1,299cc engine of the GSX3, the GSA was available initially in Club saloon and estate, Pallas and X3 forms, with the 1,129cc G Special saloon and estate and the GS Entreprise van continuing in production. Four speeds were standard on the GSA Club and Pallas saloons (with C-Matic optional), but the X3 came with a five-speed gearbox.

August 1980 saw the G-Special adopt the GSA's hatchback

configuration, to become the GSA Special, as did the equivalent estate version – both cars retaining the 1,129cc engine, with four-speed or five-speed gearbox to choice. The GS Entreprise van also gave way to a GSA version, available with either the 1,129cc or 1,299cc engine and with either a four-speed or five-speed gearbox. The GSA Special had plain jersey cloth seats and vinyl-covered door facings, while the Club had ribbed jersey inserts on the seats and more elaborate part-fabric door panels, and the Pallas ribbed jersey cloth throughout.

The following year, for 1982, the GSA Special was given the 65bhp 1,299cc engine while a new base model (available only France) called simply the GSA, retained the 1,129cc engine. Meanwhile, the 1,299cc engine received certain modifications including a transistorised magnetic-impulse ignition system that reduced both fuel consumption and emissions without adversely affecting performance.

In September 1982 the Club version of the GSA saloon (but not the estate) was deleted, and a new, cheaper, version of the GSA X3, the GSA X1, was introduced, lacking some equipment and having only a four-speed gearbox. Next, in July 1983, the base 1,129cc GSA was deleted, and the option of C-Matic transmission discontinued. A year later, the Pallas and Club estate versions disappeared.

For its final 1986 season, the range was reduced to just the GSA Special saloon and estate, the X3, and the Entreprise van, all powered by the 65bhp 1,299cc engine coupled to the five-speed gearbox. At the end of July 1986 the GSA was discontinued altogether in favour of the BX range of saloons and estates introduced four years earlier. By then a total of 2,440,610 G-series cars had been built, over 16 years – 1,874,754 of the GS, 565,009 of the GSA, and 847 Birotors – of which no fewer than 106,645 found owners in the United Kingdom. Of its successors, not even the BX (2,315,739 in 12 years) or the AX (2,425,138 in 12 years) achieved better commercial results.

Truly, the GS/GSA was the car that saved Citroën from extinction, by enabling it to overcome the crisis years of the 1970s when the marque very nearly disappeared under the weight of its financial difficulties. But more than that, it also reasserted Citroën's claim to superiority in engineering matters, by representing a benchmark against which all other cars in its class were judged, at least insofar as comfort and safety were concerned. Above all, it proved that cars of high technical quality could be produced – and sold profitably – in high quantities, and that engineering excellence was actually recognised and supported by the mainstream motoring public at large.

Buying Hints

1. Rust is a serious problem on the GS and GSA, in particular because the flat undertray hides many of the rust-traps. Check the inner wings, the rear subframe, the undertray, the floorpans and the front bumper mounting-points. The front floors are the most expensive area to repair because they are made of a spot-welded double skin and not protected internally. Also beware of surface rust on the sills, as they rot from the inside out, and so by the time rust appears the damage beneath is likely to be extensive. Turning to non-structural panels, check for rust in the front and rear wings, the front valance, the door bottoms, the tailgate (where applicable), and the leading edge of bonnet. Nice original GSs and GSAs do exist, particularly if they were treated with Dinitrol or similar from new, but they're scarce. Repair sections and body panels are available from a UK specialist, though some may be second-hand only.

2. Engines are strong but, being air-cooled, run at quite high temperatures, so need oil changes every 3,000 miles for long life. Look for clean oil and listen for noisy camshafts – irregular oil changes can cause these to wear rapidly. The crankcase breather can block and fail, causing oil leaks through the crankcase or sump gaskets – check by pulling out the dipstick with the engine running. A little smoke from cold is normal because the power unit is a flat-four and so will have oil sitting in the barrels – but it should soon clear. All G-series cars run happily on unleaded petrol.

3. Ensure the cambelts have been replaced recently or invest in a new set when buying the car, to avoid potentially terminal engine damage.

4. Erratic tickover, particularly on GSAs, with revs racing between about 600rpm and as much as 1,500rpm, means that the Weber carburettor is worn or needs setting up.

5. Gearboxes are a little crude, and they can be noisy, but this isn't really a cause for concern as they are robust enough – though the five-speed unit is weaker.

6. A slipping clutch can be expensive to remedy as it takes eight hours to replace, because the entire engine needs to be removed.

7. Listen for clonks from the driveshafts while accelerating on full lock: they're stressed when braking and accelerating because of the inboard discs.

8. The rear two sections of the exhaust are easy to replace. But if you can hear a blow and can't see where it is coming from, you have to presume that it is from the front 'Y' pipes under the engine – and these can be tricky to fit.

9. The hydropneumatic suspension is reliable, though it's worth checking the condition of the hydraulic lines: on many cars they will have been replaced with copper or Teflon-coated pipe, which is a welcome sign of continuing maintenance. Don't be put off by a bouncy ride, a sign that the spheres have lost pressure: new spheres are cheap.

10. Electronic ignition was fitted as standard from '82 onwards.

11. Interiors on virtually all models aren't that well made or durable, apart from on the desirable, 1982 limited-edition GSA Pallas SE, which only came in black or silver and had a better-quality velour interior. Some original fabric materials are available from Dutch and German specialists. Note finally that heater controls can be difficult to repair and window winder mechanisms can fail.

The CX

The CX2000 was powered by the DS20's 1,985cc engine installed cross-wise. This is the actual car tested by Autocar in May 1975 and therefore one of the first rhd examples. Note the bold Orange Tenéré colour scheme inside and out. (LAT)

The CX was undoubtedly the last true Citroën, in that it was conceived by an independent management and design team. Intended as a replacement for the D-series, it was also the last car to be designed and engineered in the tradition begun by André Lefèbvre, and remaining faithful to the principles that he laid down.

Launched in France in August 1974, the CX soon met with critical acclaim: it was voted 'Car of the Year' by a wide margin, received the *Prix de la Sécurité* in recognition of its outstanding safety features, and at the 1975 Geneva Motor Show it won the ultimate accolade from 170 international design experts, the *Style Auto* Award.

The CX quickly established itself in the European market. During its first full year of production, 1975, over 96,700 units were produced, a mere 200 or so fewer than the 96,900 DS and ID models built in 1973. But the following year, production soared to over 112,000: Citroën had another winner.

Styled (as had been the GS and SM) under the direction of Robert Opron,

The CX cabriolet conversion

For those who shed a tear over the demise of the Chapron-built DS cabriolet, the arrival of the CX must have confirmed their misery: how could the structure and shape of the new big Citroën ever give rise to an open variant? It seemed an unsolvable conundrum but in central France coachbuilder Guy Deslandes succeeded in 1983 in sculpting the CX into a two-door drophead, which he called the Orphée. With substantial body reinforcement and a polyester rear, plus an electric hood and an interior re-trimmed in leather, the conversion was not cheap, and only five cars were built. Derived from the Orphée was a one-off coupé called the Avrilly.

The Deslandes Orphée was an attempt to make a convertible out of a CX saloon. (Giles Chapman Library)

CX

1974–1989

Note: Figures given only for (in sequence) 1985 model-year CX20, CX25 GTi, CX25 GTi Turbo, and CX Turbo-diesel

ENGINE:
Four-cylinder in-line, water-cooled
Capacity
    1,995cc/2,473cc
Bore and stroke
    88mm x 82mm/93mm x 92mm
Valve actuation
    Pushrod
Compression ratio
    9.2:1/8.75:1/7.75:1/21:1
Fuel system
    Weber twin-choke/electronic
    fuel injection/diesel
Power output
    106bhp DIN at 5,500rpm
    138bhp DIN at 5,000rpm
    168bhp DIN at 5,000rpm
    95bhp DIN at 3,700rpm
Torque
    122lb ft at 3,250rpm
    155lb ft at 4,000rpm
    217lb ft at 3,250rpm
    159lb ft at 2,000rpm

TRANSMISSION:
Front-wheel drive
Five-speed manual or three-speed automatic (earlier cars have four-speed manual and option of C-Matic semi-auto)

SUSPENSION:
Front: Independent, upper and lower arms; hydropneumatic springing
Rear: Independent, trailing arms; hydropneumatic springing, interconnected with front and self-levelling

STEERING:
Rack-and-pinion, fully powered, with variable assistance and self-centring (Vari-Power/Diravi)

BRAKES:
Discs front and rear, fully powered

WHEELS/TYRES:
Michelin steel or alloy
Michelin 195/70x14 (front) and 185/70x14 (rear)
Michelin 190/65 HR390 TRX (CX25 GTi and DTR)
Michelin 210/55VR390 TRX (GTi Turbo)

BODYWORK:
Steel monocoque mounted on subframes linked by longerons.
Available as four-door saloon and (not GTi Turbo) five-door estate and Familiale

DIMENSIONS (Saloon/estate):
Length   15ft 2⅜in/16ft 3in
Wheelbase   9ft 4in/10ft 2in
Track, front   4ft 10in
Track, rear   4ft 5½in
Width   5ft 8⅛in/5ft 8¼in
Height   4ft 5½in/4ft 9⅝in

WEIGHT:
24.3cwt/27.0cwt/27.3cwt/27.7cwt (saloons)
27.4cwt/28.8cwt/29.9cwt (estates)

PERFORMANCE:
(Source: *Autocar*)
Maximum speed
    109mph (Athena)
    113mph (25Ri auto estate)
    126mph (GTi Turbo Series 1)
    112mph (CX25 DTR Turbo 2)
0-60mph
    12.5sec (Athena)
    11.9sec (25Ri auto estate)
    8.6sec (GTi Turbo Series 1)
    10.1sec (CX25 DTR Turbo 2)

PRICE INCLUDING TAX WHEN NEW
(October 1985):
£7,757 CX20 saloon
£10,669 CX25 Pallas IE
£10,669 CX25 DTR Turbo
£12,573 CX25 GTi Turbo

NUMBERS BUILT:
Definitive figures have not been established. Citroën gives a total of 1,041,560, of which 128,185 were estates. The CX Club de France gives a higher total of 1,420,460, of which 129,018 were estates and 378,670 were diesels.

The Tissier six-wheelers

Having established a successful concept with his six-wheeled DS high-speed newspaper-delivery vans, Pierre Tissier continued in the same vein with the CX – on a much larger scale. This time, over 200 vehicles were to be made, including no fewer than 80 for the Hollander newspaper distribution firm, who habitually ran their vehicles to 100,000km before pensioning them off. In addition to the van-bodied Bagagère, Tissier offered an ambulance, which retained the rear passenger doors of the CX and had a glass-fibre rear body sufficiently tall to allow medics to work standing up; in all 130 of these imposing conversions were made. Special orders included a 14-seat mini-coach, a 'CX Penthouse' motorhome displayed at the 1980 Paris Motor Show, and three special vehicles for anti-skid testing of road surfaces by the government Ponts et

Chaussées department. Never one to turn down an unusual commission, Tissier also built a special CX for Citroën-loving East German head-of-state Erich Honecker: based on a CX Presige Turbo 2, the wheelbase was extended by two feet to allow six passengers to be seated *vis-à-vis* at the rear. With its raised roofline and

Probably the most extraordinary Tissier CX was this six-wheel 'Penthouse' motorvan revealed at the 1980 Paris Motor Show. (LAT)

semi-blind extra side-windows, this was not a vehicle of any great elegance, but the issue was academic, as Honecker fell from power before he could take delivery.

the CX embraced a number of distinctive themes seen on earlier Citroëns. Most noticeable were the shrouded rear wheels enclosed by removable spats, the pronounced kick-up line running from the rear wheelarches to the tail and the use of expensive stainless steel for the bumpers and other brightwork.

The CX saloon was smaller than the DS, being 3in narrower, 1ft shorter overall and 11in shorter in its wheelbase, although with an unladen weight of 24.9cwt it was only 27lb lighter. Its streamlined shape resulted in good aerodynamic efficiency, the quoted drag coefficient being 0.38 or 0.39 (depending on source), a figure marginally inferior to that of the DS – which, however, had a greater frontal area and was thus marginally less efficient overall. It was this slipperiness that gave the car its name, 'CX' being the French term for Cd.

The CX also boasted a glass area far larger than on the DS, due largely to its huge, deeply curved windscreen,

swept by a single extra-long wiper. Another novel feature was the design of the Kamm tail and concave rear screen: this configuration allowed the airflow to scour rain and road dust from the glass so that excellent rearward vision was assured when the car was travelling at speed. The box-shaped 16.8cu ft boot opened down to the bumper for easy loading and was unobstructed by any spare wheel, this being stowed under the bonnet.

At the outset it had been envisaged that the next big Citroën would be powered by a Wankel rotary engine to be produced by the Comotor joint-manufacturing venture with the German NSU firm. But development problems and delays, aggravated by the new priorities of the energy crisis, ruled against this adventurous option. Instead, in the interest of fuel economy Citroën decided to install improved versions of the outstandingly robust and economical DS20 and DS21 power units, initially in 1,985cc (CX-2000) or 2,175cc (CX-2200) forms.

These were mounted transversely and inclined towards the front by 30 degrees. Installed in this position, the weight of the combined engine and transmission unit was concentrated slightly ahead of the front wheels. In fact the entire weight of the CX was distributed in the proportions 60:40 between the front and rear wheels, as originally advocated by Lefèbvre. One disadvantage of this arrangement was that the front disc brakes could no longer be mounted inboard, as on the DS and GS.

As expected on a big Citroën, the CX featured the same unique self-levelling hydropneumatic suspension as found on the DS and refined and simplified with such success for the GS. A lever on the console allowed the driver to select one of three height settings, the highest being used when changing a wheel. The design of the mechanical elements of the suspension, however, owed more to the GS than the DS. The front axle sub-assembly comprised two forged-

A rhd CX2200, as introduced in the UK in autumn 1975. Launched in France in January 1975, the CX2200 had a 112bhp 2,175cc engine derived from the DS21 power unit. (LAT)

Instrumentation was a development of the GS rotating-drum principle; by now the single-spoke wheel had become a Citroën trademark. (Citroën)

The clever fingertip controls used rocker switches for the indicators and flash/dip: unorthodox, but the system worked well. (Citroën)

Other special CXs

The Henri Chapron firm was waning by the time of the CX but, even so, the Levallois coachbuilder did attempt to put its stamp on the car by offering luxury interior transformations of the Prestige, with or without division. Chapron also built a roll-top landaulet CX for Citroën, and another with a three-quarter-length Plexiglas roof – this latter car being lent by Citroën to the Luxembourg royal family for the wedding in 1981 of the Grand Duke.

Heuliez, meanwhile, catered for the more practically minded, with a super-estate based on the CX hearses made by its sister company Augereau. The Evasion estate had a rear extended by 30cm (12in), and was luxuriously trimmed to please the huntin'-fishin'-shootin' clientele at

which it was aimed. The Swiss, finally, came up with the CX that many said Citroën should have produced in the first place: a hatchback. Both Beutler and Caruna offered a conversion, but the numbers made were small.

The CX was widely criticised for being a conventional saloon, and not a hatchback. But coachbuilders Beutler and Caruna both came up with hatchback conversions of the CX. (LAT)

steel transverse arms linking the hubs to the front subframe, and connected also to the front suspension units and the anti-roll bar. These arms operated as a parallelogram, but their axes of articulation were not exactly parallel. Instead, they dipped forward by 12 degrees in order to maintain a level attitude at all times and prevent lift or dive under acceleration or braking. Just as was the case with the DS and GS, the CX's front suspension was designed to follow the principle of centre-point steering; under all conditions of travel the vertical axis of the steering swivel passed through the hubs and wheels to meet the exact point of contact between the tyre and the road. It was this feature, in conjunction with Citroën's self-levelling suspension, that gave the CX driver the ability to maintain absolute directional stability and control under emergency braking, even in the event of a high-speed front tyre blow-out. Steering was by means of a manually-operated rack on the CX-2000 version, with the CX-2200 having, as an option, a development of the Diravi – or Vari-Power – system first seen on the SM

and offering just 2½ turns lock-to-lock.

Unlike the punt-chassis structure of the DS, the CX's bodyshell was a conventional monocoque, but was novel in that it was attached by rubber silentbloc mountings to two parallel longerons connecting the front and rear subframes. This unusual arrangement ensured exceptional torsional stiffness and maintained perfect alignment between the front and rear axles under all circumstances, thus making possible the highly accurate steering and exemplary directional stability for which the CX was noted.

Naturally the braking system was fully powered, with separate twin front and rear circuits energised by the car's high-pressure hydraulic system, and discs were used all-round instead of the combination of front discs and rear drums seen on the D-series. A conventional pendant foot pedal was fitted, rather than the mushroom button of the DS, this actuating a *doseur* brake control valve that distributed fluid to each of the circuits at a pressure proportional to the effort exerted on the foot pedal.

A compensating valve was fitted to the rear circuit, to ensure a more progressive action on the rear brakes according to load, so as to reduce the risk of locking the rear wheels under emergency braking.

The radically innovative interior featured a dashboard that was imaginatively futuristic yet at the same time sober and restrained: it consisted of a sweeping one-piece moulding with the instrument panel comprising a separate elliptical binnacle, this being described in one road-test report as 'a bisected flying saucer hovering above the dashboard'. This *lunule*, as it was christened in France, incorporated pods at either end containing the principal minor controls, in particular rocker switches for the indicators and headlamps, all being operated by the fingertips without the need to lift a hand from the wheel. The instruments in the binnacle comprised a speedometer and tachometer of the same revolving-drum type seen in the GS. Ergonomically excellent, this extraordinary dash-board created a sense of uncluttered spaciousness and comfort.

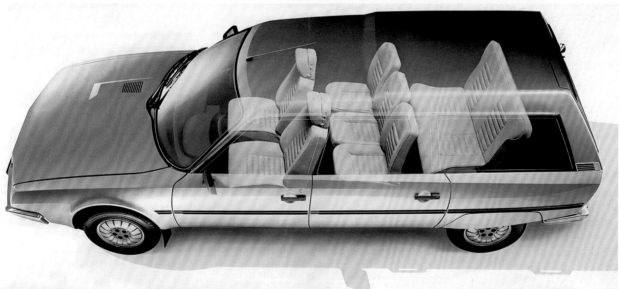

The one-piece panels cladding the interior surface of the CX's doors were also a strikingly original feature of the design. Formed from moulded plastic, padded with foam and sheathed in vinyl, they had recessed roundels for the window winders, on versions lacking electric lifters. The door catches were integrated into large pistol-grip door handles, in such a way that no potentially harmful metal fittings protruded. The seats, upholstered with jersey nylon cloth, were also of an entirely new pattern, and the result of an intensive programme of ergonomic and medical research. Though not quite so colourful as the sybaritic interiors of

Top: The CX estate was the last purpose-built Citroën estate for many years; with its extended wheelbase and raised roofline it was supremely practical. This is a 1982 car. (Citroën)

Above: Ghosted photo of the Familiale shows the car's eight-seater configuration. (Citroën)

The CX2200 Prestige was introduced for 1976. This luxurious long-wheelbase limousine used the floorpan of the CX estate. (Citroën)

the DS, the whole effect was completely original and entirely different from the sombre blacks and greys in fashion today.

In September 1975 the range was extended by the addition of the luxury CX2200 Pallas. Viewed from the exterior, the Pallas could be distinguished by stainless-steel sill covers, thin side rubbing strips, rubber overriders, metal beading beneath the windows and, of course, 'Pallas' badges on the boot lid and rear quarter panel. It also boasted distinctive stainless-steel wheel embellishers; initially, these had a six-pointed star design but from the end of 1977 onwards they took the simpler form of large, plain dishes with a small central boss. The interior of the Pallas had more elaborately upholstered seats in a superior-quality jersey nylon cloth with a ribbed rather than plain surface; leather was an option. Initially, seven colours were offered, of which three metallic shades – grey, green and bronze – were exclusive to

the Pallas. Naturally, the car also benefited from the modification to the heating and ventilation system introduced on all models in July 1975, when two extra eye-ball vents were added to the centre console, in the position previously occupied by the radio speakers; paired units were now positioned in the front doors.

December 1975 was a major milestone in the career of the CX range as it saw the arrival of the CX2200 Diesel saloon, the first diesel-engined passenger car to be offered by Citroën since the late 1930s. This version was powered by a 2,175cc compression-ignition engine producing 66bhp and rated at 9CV. With the energy crisis then at its height, the arrival of this outstandingly robust and economical diesel engine was timely indeed, and the CX2200 Diesel proved to be an immediate and substantial success. Over the next three years sales of the CX diesels mounted annually until ultimately they represented no less than 48 per cent of total production.

In January 1976 the long-awaited CX *break*, or estate, announced the previous September, became available. The last of the true purpose-

built Citroën estate cars, the *break* had a wheelbase lengthened by 9½in and a distinctive roofline with a raised rear section. With rear seats that folded to give a totally flat load space with hidden storage underneath, and with the benefits of self-levelling suspension, the *break* was in its day Europe's ultimate estate car, in terms of practical carrying capacity: with its rear seats folded down it offered an available floor length of 6ft 2ins and a total 76.7cu ft of fully usable load space. Initially two engines were offered, the 1,985cc petrol unit or the 2,175cc diesel. Available in the UK from April 1976, as the Safari, the estate was followed by an ambulance version, specially constructed by Heuliez and available only in France, and in October 1976 an eight-seater Familiale joined the range.

Also new for 1976 was the option of C-Matic semi-automatic transmission, as on the GS, while in February 1976 a new luxury CX, the Prestige, entered production, to fill the vacancy left by the demise of the DS23IE Prestige-Pallas two years earlier. Based on the estate's long-wheelbase floorpan, for greater rear legroom, the Prestige was instantly recognisable by its longer (by

The CX in competition

After the more than honourable performance in competition of the DS, it was only to be expected that the CX would be fielded in Citroën's obvious area of strength: tough endurance rallies over challenging terrain, where ruggedness was more important than outright speed or agility. And so it was to be, with the first significant result being fourth place in the 1976 Rallye du Maroc. The following year, things got into top gear. In the Acropolis Rally, a privately-entered CX2400 came in sixth, and in the London–Sydney Marathon the four CXs entered by Citroën-Australia finished third, fourth, seventh and tenth – winning the Constructors' Cup. More

importantly, though, 1977 also saw CXs in the top five places – out of only seven finishers – in the car-battering Tour Automobile de Sénégal, recognised as being one of the toughest rallies of the time. In 1978 Citroën repeated this success, its four cars being classed first, second, third, and sixth, out of the six finishers.

The same year marked an intriguing departure for Citroën: dentist Bob Neyret, famous for his exploits in the DS, entered an all-female three-car team in the Monte Carlo, sponsored by a toothpaste brand and running diesel CX2200s. The result was a class win – just as a CX2500D won its class in that year's Tour de France. Meanwhile Citroën's hat trick in the

Tour Automobile de Sénégal came in 1979, with a largely-standard 2400GTi winning the rally: nobody could say that the CX wasn't tough! The following year saw a GTi win the Rallye du Maroc, but this marked almost the end of the CX's frontline competition career, as Citroën decided to switch its efforts to the Visa. As a reminder of the CX's potential, however, 1981 saw a CX win the accolade of being the first two-wheel-drive touring car to finish the punishing Paris–Dakar rally.

In 1977, a team of four CX2400s – one of them driven by Paddy Hopkirk – gained the Constructors Cup for Citroën in the second London–Sydney Marathon. (Citroën)

7in) rear doors and by the broader stainless steel C-pillar. Internal refinements included rear footrests, air conditioning and button-backed seats in jersey cloth or optional leather, while, externally, black or metallic paintwork, additional beading around the front and rear lamps, Pallas-style wheel trims and a (latterly optional) vinyl roof were to be found. Available in the UK from August 1976,

the Prestige was initially offered only with a new carburettor-fed 2,347cc engine delivering 115bhp DIN.

For 1977 this unit replaced the 2,175cc engine in the standard CX, the resultant CX2400 being available in Super and Pallas forms, with either four-speed manual or C-Matic transmission. Electronic fuel injection returned beneath Citroën bonnets in May 1977 when the high-performance

128bhp CX2400 GTi saloon, capable of 118mph, was introduced; shortly afterwards this engine was made standard in the Prestige and became available as an option in the Pallas. Equipped with a five-speed gearbox, as was to become an option on lesser CX2400s over the course of the 1978 model year, the GTi was distinguished by a special steering wheel, front fog lights, alloy wheels

Above: Introduced in July 1979, the CX Athena and Reflex saloons were budget-priced models powered by a completely new 106bhp all-alloy 1,995cc ohc engine manufactured by the PSA-Renault joint-venture Douvrin factory. Top speed of both cars was 109mph. This is the Athena. (Citroën)

The CX2400IE Pallas, introduced in December 1977 – a luxury range-topper, powered by the same engine as the GTi but with C-Matic semi-automatic transmission. All the usual Pallas exterior features are visible here, including stainless-steel sill covers, rubber bumper inserts, and full-diameter wheel embellishers. (Citroën)

Driving the CX

More conventional, less Citroën? Not really: the CX still exhibits the same delightful idiosyncrasies of the DS and the SM, albeit tempered somewhat. Indeed, there are those who have described it as an SM for the real world. It's certainly true that as with the SM you need time to adjust to the way a CX should be driven: the Vari-Power steering and the hard short-travel brake pedal demand the same gentle touch, even if the steering is less extreme than in the SM.

Obviously the nature of the CX varies from model to model, depending on the engine fitted. Certain characteristics, all the same, are constant. The Vari-Power steering is deliciously seductive once you've mastered it. Manoeuvring is wonderfully easy, with an engaging hiss or two as the steering goes about its business, while on the open road the mechanism loses assistance to give reassuring weight allied to an incredible sense of security owing to the constant self-centring action. The

brakes have superb stopping power, and getting the measure of the pedal action is something you'll soon master.

The CX rides with traditional Citroën comfort, but without the exaggerated roll of the DS. The self-levelling action is particularly invaluable in the estates, which can carry an enormous amount of luggage or tow a heavy trailer or caravan without developing a nose-up attitude.

The 2-litre engines, whether of Citroën or Douvrin origin, provide relatively leisurely performance, while the 2.2-litre versions of either type have a bit more pep, especially in terms of mid-range power. The un-blown 2.5 diesel has fairly leisurely responses at low speed but cruises with ease and refinement, while the turbo-diesel has genuinely sprightly performance and thoroughly satisfactory refinement – a combination made all the more attractive by modest average fuel

consumption figures in the 30–33mpg range. Another attractive power unit is the fuel-injected 2.5-litre, which is refined and more than adequately powerful – even if 24mpg is the best you're likely to wring from it. This unit is particularly well suited to the automatic gearbox, which offers smooth and responsive shifting; in contrast, the manual gearbox alternative is nothing special, having a light but slightly imprecise action. As for the GTi Turbo, the extra torque, near-total lack of turbo-lag and the enhanced performance put it in a different league: if you want a BMW-eating Citroën, the Turbo is a tempting proposition.

Whichever model you choose, the CX has a distinctively Citroën character, enhanced by such details as the unusual but ergonomically excellent switchgear. Just don't expect Mercedes levels of build quality: equally characteristic, alas, is a certain flimsiness and lack of durability in the interior fittings.

with Michelin XVS tyres, and matt-black window frames. Appropriately, the car boasted a more sporting interior, with black dashboard and carpets and sports seats with integral headrests, optionally in a flamboyant two-tone black and buff leather.

Production of the CX exceeded 112,000 units in 1977, for the second year running; the following year, 1978, it was to hit 132,000, of which 70,116 were sold in France and 7,000 in the UK. In spite of the problems of the energy crisis, the CX had succeeded in establishing itself as a formidable *grande routière* in the French tradition.

It was surely this same demand for relaxed and economical high-speed motorway cruising that led to the arrival in February 1978 of two improved diesels, the CX2500D saloon and estate. With capacity increased to 2,500cc, power output rose by more than 13 per cent to 75bhp while, more

importantly, maximum torque was increased by 20 per cent to 111lb ft, delivered at the much lower engine speed of 2,000rpm. A four-speed gearbox and a higher final-drive ratio were fitted, while Vari-Power steering was made standard. Truly, the CX2500D represented the ultimate in diesel-car development for that era: official EEC tests recorded 32.5mpg at a constant 75mph and 34.5mpg on the urban cycle, yet when fitted with the five-speed gearbox – optional from summer 1978 – the Citroën was the world's fastest non-turbo diesel, good for a 96.9mph maximum speed.

By July 1979, Vari-Power steering had become standard on most models. This date also marked a new step forward in the evolution of the range, with the introduction of the four-speed Reflex and the much better-equipped Athena, with standard five-speed gearbox for the

UK. Replacing the CX2000, these two newcomers were powered by a modern 1,995cc all-alloy single-ohc engine manufactured by the joint Peugeot-Renault-Volvo plant at Douvrin; the same unit was found in the Renault 20 and Peugeot 505. Rated at 106bhp, it gave the Reflex and Athena lively acceleration (0–60mph in 11.7secs) and a top speed of 109mph.

The Athena had ribbed rather than plain jersey cloth seats, plus tinted glass and electric front windows, and Vari-Power steering was standard, while externally it had Pallas-type wheel embellishers and rubbing strips in contrast to the cheaper Reflex's simple plastic wheel covers and matt-black window frames. Three months later, another interesting innovation appeared for the 1980 season – the CX2500 Diesel Limousine, which was not sold in the UK. This combined the long-wheelbase Prestige body with the

Easily identifiable by its special alloy wheels, this is the CXGTi Turbo introduced in France in September 1985. Powered by a turbocharged, fuel-injected 2,500cc Citroën pushrod petrol engine, top speed is 137mph. (LAT)

engine and five-speed manual transmission of the CX2500 diesel saloon. All the motoring commentators were agreed that this truly luxurious diesel car had little real opposition, at a time when rival diesel models were generally more spartan, and aimed essentially at the taxi market.

In 1979 Citroën production reached a post-war record of 815,173 units (with 375,395 exported) of which no fewer than 123,391 were CX models. But in the new decade this tally would

prove impossible to sustain. During 1980, for the first time since 1975, annual CX production fell below 80,000 units, to a total of 77,237 of all types – 42,578 petrol and 34,669 diesel. The signs were that, if only temporarily, big cars like the CX were falling from favour, particularly in France, where taxation penalised engines larger than 1700cc–1800cc.

The process of improvement went on regardless, however, and in July 1980 a new paint shop was installed at Aulnay, designed to achieve a significant improvement in the corrosion resistance of the CX's coachwork. The measures introduced included injecting cavities with a rust-inhibiting treatment, fitting rigid rubber sealing strips on the door bottoms, and applying a final coat of clear lacquer to the paintwork. Among

detail improvements for 1981 the CX2400 petrol engine was boosted from 115bhp to 120bhp, and the five-speed gearbox was fitted as standard to the CX Pallas and CX2500 Diesel, while the CX2400 GTi was given a new interior with improved seats, a boot lid spoiler, and a matt-black finish for exterior fittings such as the window-frames, door-handles and C-pillar trim panel – this last being widened. Also for 1981, the C-Matic semi-automatic transmission was discontinued and the CX2400 Pallas and Prestige were given the option of a fully automatic three-speed ZF gearbox.

Throughout the end of 1981 and beginning of 1982, the CX Reflex Safari Estates and Familiales were introduced in the UK market, based on the vehicles that had appeared earlier in France. The models were the CX

A rhd Series One GTi Turbo of 1985. Note the prominent rear spoiler and special alloy wheels exclusive to this model. (LAT)

The revised fascia and console of the Series Two CX range introduced in September 1986. The unusual 'lunule' dashboard was retained, but now featured conventional round-dialed instruments. This is the GTi Turbo version (LAT).

Reflex (1,995cc petrol), the CX Reflex D (2.5-litre diesel), the CX Reflex 2.4 Auto (2.4 carb) and the CX Reflex IE (2.4-litre fuel-injected). Competitively priced, they shared a common level of trim and equipment.

For 1982 the 2,347cc estates became fuel-injected, and gained the option of the ZF automatic gearbox, while the front wheelarches of all models were flared to accept new Michelin TRX high-speed tyres, henceforth standard on the GTi and optional on the CX2400 Pallas and Prestige. At the same time all the saloons received the enlarged C-pillar panel introduced earlier on the GTI. In all cases except the CX Prestige, this was made from matt-black plastic.

In the autumn of 1982, the entire CX range was reorganised, a process that involved equipment improvements and the renaming of certain models. For example, the Reflex and Athena names disappeared, the CX Reflex becoming the CX20 and the CX Athena the CX20TRE. Following on from this, 1983 saw power increased for both petrol and diesel CXs. First to arrive, in April was a 2500 turbo-diesel offering 95bhp DIN and 159lb ft of torque at 2,000rpm. Then in July the 2,347cc fuel-injected petrol engine

The only really new offering among the revised Series Two CX models for 1986 was the CX22TRS, powered by an ohc Douvrin engine enlarged to 2,165cc. Note the exterior changes introduced on the Series Two cars, including plastic bumpers and a lowered 'kick-up' line over the rear wheelarch. (Citroën)

gave way to a 2,500cc unit developing 138bhp and featuring a computerised solid-state electronic ignition system that dispensed with a distributor, rather than the transistorised magnetic-impulse ignition previously used. Both these new engines were additionally offered in high-spec estate models, known in the UK as the CX25 TRi Safari when in petrol form, and as the CX25DTR Turbo Safari when fitted with the turbo-diesel. At the other end of the range, May 1984 saw the introduction of the budget-priced CX20 Leader limited edition,

which was not sold in the UK. Distinguished by its two-tone metallic grey paintwork, with a contrasting dark grey strip along its lower flanks and a decal on its front doors, it also boasted tinted glass, a rear spoiler and its own individual pattern of wheel embellisher. That year, only 700 were produced, but the model continued for the next five years at an average of 2,000 units per year, until a total of 9,700 examples had been manufactured.

In September 1984, heralded by a spectacular advertising campaign featuring American model/singer Grace Jones and using the slogan C'est démon! ('It's Devilish!'), came the CX25GTi Turbo. Adding a turbocharger to the petrol engine boosted output by 22 per cent, to 168bhp, and torque by 40 per cent, to 217lb ft at 3,250rpm, translating into a maximum speed of 138mph and a 0–60mph time of just

7.9 seconds – making the five-speed Turbo a true high-performance saloon and the fastest French car of its day. Appropriately, in addition to its unique new alloy wheels carrying a 'T' symbol and fitted with ultra-low profile Michelin TRX tyres, the GTi Turbo was kitted out with a large rear spoiler plus matt-black door handles and window frames. The Turbo 'T' motif was also to be seen as a badge on the bonnet air-intake. An all-black interior featured special sports seats with integral headrests, upholstered in a chevron-patterned velours, and there was a revised dashboard with conventional round instruments. Equally fittingly, the following March ABS braking became optional on the Turbo, the first time it had been offered on a French vehicle.

By the end of June 1985, eleven years after the commencement of production, no fewer than 912,500

CX in the United States

The CX was never imported into the USA by Citroën, but individuals and independent companies brought in cars over the years. The best-known was CX Automotive of New Jersey, who modified the car to meet US lighting regulations by fitting twin round headlamps and even went as far as to have it crash-tested. Mostly CX Automotive imported Series IIs, which were sold with a 'CXA' badge; as the venture was strictly unofficial, the Citroën name was removed from the car, along with the chevrons normally adorning the grille.

CXs had been produced, of which 42.3 per cent had been exported, principally to Germany (90,610), Italy (63,433), Belgium (48,429) and Great Britain (39,848); 81 per cent of this total had been saloons and 19 per cent estates, 53 per cent of CXs produced up to this point being petrol-engined and 47 cent diesel powered. Even so, annual production – which had peaked at 132,675 vehicles in 1978 – was falling at an ever-accelerating rate, largely as a result of declining demand in its home country, where it was under strong attack from Renault's attractive 25 model; indeed, of a total of only 41,949 CXs built in 1984, a mere 17,847 found customers in France. Clearly it was time to attempt to rekindle interest in Citroën's big car.

Accordingly, July 1985 saw the revamped Series Two CX models, facelifted inside and out. The salient

Last of the line – a 1987 CX GTi Turbo 2 equipped with an intercooled version of the turbocharged 2,500cc engine. Top speed was an impressive 138mph. (Citroën)

external changes were wraparound body-colour plastic bumpers front and rear, a broad waistline rubbing strip, black plastic sill covers, and the elimination of much of the stainless-steel brightwork; additionally all saloons but the 20RE and 25RD received the rear spoiler of the GTi. Internally the dashboard and centre console were more closely integrated in a revised one-piece structure housing an improved heating and ventilation system with relocated vents and with orthodox round instrument dials; restyled, the idiosyncratic but logical finger-tip controls remained, but in an unworthy concession to conventional tastes mock wood inserts appeared in the

Buying Hints

1. The most important thing to bear in mind is who you're buying the car from: a CX being sold by an enthusiast Citroën Car Club member is more likely to have been maintained properly. Look for a full (recent) service history, ideally from a Citroën specialist: it's vital.

2. All CXs rust, though Series One cars produced before early 1981 are much worse and have become scarce. After this date Citroën opened a new paint shop and applied better rust-proofing techniques, redesigning some areas of the car with this is mind. The easiest way to tell these better-protected cars is by their slide-out ashtrays; before this the ashtray was a round ball that looked like an air freshener. Series Twos are less rust-prone.

3. Higher-specification models such as the TRi, Pallas or Prestige are more desirable but can have a lot of extra electrical equipment such as central locking and cruise control, so check that it all works. The Prestige Turbo 2 is the ultimate – only five were sold in the UK

4. On pre-'81 cars, there's a rubber seal between the inner and outer skins of the front wing, and the area around this corrodes, as do the front and rear areas of the wing itself. The rear wings are worse, and the inner rear wheelarches rot too. Unlike the DS, the panels aren't bolted on – so replacement isn't really a viable option. Other rust-prone areas are the door bottoms, the base of the

windscreen pillar (which can't be repaired) and the leading edge of the bonnet. The underside is better, though you should check the floorpans, chassis longerons (poor on '81–'83 examples) and sills: just set the suspension to maximum and look underneath. Post-October '81 cars, identified by flared front wheelarches, are much better, but you still need to check the bonnet, lower edge of the boot and the rear wings in particular.

5. On Safaris and Familiales, examine the rear of the roof where the tailgate hinges as serious rust can take hold in this area. Also check the rot-prone tailgate, as these are costly: second-hand ones will probably be rusty too.

6. Like all hydropneumatic Citroëns, the system is reliable and cheap to maintain so long as it has been correctly maintained – look for clean green LHM fluid in the reservoir. The ride should be exceptionally smooth: if it's hard or choppy, the spheres need to be repressurised or replaced. The car should rise to its normal height within 15 seconds: if you press down either bumper at each end, the body should glide up and down. If there's a constant clicking from the belt-driven pump, the main accumulator sphere probably needs replacing; heavy steering at parking speeds is another sign of this. Also check the condition of the hydraulic pipes under the car (along the chassis longerons and rear subframe): they're made of steel, not copper, and can corrode badly.

7. The condition of the rear suspension arm bearings should be checked. With the suspension on its highest setting, check the inclination of the rear wheels from the back of the car and, if they aren't vertical, the bearings need replacing – which can cost £200–£300 per side. Other tell-tales are creaking noises and bangs in normal driving.

8. As the front discs do 75 per cent of the braking, the rear discs and callipers can corrode, so should always be checked. Don't be surprised if the handbrake isn't effective: it works well when it's adjusted, but this doesn't last long. It typically needs to be adjusted two to three times per year.

9. The early 1,985cc, 2,175cc and 2,347cc pushrod engines, carried over from the DS, are virtually indestructable and with regular oil changes typically last 300,000 miles. The all-alloy 1,995cc and 2,165cc overhead-cam 'Douvrin' engines are also reliable, so long as the rubber timing belts have been changed every 40,000 miles; they are also more economical. Later fuel-injected cars may have up to three ECU modules, which aren't cheap to replace, though second-hand units are readily available. Earlier diesels last longer, the 2,500cc unit being the best, though they should ideally have had oil changes every 3,000 miles (Citroën recommended 6,000 miles). Turbo-diesels are more troublesome: their heads can crack and, if heavy breathers, probably

doors of some models. New patterns of trim and upholstery completed the package, the CX25 GTi Turbo retaining its grey/black interior and special sports front seats with integral headrests, and with black leather trim remaining optional.

Engines and other mechanical

elements were essentially unchanged, although a detail enhancement on all models was that an electric servo-motor now controlled ride-height adjustment, replacing the manual lever previously used. Additionally the ride was made firmer on most models by the incorporation of modified

damper valves plus stiffer anti-roll bars. Indeed, of the grand total of 24 Series Two models, only two, the CX25 Prestige Turbo saloon (a flagship model not offered in the UK) and the CX22TRS saloon, were actually new. The CX25 Prestige Turbo featured the turbocharged 2,500cc fuel-injected

have worn piston rings and bores; the 2.5-litre Turbo 2 suffers from porous bores, due to defective castings and high internal pressures generated in the engine. On all CXs, check the engine mounting links.

10. Walk away from a car with a slipping clutch, as replacement is an engine-out job that takes more than 13 hours. Manual gearboxes are strong and synchro problems are rare; the oil coolers on automatics can develop leaks but these can be repaired.

11. Plastic bumpers on S2s often tear. Like the GS, the comfy cloth-trimmed interior isn't that hard-wearing – some higher-spec cars have leather interiors, which are more desirable. As on many Citroën models, the alloy wheels deteriorate badly and the rims corrode with age, allowing air to escape. Look out for metric-sized wheels too, shod with authentic Michelin TRX tyres, which are now extremely scarce and can cost up to £200 each (for a GTi Turbo tyre). Michelin still makes TRXs at its Historic Tyre Division, but only in certain sizes.

12. Unfortunately, Citroën doesn't support its classic models nearly as well as some German marques. Routine service items are stocked, but many parts – such as body panels and trim – have been deleted, so you'll only be able to get them from specialists (who may charge according to their rarity), though second-hand items are generally available.

engine previously available only in the CX25 GTi Turbo saloon, while the CX22TRS was equipped with a much improved version of the Douvrin 'four', its capacity increased from 1,995cc to 2,165cc and its output boosted from 106bhp to 115bhp; this unit, matched to the five-speed gearbox, raised top

speed from 109mph to 116mph with little penalty in fuel consumption. The CX22TRS boasted a particularly high level of trim and equipment, including grey herringbone tweed upholstery, tinted windows, rear seatbelts and head restraints and also a rear spoiler. In the UK that year (1985/86), a reduced range of five saloons and three estates was offered, comprising naturally-aspirated CX20RE and CX22TRS saloons, the fuel-injected CX25GTi automatic saloon, the CX25GTi Turbo and the 2,500cc CX25 Prestige automatic, plus the CX20RE Safari estate saloon car and Familiale, the CX25Ri Familiale and the CX25TRi Safari estate, and finally the CX25DTR Safari. That season also, the Pallas appellation was abolished in the UK, as in France.

In July 1986, an intercooler or air-to-air heat exchanger was fitted to the turbocharged petrol models, which were renamed CX25GTI Turbo 2 and the CX25 Prestige Turbo 2 respectively; at the same time ABS braking was made a standard fitment on both cars. Nine months later, in April 1987 – the year in which the millionth CX rolled off the Aulnay production line – the Series Two CX25 Turbo-diesel saloon and estate were also given an intercooler and renamed the CX25 Turbo 2 Diesels. By increasing the density of the air that entered the combustion chambers, the intercooler boosted power by 26 per cent to 120bhp, making the Citroëns simply the fastest diesel vehicles in the world. The saloon version had a top speed of 121mph, a 0–60 mph acceleration time of just 10.4 seconds and yet returned an average fuel consumption of 58mpg, according to Citroën.

Sadly, despite the popularity of these impressive turbo-diesel models among high-mileage, long-distance motorists throughout Europe, the arrival of the Series Two CX failed to arrest the car's decline; in 1984, the last year of the Series One CX, 41,849 units were produced, but in 1985 output fell again to 38,696 vehicles, in 1986 to 35,409, in 1987 to 35,630 and in 1988 to a slender 23,979 units. Clearly, the imminent arrival of the

new XM saloon, due to be launched in 1989, was having a discouraging effect on buyers, and the end of the road was now in sight for the CX range. However, as a final gesture towards the CX's British fans, in May 1988 the CX22TRS was offered in a special limited edition only available in the UK, the Croisette. Fitted with ABS as standard and finished in Pearl Grey only, with grey side mouldings instead of the normal black, this car also featured sports seats upholstered in a special dark grey cloth unique to this model. The standard CX22TRS also continued in the catalogue for the final 1989 model year, however, but enhanced by the so-called VIP interior pack (in effect, the sports seats and chevron-patterned velour upholstery from the GTi) plus an electrically-operated sunroof, alloy wheels and ABS brakes as standard.

So it was that the last CX saloon left the Aulnay factory in May 1989, entirely without ceremony, to conclude a career that had lasted for no fewer than 17 years. Exactly 1,041,560 examples had been built since the first car had rolled off the lines in 1974, of which just 46,412 had found owners in the United Kingdom. Although the saloons had vanished from the showrooms, the CX story was not completely over, all the same: in the absence of an immediate replacement in the XM range, the CX estates continued in production for a further two years until the belated launch of the XM *break* in June 1991. These 1990 and 1991 model year estates were built exclusively by Heuliez and marketed in France as the Evasion. Four versions were made available for the UK, all to special order; these were badged as the CXTGE Safari (equipped with the 2.2-litre Douvrin engine), the CXTGI Safari and Familiale, which replaced the CX25TRI Safari and the CX25RI Familiale, and the CXTGD Turbo Safari, which superseded the CX25DTR Turbo 2 estate. Production of rhd vehicles for the UK market actually ceased in January 1991, but assembly of lhd *breaks* and ambulances continued until later in the year.

Citroën in *the* PSA *era*

In July 1974, three months before the introduction of the CX, Citroën underwent another enforced change of ownership and management. After 40 years of Michelin rule, it came under the control of former rival Peugeot, in a reorganisation that altered, once again, the ethos of the marque. Symbolically, the old Quai de Javel factory, the last link back to the André Citroën era, was closed that same year.

During the 1960s Michelin had talked to various continental motor manufacturers about possible collaboration – and even considered divesting itself of Citroën altogether. The most notable outcome of these negotiations was a short-lived association with Fiat between 1968 and 1973.

The severe losses caused by the collapse in sales of both cars and tyres in 1974 as a consequence of the

Star of the show at the 1982 Paris salon was the new BX, the car that was to revive Citroën's fortunes. This is the BX16 TRS. (Citroën)

The MkI Visa had a choice of two engines – a Citroën 652cc air-cooled flat-twin (Special and Club) and a 1,124cc four-cylinder water-cooled Peugeot unit on the Super. This is a Special. (Citroën)

oil crisis made this policy all the more pressing. Having invested heavily in the development of the GS, SM and CX, and in brand new production facilities at Aulnay-sous-Bois and elsewhere, Citroën was more exposed than most other car firms to the downturn, and once again drastic action was needed.

The managerial reorganisation and financial restructuring begun in 1974 and concluded in 1976 were radical indeed, and involved the sale to Peugeot of an 89.95 per cent stake in Citroën. With French government backing, the two ostensibly incompatible marques were merged in a shotgun marriage to become the PSA group, entirely controlled by Peugeot. The aim was to create a truly global French-owned automobile enterprise to compete on equal terms with the major American and Japanese multinationals. While pooling components such as engines and floorpans, the cars would retain their own distinct identity, it was stressed.

So it was that the Citroën marque

survived misfortune yet again, but this time in the hands of a company whose management was cautious, conservative and bureaucratic, motivated not by adventurous, avant-garde design but by the rigorous disciplines of cost accountancy and marketing. Consequently, the centre of gravity of the firm swung away from the *Bureau d'Etudes*. Not surprisingly, the clash of corporate cultures led to a number of departures among Citroën's key design and engineering staff, including that of styling chief Robert Opron.

The first product of the takeover was the Citroën LN of 1976, a hastily conceived amalgam of a Peugeot 104 coupé bodyshell and the 602cc 2CV air-cooled engine, mated to a GS gearbox. Basic in its equipment and more of a 2+2 than a full four-seater, the LN proved a comfortable and competent runabout; top speed was a whisker short of 75mph. In 1978 the revised 652cc flat-twin fitted to the Visa replaced the 2CV unit, power rising from 32bhp DIN to 36bhp and

the car being renamed the LNA. For 1983 the transverse-mounted 1,124cc water-cooled Peugeot 104 engine became available, and it was this version that was eventually imported into the UK, between 1983 and 1986. Very few LNAs were sold in Britain, but 281,206 LNs and LNAs were built in all, a respectable enough figure for what was essentially a stopgap.

It had been promised that the LN would be the first and last Citroën to be nothing more than a facelifted Peugeot, and accordingly when the Visa appeared in October 1978 to replace the Ami 8 it had its own unmistakably Citroën appearance – too distinctive, indeed, for most tastes, due to its unusual combined polypropylene grille and bumper. With a solitary large screen wiper, single-

Hot Visas from mild to wild

In its bid to raise the profile of the Visa – and have an effective presence in rallying – Citroën developed various hot Visas over the years, as did several outside specialists. The first version of note was the 200-off Group B Trophée, which was built in conjunction with Heuliez and boasted a 100bhp twin-Weber 1,219cc power unit. From this was spawned the Chrono, of which 2000 numbered road versions were

The Visa Mille Pistes was a 4wd rally special – and the ultimate hot Visa. (LAT)

made, with 93bhp 1,360cc engines, plus 200 rally specials and 20 1,434cc 'evolution' rally cars pushing out 134bhp. The cars had smart screw-on wheelarch flares and were finished in white with red and blue striping, but this proved too aggressive for the Dutch – for whom the cars were de-striped and sold as GT Spirit 330s. Effectively replacing the Chrono was the Mille Pistes, which was Citroën's ultimate hot Visa, with 4wd and a 1,434cc engine developing 112bhp or 147bhp in 20-off 'evo' form.

Meanwhile, Lotus developed a mid-engined Visa for Citroën, with a 210bhp Esprit Turbo engine, SM gearbox (as used in the Esprit), and rear-wheel drive only. Other mid-engined Visas to see the light of day included cars with CX powerpacks, one 4wd car with the Talbot Tagora four-cylinder engine and hydropneumatic suspension, and another all-wheel-driver with a mid-mounted PRV6. Another tack was to try two engines, and Citroën built three twin-engined Visas as experimental rally cars.

spoke steering wheel and bold but effective satellite-pod controls, the new car made a strong claim to be a true Citroën, but underneath the striking lines and the imaginative interior was the floorpan and suspension of the Peugeot 104.

Initially available in three different

forms, a 652cc flat-twin Special or Club and a 1,124cc Peugeot-powered four-cylinder Super, the Visa had its origins in design studies begun well before the merger. Formerly, back in the days of the liaison with Fiat, it was to have been based on a Fiat floorpan, but when the collaboration ended it

was redefined around new Citroën underpinnings using torsion-bar suspension all-round and either a 2CV-derived flat-twin engine or the GS's flat-four. The arrival of Peugeot put paid to this plan, but, even so, the original Citroën design ended up being built in Romania by a joint venture

If the Peugeot takeover hadn't happened, the replacement for the Ami 8 would have been the Axel, a car that ultimately reached production in Romania in an ill-fated collaboration with the Ceaucescu dictatorship. The attempt to sell this shoddily assembled but mechanically interesting vehicle in France was a fiasco. (Citroën)

In MkII form the Visa won success – in GTi form it was a real hot-hatch 'sleeper'. (Citroën)

between Citroën and the Romanian government. Known as the Oltcit, it was introduced in Romania in 1981, powered by the 652cc air-cooled twin from the Visa or either the 1,129cc or 1,299cc version of the GS engine, together with a GS transmission and inboard front disc brakes. Between

1984 and 1988, this car – perhaps the marque's last true Citroën-designed model – was also sold in France, by Citroën, in four-cylinder form, under the name Axel. Unfortunately, despite its engineering heritage, lamentable build quality meant that only 13,175 examples found customers there.

Meanwhile, after less than three years in its original form, the Visa range was relaunched in March 1981 as the Visa II, with a redesigned front end and a lightly remodelled rear – a low-budget restyle carried out by independent coachbuilder Heuliez in response to worryingly poor sales.

The BX estate was particularly popular in the UK, thanks to its self-levelling suspension that made light work of carrying heavy loads or towing a trailer or caravan. (LAT)

This revision marked the start of a long and successful career for the Visa – a career that continues today albeit only in C15 van form. Sold in the UK from 1979 to 1989, the saloon range expanded considerably – losing the 652cc twin-pot on the way, in favour of a 954cc Peugeot 'four' de-tuned for minimum fuel consumption. The performance version, which had begun as the 64bhp Super X of 1,219cc, evolved into the 1,360cc Visa GT, developing 80bhp, and finally into the 1,580cc GTi introduced for 1985. Created by the simple expedient of dropping in the entire Peugeot 205GTi power pack – hence the plastic wheelarch extensions to cope with the wider track – the fuel-injected GTi delivered 105bhp in its initial form,

rising to 115bhp for 1987. The GTi had a more workaday sister in the Visa 17D, introduced in spring 1984 and using the responsive but outstandingly economical 1,769cc XUD diesel unit of the Peugeot 205D. This engine was also employed in the Visa-based C15 light van, introduced in 1984 and available in the UK from 1985 with a choice of either the diesel engine or a 1,124cc petrol unit. Still in production, in Spain and Morocco, over 750,000 examples have been sold to date. The Visa saloon, meanwhile, was withdrawn in 1988, after more than 1.2 million had been made.

The means by which the Citroën's individuality could be preserved within the merger, while keeping the financial benefits of collaborative component-sharing, was demonstrated for the first time with the arrival, in September 1982, of the new medium-class BX as the replacement for the GSA. Although it appeared at first sight to be a 100%

Citroën production, the BX was based on the Peugeot 405 floorpan, and used transversely-mounted Peugeot engines. It had originally been proposed at the planning stage that Citroën's hydropneumatics would be discontinued in favour of conventional coil-spring suspension. But faced with the combined revolt of Citroën's Vélizy design centre and the entire dealer network, Peugeot relented and agreed that hydropneumatic suspension would be preserved as a distinguishing Citroën feature.

However, as installed on the BX, it was modified in a hitherto unthinkable way, by the use of a hybrid MacPherson strut arrangement at the front, with trailing arms at the rear. The oleo-pneumatic spheres were retained, and thus also the self-levelling function, but the revised front suspension geometry enforced by this simplification meant that the principle of centre-point steering was

The BX 4TC

In the mad and short-lived 1980s world of Group B rally cars, the rules were not hugely complicated: pretty much anything was permissible, so long as you built 200 road-going examples. The result was the arrival of the tailor-made rally-car, in the shape of the Metro 6R4, the Lancia Delta S4, the Peugeot 205 Turbo 16, the Ford RS200, and suchlike. Citroën's entry to the party was with the BX 4TC. Instead of electing to use a mid-engined layout, it decided to keep to a frontally-mounted engine. The idea – alas fallacious – was that if the resultant car appeared to be a practical four-seat saloon, then the 200 road-cars required for homologation could be sold off more easily. With the 'PRV' V6 too big to fit the BX and the XU-based 205 Turbo 16 engine being rejected as too small, Citroën competitions chief Guy Verrier turned to an old PSA favourite that had started life in one of Europe's least-loved cars. This was the alloy-head ohc 'four' which had originally equipped the Chrysler 180, and had gone on to be used in the Peugeot 505, and in Talbot's Murena and ill-fated Tagora. Robust and happy to be turbocharged, it was mounted longitudinally in the BX shell, and in 2,141cc turbo configuration kicked out 200bhp – good for a 7.5-second 0–60mph time. Drive went to all four wheels, of course, and hydropneumatic suspension was retained. Built by Heuliez, the 200

'homologation' cars, all in white, were completed by the beginning of 1986 . . . in the course of which year Group B was abandoned, following Henri Toivonen's high-speed death on the Corsica Rally. The 4TC never had a chance to prove itself, and Citroën, in common with other manufacturers, was left with numerous rally hybrids nobody wanted to buy. An interesting spin-off from the project was the 4TC-based Bertone Zabrus showcar.

Top: The bulging wheelarches of the BX 4TC homologation special hide a completely re-thought chassis with four-wheel drive and a longitudinal Simca/Talbot engine; the suspension remains hydropneumatic. (Citroën)

Above: Bertone's Zabrus concept car was based on the BX 4TC. (Bertone)

The Heuliez Dyana

For those who found the BX estate too awkward-looking – or too familiar – the company responsible for building it, Heuliez of Cerizay, could offer a rather more exclusive alternative: a two-door estate called the Dyana. Doing away with the saloon rear doors that merged so clumsily with the estate roofline, the two-door was undeniably elegant. It was available in all the regular BX formats, and could optionally be fitted with a rearward-facing children's bench in the boot; additionally a two-seat Entreprise version was available.

Heuliez came up with this elegant three-door BX estate, called the Dyana; various different versions were offered, including a two-seater Entreprise, and a rearward-facing children's bench seat was available. (Citroën)

abandoned. Citroën's fully powered all-disc braking system was also retained, but the power steering, when this was eventually introduced, was to be of the conventional hydraulic-ram type.

The BX also looked completely different from previous Citroëns, with angular lines that contrasted totally with the fluid silhouettes of the Opron era. The new style came from Italian styling house Bertone; this was the first time that a Citroën had been shaped by an outside concern. Designed for extreme lightness, and for simplicity of construction, the body comprised only 334 elements, instead of the 531 used on the GSA, and had bonnet, tailgate, bumpers and rear quarter panels made from plastic.

Launched in the UK with the slogan 'Loves Driving, Hates Garages', the BX was intended to appeal to motorists who had never owned a Citroën, and who were intimidated by the perceived complexity of hydropneumatic suspension. Service intervals were extended to 12,000 miles or a two-hour inspection once a year. Initially, three versions of the BX saloon were offered: the BX (62bhp 1,360cc engine and four-speed gearbox), the BX14 (72bhp 1,360cc engine and five-speed box) and the BX16 (90 bhp 1,580cc engine and five-speed box). In September 1983 came a diesel version, the BX19D, powered by an all-new 65bhp 1,905cc XUD-series unit; three years later this was joined, in September 1986, by the BX17RD, powered by the 1,769cc diesel engine from the Visa. Ultimately the BX diesel range proved to be an enormous success for Citroën – 295,000 units were produced in 1987 alone. Indeed, the BX Diesels became the most popular single diesel car ever sold in the UK, revolutionising public perception of the compression-ignition engine among British motorists. From September 1988 the 1,905cc diesel was also available in turbocharged form.

The range was soon augmented by a series of sporting versions. The first, introduced in July 1984, was the BX19GT, equipped with a 105bhp 1,905cc petrol engine. Next, in March 1985, came the BX Sport (not sold in the UK) powered by a specially prepared 126bhp version of the 1,905cc unit. This was eventually followed, in July 1986, by the 125bhp fuel-injected GTi, which was supplemented in turn by the 160bhp GTi 16-Valve in July 1987.

In the meantime the long-awaited estate car version had arrived, early in 1985. This was available in five separate versions, powered by the same petrol engines as the saloon, plus the 1,905cc diesel of course. At its zenith the BX range offered no fewer than 23 different permutations – 15 saloons and eight estates – to cover virtually every purpose and pocket. In 1986 the range was re-vamped, the most notable revision being a new, more conventional dashboard and instrument panel.

By the time that the BX was finally withdrawn in 1993, 2,315,739 had been sold world-wide, of which 219,529 had found owners in the UK. Like the GS and GSA before it, the BX was a success that saved Citroën from extinction.

When it arrived in 1986, the replacement for the 2CV, the AX supermini, was widely regarded as a disappointment by Citroënistes who were still hoping for a radical go-anywhere, do-anything vehicle that would serve the needs of the third world as well as the consumer society of western Europe. Launched in France with the slogan 'Revolutionary', the AX was anything but that: in both conception and construction it was entirely conventional, down to its self-cancelling indicators. PSA had aimed the AX squarely at the urban female drivers of France who in customer clinics had expressed a marked lack of interest in owning anything more unusual than such alternatives as Peugeot's own 205 model. With all traces of quirkiness having been eliminated, the AX's most interesting technical feature – other than its impressive 0.31 Cd – was its ultra-low weight. Ranging between 12.6cwt and 13.7cwt, it was approximately 2cwt lighter than the average for its class, a saving produced by a 30 per cent reduction in the amount of steel used compared to normal industry levels, helped by the rear tailgate being a composite structure formed entirely of glass and moulded plastic. The intention, of course, was to be able to claim impressive fuel economy (72.4mpg at a constant 56mph for the AX11) by virtue of a high power-to-weight ratio. But the strategy backfired and the AX was criticised for its flimsy build. Its bland styling, banal interior, indifferent ergonomics and uncomfortable seating were also panned by the critics – but at least it had an effective heating and ventilation system, a benefit not previously noted on a Citroën.

Available initially in three three-door versions (but with five-door variants following one year later), the AX was powered by the familiar four-cylinder water-cooled PSA engines also used in the 205 – an economical 45bhp 954cc unit (AX10), a 55bhp 1,124cc (AX11) mid-ranger, and a more powerful 70bhp 1,360cc unit (AX14) that in uprated 85bhp form also propelled

the AXGT. In April 1987, the AX Sport (not sold in the UK) joined the range, powered by a high-performance 95bhp 1,249cc engine. Weighing only 14.2cwt, it could reach 116mph. This arrival was closely followed by the appearance of the AX Diesel in September 1988, equipped with a 53bhp 1,360cc compression-ignition engine and offering one of the lowest fuel-consumption figures in Europe, a touring figure of close on 50mpg being achieved by *Autocar* magazine.

By January 1990, the AX was well-established, with over a million examples having been produced. For 1993, the model was lightly restyled and given an improved interior, though there were no significant mechanical modifications; at the same time the AX Sport was replaced by the AX GTi, equipped with a fuel-injected version of the 1,360cc engine. Production of the AX ended in July 1998, by which point a total of 2,424,808 had been constructed.

When the time came to replace the CX as Citroën's flagship, once again a contest was staged between the company's Vélizy design centre and Bertone. Yet again, the Bertone proposal won and the result, an all-new executive-class saloon named the XM, was unveiled at the 1989 Frankfurt Motor Show. Although the XM was subsequently voted

European Car of the Year, this time the result was less successful both aesthetically and commercially, for Bertone's five-door, five-seater hatchback was a curious compromise between the ancient and modern, an inharmonious composition of contradictory themes that pleased neither the conservatives nor the progressives. To the regret of die-hard Citroënistes, the XM also regressed to the use of quasi-strut suspension geometry and conventional power steering; only lhd examples of the top-of-the-range V6 XM models briefly inherited the CX's Diravi system.

The XM saloon arrived in the UK in autumn 1990, with an estate following a year later. Notable for its adjustable, computer-controlled Hydractive oleo-pneumatic suspension – another Citroën innovation – the XM saloon was initially available in five forms: a 1,998cc four-cylinder carburettor-engined model with manual transmission, a 1,998cc fuel-injected model with either manual or automatic transmission, a 2,088cc 2.1-litre turbo-diesel, a 2,975cc 3.0-litre V6 with either manual or automatic

To replace the CX as its flagship, in May 1989 Citroën announced the XM saloon, which duly captured the Car of the Year award in 1990. An estate followed in 1991. (LAT)

The Activa research programme

Despite the uncertainties surrounding the future of Citroën's hydropneumatic technology following the Peugeot takeover, from the early 1980s onwards an extensive research programme was maintained to develop a number of associated concepts and technologies including 'drive-by-wire' four-wheel steering and computer-controlled suspension.

The Activa research vehicle – first revealed to the public in 1988 – played an important part in this programme. A fully working prototype rather than just a show-car, the Activa was powered by a fuel-injected quad-cam 3,000cc V6 with four valves per cylinder. It also featured permanent four-wheel drive delivered through a four-speed automatic gearbox.

Naturally, its anti-lock disc brakes were fully powered by Citroën's high-pressure, load-sensitive, anti-dive hydraulic system, while its self-levelling hydropneumatic suspension incorporated a speed-sensitive, semi-active computer-controlled device to adjust suspension damping and ride-height adjustment on the move. By providing constant monitoring and adjustment of anti-roll-bar stiffness, this device ensured level cornering regardless of vehicle speed or steering angle.

The steering was also novel: hydraulic servo motors turned each pair of wheels, both front and rear, independently through 30 degrees to left or right so that the vehicle could move sideways in a crabwise fashion to facilitate parking. The Activa's pillarless four-door bodywork also

Activa showcased Citroën's advanced hydropneumatic systems – which found their way into the Xantia Activa and the C5. (LAT)

broke new ground, as did its highly sophisticated electronic navigation and traffic information systems.

The ideas introduced in the Activa soon found their way into full-scale production on the XM range of 1989, in the form of Citroën's first-generation Hydractive 1 electronically-monitored and actuated suspension system. Effectively, this reacted automatically to driving style and road conditions, responding to steering-wheel and accelerator movements, braking effort, body movement and vehicle speed, and adjusting the suspension accordingly; additionally the driver could over-ride the system should he want firmer, more sporting responses. These concepts were refined in the Activa 2 prototype, displayed at the 1990 Paris Motor Show, and ultimately led to the Xantia Activa of

1993, the first production vehicle to employ Citroën's second-generation Hydractive 2 intelligent roll-control system. Currently, as installed on the latest C5 saloon and estate car models introduced in 2000, the third-generation self-levelling Hydractive 3 system goes one stage further, adjusting ride-height upwards or downwards automatically on the move, according to speed and the condition of the road surface, as foreseen by the original Activa prototype 12 years previously. The system is claimed to endow the C5 with levels of handling, roadholding and ride comfort not to be found even on expensive luxury vehicles costing two or three times more.

transmission, and finally a top-of-the-range high-performance variant equipped with a 200bhp 24-valve fuel-injected V6, capable of 146mph and only available with manual transmission. In January 1996 the XM was relaunched as the Series II with a restyled front and a new dashboard. By this time three new engines were

available, a 1,998cc 16-valve injected petrol engine, a 2,138cc turbo-diesel and a 2,446cc turbo-diesel.

Alas, not even the most partisan of Citroën fanatics could claim that the XM was a success. Ultimately, by the time that it was discontinued eleven years later in 2000, only 333,775 had been made. A respectable 96,000 were

produced in 1990, the first full year of assembly, but this fell to 49,000 in 1991, to 20,000 in 1993 and 1994, to 12,000 in 1996 and to a paltry 7,500 in 1998. Early technical problems, especially with its complex electronics (caused by inferior wiring connectors), gave the XM a reputation for poor reliability and excessive – indeed, punitive – depreciation, from which it never recovered. The XM failed entirely to capture its expected share of the market, let alone regain for Citroën its customary position as the arch-exponent of high-quality engineering and the leader of the avant-garde.

When taking over the Double Chevron marque, Peugeot had expressed its intention to make Citroën more accessible to the ordinary motorist by eliminating its customary quirks and eccentricities – though the relentless trend to standardisation and uniformity imposed throughout the motor industry during the 1980s and early 1990s was not envisaged at this point. Undoubtedly, this move towards the centre ground proved counter-productive, losing Citroën more loyal supporters and devotees than it won. Between 1974 and 1998 its share of the French domestic market fell from 18.6 to 11.6 per cent, although the

decline was masked in part by improving sales in foreign markets such as the UK.

Plainly, the authentic Citroëns such as the Traction Avant, the 2CV, the DS/ID – and even the GS/GSA and the CX – have all survived the test of time to establish themselves as icons of automobile design. But what about the more recent PSA cars, such as the ZX, Xsara, Xantia and Saxo, which fall beyond the scope of this book? Will they also be recognised as true classics in their turn, generating as much interest, pride and affection among enthusiasts as their predecessors? The question is open to debate.

In 1997 long-time PSA boss Jacques Calvet, a banker and financial specialist, retired and was succeeded by Jean-Martin Folz, an engineer and industrialist of wide experience who had trained in the customary French tradition at the Ecole Polytechnique and the Ecole des Mines. Fortunately,

the new and enlightened policies adopted by Folz have already begun to restore the marque's reputation for originality and individuality, so that its popularity and sales are now on the increase again among a new generation of European motorists. Bold and original new products such as the C2, C3, Picasso and Pluriel uphold the heritage of creativity and imagination, and exhibit once again the refreshing non-conformity that characterised Citroën products in the past. There is a new buzz at the company as its reputation – and sales – experience a dramatic revival around the world. All the same, those enthusiasts who hope or expect that this renaissance may lead to the arrival of a modern-day DS are perhaps over-optimistic: that miraculous creation came about through an extraordinary conjunction of events, circumstances, influences and talents that can never be repeated.

Acknowledgements & Bibliography

Special thanks are due to the following: Fred Annells, Leonardo Bertoni, Malcolm Bobbitt, Roger Bradford, Neill Bruce, Marc-Antoine Colin, Stephen Cooper, Jerry and Sylvia Hathaway, Wouter Jansen, Jan de Lange, Karl Ludvigsen, Olivier de Serres, Jim Sheehan, Ken Smith, Tony Stokoe, Nigel Wild, Anne-Marie Michel, Gro Hoeg and Annick Rouauld of Automobiles Citroën in Paris, and Julian Leyton of Citroën UK Ltd.

The buying advice sections were compiled with invaluable help from Pete Abbott (2CVGB Spare Parts Organisation), Roger Bradford (The CX Centre), H-type specialist Simon Doe (Le Cube Utile), Steve Hill (Deux Chevaux et Charette), Rob Moss (Chevronics), SM group SeMantics, and Méhari specialist Garage Ciercoles of Cazals; special thanks to David Evans of Classic & Sports Car magazine for his assistance. The author also acknowledges the contribution of series editor Jon Pressnell to the buying advice sections on the Traction Avant and DS.

The majority of the illustrations are from LAT Photographic or are contemporary Citroën press photographs from the archives of Citroën France and Citroën Netherlands, or from the Neill Bruce/Peter Roberts Collection, the Ludvigsen Collection or the author's own archives. Other material was kindly provided by Brian Scott Quinn, Neill Bruce, Paul Debois and Jon Pressnell.

Other books by this author include: Original Citroën DS, André Citroën – The Man and the Motorcars, Citroën 2CV, Engines & Enterprise – The Life and Work of Sir Harry Ricardo, Citroën from A to X, Eighty Years of Citroën in the United Kingdom.

Books on Citroën matters published in English, currently (or shortly to be) in print, include:

Citroën 2CV (Sutton Publishing, 2001) John Reynolds. ISBN 0-7509-2609-0. Covers the design and production history of the 2CV and other A-Series models from 1949 to 1990.

Citroën DS – The Complete Story (Crowood, 1999) Jon Pressnell. ISBN 1-86126-055-5. Covers the production history of the D-Series cars from 1955 to1975.

Citroën Traction Avant – The Complete Story (Crowood, 2004) Jon Pressnell. ISBN 1-86126-614-6. Covers the production history of the Traction Avant from 1934 to1957.

The Citroën (Shire Publications, 2003) Jonathan Wood. ISBN 0-7478-0563-6. Covers in brief the story of the Citroën marque from 1919 to the present day.

Eighty Years of Citroën in the United Kingdom (Dalton Watson, 2004) John Reynolds. ISBN 1-85443-137-4. Covers the imported RHD vehicles sold in the UK between 1923 and 2004, including the cars assembled at the Citroën Works at Slough from 1926 to 1966.

Index